OUT WHERE THE WEST BEGINS

OUT
WHERE
the
WEST
BEGINS

PROFILES, VISIONS
& STRATEGIES
OF EARLY WESTERN
BUSINESS LEADERS

PHILIP F. ANSCHUTZ

WITH WILLIAM J. CONVERY AND THOMAS J. NOEL

CLOUD
CAMP
PRESS

International Standard Book Number 978-0-9905502-0-4

Library of Congress Control Number: 2014951108

CLOUD CAMP PRESS, LLC

555 Seventeenth Street

Suite 2400

Denver, Colorado 80202

PUBLICATION LIAISON: Darlene Dueck

DESIGN AND EDITING: Carol Haralson

PHOTOGRAPHS OF ARTWORKS: William O'Connor

PAGE 12: *The Departure of Columbus from Palos in 1492*, Emanuel Leutze, 1855

PAGES 20-21: *Trading Post (Bent's Fort, Colorado)*, Harold Von Schmidt, 1937

PAGES 58-59: *In the Sagebrush*, Carl Rungius, c. 1900

PAGES 116-117: *Oregon Trail*, Albert Bierstadt, c. 1871

PAGES 218-219: *Days of the '49ers*, Dean Cornwell, 1926

PAGES 274-275: *Wheat Threshing on the High Plains*, Thomas Hart Benton , 1969

PAGES 324-325: *The Cinch Ring*, Charles Russell, 1909

PAGES 360-361: *The Great Royal Buffalo Hunt*, Louis Maurer, 1895

Collection of the American Museum of Western Art, Denver

FRONT COVER AND PAGE 2: MAPS OF NORTH AMERICA IN THE EARLY 1800S.

Courtesy of Oldmaps.com.

Printed in Canada by Friesens Printing

Dedicated to my mother,

MARIAN PFISTER ANSCHUTZ

I will always be grateful that she
imparted her great love of history to me.

~

Philip F. Anschutz

CONTENTS

ACKNOWLEDGMENTS

With my full appreciation to Bill Convery, State Historian at History Colorado, Tom Noel, Professor of History at the University of Colorado Denver, and Darlene Dueck, Curator of the American Museum of Western Art, for their valued guidance and assistance in the preparation of this book, I wish to dedicate the book to my mother, Marian Pfister Anschutz. As a young woman, she was a schoolteacher who taught eight grades in a one-room country schoolhouse in the bleak northwest corner of Kansas. She exerted a powerful and positive influence over my life. She sparked my interest in art, music, and history at an early age, and her fondest hope was that someday I might become a professor of history at Ft. Hays State Teachers College (which she attended) in Hays, Kansas. I don't believe she held anything against a business profession, but possibly harbored some suspicion that I had limited aptitude and skill for it.

I dedicate this book to my mother both for all her assistance in my life and as a small apology for getting into the wrong line of work!

—*Philip F. Anschutz, 2014*

The Departure of Columbus from Palos in 1492, Emanuel Leutze, 1855.

FOREWORD

Philip F. Anschutz

AMERICA ~ THE LAND OF THE FUTURE ~ IT IS A LAND OF DESIRE .
— *G.W.F. Hegel, 1831*

THERE ARE NO WORDS THAT CAN TELL THE HIDDEN SPIRIT OF THE WILDERNESS,
REVEAL ITS MYSTERY, ITS MELANCHOLY, AND ITS CHARM.
— *Theodore Roosevelt, 1910*

THE GOLDEN AGE OF DISCOVERY FOLLOWED THE SUN WEST. — *P. S. Anbar, 1918*

THE WEST IS A LANDSCAPE THAT HAS TO BE SEEN TO BE BELIEVED . . .
AND BELIEVED IN ORDER TO BE SEEN. — *N. Scott Momaday, Kiowa poet*

*W*ho created the American West? That is the question I
began with in thinking about this book. I was interested in both the perception and the reality—but especially the reality. Long a student and admirer of the American West,
its history, its art, its culture, its cast of personalities, I'm aware that in
the West a great confluence of events and people combined to create
something unique in the annals of human history.

Like all great moments in history, the West is about people, so I
decided to focus on those who made important early contributions to
the region's development, turning their visions of what might be into
realities. Next it was necessary to provide the proper framework for
the book and to develop the criteria for its subjects. Given the great
number of candidates and breadth of choices, I was faced with a series
of decisions in order to reduce the scope and the number of profiles to
approximately fifty individuals who seemed most critical. The criteria
for selection had to be refined, and the time period narrowed to the
most critical years.

What type of men were they to be? Explorers, politicians, doctors, teachers, inventors? These professions and many more all made important contributions, but it will come as no particular surprise to my friends that I selected entrepreneurs and businessmen to write about.

And for the most obvious reason: at that particular moment in time when the country was on the verge of an explosion of growth, government interference and involvement were at a low point, new technologies and inventions were being created, vast new frontier lands in the West were available, people were becoming more mobile and willing to move, and investment capital was coming into the market, no other group of individuals could have had such a far-ranging impact. They were willing to take the risks, marshal the resources, and organize and lead the considerable efforts required.

For the last fifty years I have read their biographies, learned their histories, thought about their strategies and contributions, and have even purchased some of the companies they founded and extended their business strategies further.

The book has evolved into some fifty individual profiles of entrepreneurs and businessmen covering a period of about 120 years (1800 to 1920). In historical terms this time period is short—a mere blink of an eye—when compared to the magnitude of what was achieved in the broad perspective of history.

The well respected history professor Frederick Jackson Turner argued in his highly regarded essay "The Significance of the Frontier in American History" that the closure of the American frontier occurred in 1890. This was made somewhat official by a declaration from the superintendent of the U. S. Census in that same year (1890) that "there can no longer be said to be a frontier line and hence the country's westward movement can no longer have a place in the census reports." In addition, Henry Ellsworth, U. S. patent officer in 1843, was reputed to have said that "everything that can be invented has been invented." I mention these observations only as perspective, as history has a way of embarrassing those who might be tempted to make premature statements without properly accounting for the passage of time.

The arbitrary dates I have chosen for this book, 1800 to 1920, simply assisted in my defining a framework for when the American West was largely discovered, explored, settled, civilized, and then transformed into a major economic power in its own right. In this short period the West was transformed from an idea into a place of great relevance to America.

The individuals selected were bold men of vision and considerable energy. They were able to accept both the concept and the burden of high levels of risk. Most risked their reputations and capital—some even their lives. They are examples of countless and nameless others who did the same, but upon whom good fortune never chose to shine.

The individuals selected were not chosen necessarily as being good role models—a few were not, even judged by the standards of their time. Nevertheless, these individuals had a vision and the ability to see it implemented; they had focus, discipline, and work ethic. Many had charitable instincts, willingness to give back to their communities, and religious commitment. I remain impressed with the rather high percentage of them who actually were the role models I had hoped for. Few escaped some controversy in their lives. Yet all created companies or ventures that were innovative, productive, and contributory in some manner to the founding and expansion of the American West. For the most part, they were multi-dimensional as to their interests, skills, and investments. In addition to establishing individual ventures, many of them helped to establish and then define whole industries (Ford, Giannini). A few went beyond the limits of business to establish towns, cities, and even whole regions of the country (Evans, Palmer, Young). Some contributed to defining the enduring perception of the American West (Holliday, Harvey, Cody, Laemmle). While almost all believed in giving back to society and in sharing the benefits of their success, a few went on to help define philanthropic and philosophical guidelines for the future (Carnegie—his essay of 1889, "The Gospel of Wealth").

The selection criteria for the individuals focused on these key components: What they did; what their vision or strategy was; whether the individual had the requisite skills to turn the idea into a reality; whether the idea itself had long-lasting value and impact; and why it was important to the American West. The importance was judged by a number of factors ranging from expansion, settlement, and creation of an established society and population base to creating livelihoods, jobs, and improvement in the quality of life for its inhabitants.

The key industries studied, many of which were already in existence (but not yet established in the American West) were positioned to have the greatest impact. They were trading, farming and ranching, transportation, real estate, mining, manufacturing, and banking. They were (and needed to be) interdependent upon each other in order for such remarkable progress to be made in such a short period of time. The ability to transfer skills and build infrastructure rapidly in order to drive and support growth was a key factor. The fact that these industries were interconnected is but yet another reason why entrepreneurs and businessmen were uniquely positioned at this particular moment in history to emerge as early contributors and leaders.

The question posed in the first sentence of this foreword was "Who created the American West?" As in most of history, there is not a single answer. Numerous people, facts, perceptions, myths, images, and desires collided and interwove, and they can tend to get a bit confused. It is undoubtedly true that it was a combination of all of the above, both facts and fancy, that led to what was ultimately created.

As for who created the "western image," the popular perception that the American West was created in part by countless artists, writers, poets, photographers, historians, politicians, and others, is true. It has been messaged, re-messaged, enforced and reinforced over time by numerous events, generations, and the media—and that process continues today. But what is lost to history is the fact that the earliest and certainly best organized and best financed promotions of the American West were by the very companies and businessmen who led in the development of the West in the first place.

Whether for public relations, governmental objectives, or mainly just good advertising in order to sell what needed to be sold, individual companies initiated the first formal efforts and paid to create the images and perceptions. Whether it was railroads selling tickets to passengers or land to settlers, manufacturers selling farm equipment to farmers; real estate developers selling land to investors and homes to newcomers; mining companies advertising for new workers; gun companies selling guns; beer makers selling beer; movie makers selling entertainment—the list goes on and is extensive. But the point is that the public at large developed a favorable perception of the American West (mostly accurate, but with plenty of imagination as well), created and driven at the start by the very men who helped build the West, so in a certain sense the perception and the reality began to merge into one.

When attempting to explain the appeal of the American West, the broad themes really haven't changed much over the past 200 years. They include exploration, adventure, idealized places, incomparable vistas, glory, wealth and riches, freedom, quality of life, personal fulfillment, new opportunities, and second chances.

Accompanying this foreword, the reader will find a painting by the artist Emanuel Leutze depicting Columbus's departure from the Old World ... pointing west towards the New World. (Forget the fact that he thought he was headed to one place, ended up in another, and for different reasons than he initially envisioned.) The world already well knows, I suspect, that if one is focused on being an entrepreneur (and possibly a visionary), luck definitely helps, but being positioned for good luck to occur is often paramount. Many individuals in the book started their early careers headed in one direction with one goal and ended up in an entirely different place and with a different goal—but, then again, "Good fortune favors the bold"!

The reason this painting is included is to help portray a final question occurring to me about this book, namely, "Where did it all start?" I have decided (perhaps simplistically) it began with the voyage of Columbus. A clean break from the old, and a new fresh start with endless possibilities ahead . . . to the West! The phrase "Empire follows the sun West" was never more true than in the discovery of America, followed by the discovery of the American West.

For America, the period of 1800 to 1920 was an unparalleled time of broad expansion and growth driven by extraordinary factors unlike almost any other in history. It was a period of empire building and empire builders. The risks were high, but then too, the opportunities and rewards were high as well. The men in this book made a lasting impact on the American West.

Out Where the West Begins

Out where the handclasp's a little stronger,
Out where the smile dwells a little longer,
That's where the West begins;
Out where the sun is a little brighter,
Where the snows that fall are a trifle whiter,
Where the bonds of home are a wee bit tighter,
That's where the West begins.

Out where the skies are a trifle bluer,
Out where friendships are a little truer,
That's where the West begins;
Out where a fresher breeze is blowing,
Out where there's laughter in every streamlet flowing,
Where there's more of reaping and less of sowing,
That's where the West begins.

Out where the world is in the making,
Where fewer hearts in despair are aching,
That's where the West begins;
Where there's more of singing and less of sighing,
Where there's more of giving and less of buying,
And a man makes friends without half trying—
That's where the West begins.

—Arthur Chapman

MANUEL LISA

INDEFATIGABLE SPANISH TRADER {1772–1820}

Daring and energetic, boastful, blustering, scheming—Manuel Lisa was the first, most colorful, and, arguably, most imaginative businessman in the upper Missouri River fur trade. Hiram Chittenden, the grandfather of fur trade historians, called Lisa "the most active and indefatigable trader that St. Louis ever produced." A self-made man and a fierce competitor, Lisa was the first St. Louis trader to probe the Santa Fe Trail and the first to test the commercial potential of the Rocky Mountains after Lewis and Clark's return. He played a key role in the St. Louis and the Missouri River trade between 1807 and 1820, building the first trading post in today's Montana. Virtually all subsequent traders followed his business model of establishing fixed posts deep in Indian country. The energetic trader ascended the Missouri no fewer than twelve times, spending a cumulative eight years in the wild. Lisa once boasted to William Clark, "I put into my operations great activity. I go a great distance while some are considering whether they start today or tomorrow."

Despite his frequent travels, Lisa enjoyed affectionate relations with his wives and children. In family matters, Lisa adopted the pragmatic approach common among Creole traders, taking one spouse in St. Louis and a Native American one in the field. His first wife, Polly Charles, was the widow of a frontier settler who died in an Indian raid. Following Polly's death in 1817, Lisa married Mary Hempstead Keeney, the widowed sister of a St. Louis business associate. Neither union produced surviving children. Lisa's genuine affection for both his American wives did not prevent him from marrying Mitian, an Omaha Indian woman, which strengthened his commercial ties to her tribe, in 1814. Their daughter, Rosalie, was Lisa's only offspring who survived to adulthood.

Lisa was born in 1772, in Spanish New Orleans. His father, Cristoval de Lisa, was a native of Murcia, Spain, and his Spanish mother, Maria Ignacía Rodríguez, of colonial St. Augustine, Florida, the first city planted by Europeans in what is now North America. Cristoval, a Spanish colonial bureaucrat, ranked as a sergeant in the colonial militia and likely worked as a New Orleans customs official. Little is recorded of Lisa's youth, but by the early 1790s the self-billed "merchant of New Orleans" was already familiar with the Mississippi and Ohio River trade. As the owner of a small trade boat, then proprietor of a store in Vincennes, Indiana (America's westernmost settlement at the time), Lisa learned firsthand the dangers of commerce. Whether contending with rivals willing to murder the competition to get ahead or bargaining with unpredictable Indian tribes hundreds of miles from home, Lisa relished the (literally) cutthroat nature of his business.

The take-no-prisoners nature of frontier commerce sharpened his business sense even as it dulled his scruples. Biographer Richard Oglesby noted that "Lisa always was present and active when there were any prospects of profit, and usually was far away when expenditures were to be made." Enemies—and Lisa made many—considered him an unscrupulous, litigious braggart. He drove his employees mercilessly. He complained incessantly that his competitors were conspiring to ruin him, while himself scheming to foil them. He never hesitated to file legal and ethical complaints against his competitors, yet regularly violated legal and ethical codes when it granted him an edge.

Lisa especially irritated authority figures. A talented opportunist who bridled against regulatory restrictions, Lisa railed against government oversight and dodged official regulations whenever it served his interests. Spanish authorities found that paying off the entrepreneur with favors did little to silence his complaints; the lieutenant governor of Spanish Louisiana eventually jailed Lisa for using abusive language. Captain Meriwether Lewis cursed his sharp business practices, claiming that Lisa and a partner gave him "more vexation and trouble than their lives are worth." Louisiana's first American governor, James Wilkinson, called Lisa the "Black Spaniard" and condemned his "despicable intrigues."

On the positive side of the ledger, Lisa poured boundless energy into his endeavors. In his comprehensive survey of the fur trade, historian Hiram Chittenden wrote, "Privation, hardship, incessant toil, were [Lisa's] constant portion." He led from the front, taking a hand at the oars, wrestling his keelboats upstream against the Missouri River current, leading his boatmen in song, and encouraging them to perform beyond their capabilities. Lisa, Chittenden wrote, "never shrank from any work that he demanded from his men." His Indian customers regarded him as brave and fair, and he possessed a talent for mollification, intuiting the exact amount of honey required to win over an opponent. Lisa's boatmen sometimes complained about their hardships, and his partners never fully trusted him. But he was respected, because no one else could ferry people and goods safely up and down the treacherous Missouri like he could. In fairness, it may be said that he entertained no fewer scruples than his rivals; Lisa simply played a better game, and he was a better leader of men.

It's hard to exaggerate how remote St. Louis really was when Lisa finally settled there in 1799. Wilderness lay on all sides, and only a handful of voyageurs had dared venture up the Missouri, Arkansas, or Platte Rivers. No one had a clear picture of the geography drained by the western tributaries of the Mississippi or exactly who lived there. St. Louis in 1799 was a Spanish possession with a largely French population. Brothers Auguste and Pierre Chouteau dominated commerce. Abetted by exclusive trade licenses from the Spanish government, the Chouteaus rested comfortably on their reputation as St. Louis's oldest and richest trading clan. This combination of mystery and monopoly was an irresistible draw for Manuel Lisa.

Lisa had hardly settled in St. Louis before he led an insurgency against the status quo. Unhappy with the Spanish mercantilist policies that gave the Chouteaus trade monopolies with local tribes, he convinced nearly three dozen St. Louis merchants to sign his petition denouncing government licensing. As a lower-class Spaniard, Lisa believed free trade would give small independent businessmen a fighting chance. "We would see industry revive," he wrote. "Speculations would quickly follow one another; and various enterprises would be formed which would tend to regenerate the country and make it flourish." Convinced that he could compete on any level playing field, Lisa pushed with all his might against the rigid social hierarchy of colonial Spain.

Lisa's tilt at mercantilism only earned him a severe rebuke from the Spanish government. Unable to pry open the marketplace, the wily trader angled to swipe the Chouteaus' vaunted trade monopoly with the Osage tribe for himself. The Chouteaus had initially won the franchise by subsidizing a military post near the Osage villages, but they were unable to meet their fiscal obligations, even requesting a government loan to help them supply the fort. Lisa switched from championing free trade to offering his own exclusive services to the Spanish government. In 1802, two years before the Chouteaus' license was set to expire, he petitioned against the Chouteau-Osage alliance and offered generous considerations in exchange for a five-year permit. Proffering his boundless love for the Spanish crown, he promised to build a flour mill for the good of the community and coyly offered a thousand-dollar "gift" to the royal treasury. His protestations of love and patriotism, lubricated with hard cash, persuaded officials to take away the Chouteaus' monopoly and award it to the upstart Lisa.

Louisiana's transfer to France in 1800, and then to the United States in 1803, radically changed the commercial rules of engagement. The Americans ended the practice of licensing and sponsored official military explorations, led by Lewis and Clark, Zebulon Pike, and others, to chart out the potential roads, resources, and markets of the upper Missouri and Arkansas River country. Lewis and Clark's triumphant 1806 return from the Pacific Coast in particular set new speculative fires alight in Lisa's imagination.

Experienced and well connected, Lisa next organized daring new ventures into the unknown. In 1807 he drew fire from the new American governor, James Wilkinson, for launching an illicit trading expedition to Santa Fe. (Perhaps forewarned of Wilkinson's wrath, Lisa called the venture off.) At the same time, he began outfitting a voyage up the Missouri River to the Rockies. Hiring some fifty or sixty men, including several experienced Lewis and Clark men, as guides, the St. Louis merchant and his partners loaded two keelboats with trade goods and equipment. He imagined building a string of permanent trading forts secure enough to defend his employees and their wares from Indian raids in the heart of Indian country. Except perhaps for John Jacob Astor, no American had imagined trading on such a continental scale, and none—not even Astor—had yet risked so much or gone so far.

Setting out in April 1807, Lisa personally led the expedition past the Arikara and Mandan villages of North Dakota and into the Crow and Blackfeet homelands. His very presence threatened to upset the delicate economic balance between the Indian traders of lower

Missouri villages and their upstream customers. Marshalling all his skill at bluster and diplomacy, Lisa forged lasting trade alliances. He alternately distributed presents to willing headmen and threatened force to intimidate tribes who challenged his passage. Under his supervision, the company built Fort Raymond, named after Lisa's newborn son, at the confluence of the Bighorn and Yellowstone Rivers in present-day Montana.

Lisa's success made it easier to secure capital for a second expedition. With the enterprising Spaniard at their head, St. Louis's leading merchants organized the St. Louis Missouri Fur Company, attracting local power brokers such as Benjamin Wilkinson (brother of the first American governor of Louisiana), Reuben Lewis (brother of the then-current governor, Meriwether Lewis), William Clark, and the Ste. Genevieve lead mining magnate Andrew Henry. After careful consideration, even Lisa's old enemy Pierre Chouteau signed on.

Backed by St. Louis's most powerful families, Lisa ascended the river again in 1809. This time the company included thirteen keelboats and more than 300 men, including French voyageurs, Delaware and Shawnee hunters, and American riflemen and traders. The Missouri Fur Company built new posts and returned the Mandan chief Shehaka, long blocked by his Indian enemies downriver, to his North Dakota home.

Thomas James, an American soldier of fortune who captained one of the keelboats, recorded his surprise and resentment at meeting a Spaniard with such drive and enterprise. In his account, "Liza [sic] and some of his colleagues lorded over the poor fellows most arrogantly, and made them work as if their lives depended on their getting forward with the greatest possible speed." Unused to Lisa's driving pace— matched by that of the expedition's fierce French voyageurs—many of the Americans employees remained surly throughout the journey.

The Missouri Fur Company established new forts in today's Wyoming, near the headwaters of the Missouri in Montana, and across the Continental Divide. Their trip was unprofitable. A costly fire consumed one post, destroying thousands in furs and supplies. Lisa's trapping parties faced constant resistance from the Blackfeet, who opposed virtually all American incursions into their territory. Blackfeet warriors hunted Missouri Fur Company trappers wherever they could find them, often mutilating the dead and selling their horses, equipment, and pelts to the Hudson's Bay Company. On one occasion, they captured and stripped Missouri Fur Company employee John Colter, ordering the naked mountain man to race for his life. The desperate Colter outran the Blackfeet; his subsequent eleven-day al fresco hike to Lisa's trading post entered the legends of the mountain men. By 1810 Lisa realized that unlocking the immense wealth of the Rockies required more capital and supplies than St. Louis traders could marshal. Lisa beat the bushes for new suppliers, traveling to Detroit, Montreal, and Philadelphia. Unsuccessful, he gloomily conceded that the company would be unable to provide its posts with trade goods and equipment for the 1810–1811 season.

At this vulnerable moment, John Jacob Astor struck. The New Yorker sent agents to St. Louis to prepare for a leap across the Continental Divide to the Columbia. The deep-pocketed Astorians drove up wages and prices for goods, and they got a head start over Lisa's hastily-organized rival expedition. Lisa used every trick he knew to hinder the Astorians, attempting at one point to serve an arrest warrant on the Astorians' interpreter. Failing that, the wily trader exploited his knowledge of the Missouri's geography, using shortcuts and sniffing out calm eddies to snatch a few hours here, a few miles there, to make up for his opponents' lead.

Certain that Lisa intended to forge ahead in order to turn the upriver Indians against them, the Astorians drove on, ignoring Lisa's implorations for them to wait. For his part, Lisa drove his oarsmen on, sometimes keeping them at work deep into the night. He asked no less of himself, taking turns at the oars, guiding his boat by the stars, feeding his *engagés* Herculean meals to keep their strength up, and leading them in song to maintain their spirits. After sixty days of chase, the two groups combined.

Perhaps Lisa realized that Astorians could fulfill his desperate need for horses and supplies. Better to work together on good terms to ensure peaceful travel through potentially hostile territory. The leader of the Astorians concluded otherwise. Lisa only wanted to catch up, he believed, in order to forge ahead and rile up unfriendly Indians.

The combined economic might of the St. Louis bourgeoisie was not enough to compete with Astor. Although the Missouri partners considered an alliance with the New York magnate, they instead kept him at arm's length. But then, neither had they much use for Lisa. When the Missouri Fur Company reorganized in January 1812, Manuel was removed from the board of directors. Investment capital dried up in the face of rumors of approaching war with the British, which meant British-influenced Indians would be hostile. The directors disbanded the Missouri Fur Company in January 1814.

Lisa was the only active trader on the upper Missouri during the War of 1812, defying his former partners by continuing to operate under the Missouri Fur Company banner. But wartime hostility of the upper Missouri tribes, encouraged by British agents, caused him to close his advance posts. From his remaining base at Fort Lisa, near Council Bluffs, Iowa, Lisa served as a United States Indian agent, successfully encouraging local tribes to launch war parties against the British and their Indian allies. Lisa spent much of the later 1810s rebuilding his lost empire, eventually reopening trade as far as the Mandan villages, near today's Stanton, North Dakota. By 1816 the trader again advertised in St. Louis newspapers for investors seeking to profit from trade ventures beyond the Platte River. Conditions had improved enough by 1818 that Lisa was actively planning new posts beyond the Missouri headwaters.

A sudden illness struck Lisa on his way back from a Missouri trading expedition in the spring of 1820. His prodigious energy flagged rapidly. On August 12, 1820, Lisa perished "without distressing struggles." Lisa's passing left a void in the fur trade that remained unfilled until the emergence of the Rocky Mountain and American Fur Companies in 1822. Yet even in death, Lisa's impact was profound. The St. Louis trader was among the first Americans to exploit the vast beaver country at the foot of the Rockies, successfully building an extensive trade network without the deep reserves of an Astor. He had risen from practically nothing, shouldering aside St. Louis's trading elites to become one of the Gateway City's leading citizens. As an Indian agent, he fought to protect Native American land rights, and he earned the respect of his Indian clients. Lisa trained a cadre of traders who carried on his legacy for another generation. And perhaps most importantly, his ventures aided the young United States. Lisa's outposts strengthened American claims to lands contested by Spain and Great Britain, and he supplied goods and information to government explorers such as Lewis and Clark and Zebulon Pike as they charted the boundaries of America's new western territories.

Lisa's restless enterprise left behind few physical monuments. Heavily leveraged in order to continue expanding, the Spanish trader was always exceedingly generous when providing for his retired and disabled employees. Nearly everything he had acquired was sold off to pay his outstanding debts. Instead, he left behind a model business strategy for others to follow. Certainly not without controversy, his early enterprises nevertheless succeeded through his energy, organization, and leadership skills.

Chittenden, Hiram. *The American Fur Trade of the Far West*. 2 volumes. New York: F.P. Harper, 1902.

Clark, William. Manuscript Collection. Missouri Historical Society.

Douglas, Walter B. *Manuel Lisa,* annotated and edited by Abraham P. Nasatir. New York: Argosy-Antiquarian Ltd., 1964, 1911.

James, Thomas. *Three Years Among the Indians and Mexicans*. St. Louis: Missouri Historical Society, 1916.

Lisa, Manuel. Papers. Missouri Historical Society.

Oglesby, Richard E. *Manuel Lisa and the Opening of the Missouri Fur Trade*. Norman: University of Oklahoma Press, 1963.

Pike, Zebulon M. *The Southwestern Journals of Zebulon Pike, 1806-1807*. Edited by Stephen Harding Hart and Archer Butler Hulbert. Albuquerque: University of New Mexico Press, 2006.

WILLIAM HENRY ASHLEY

REINVENTING THE FUR TRADE {1778–1838}

Politics, not the fur trade, was William Henry Ashley's greatest love. Ashley's direct involvement in the Rocky Mountain Fur Company, which he founded with his longtime business partner Andrew Henry in 1822, lasted fewer than ten years. Yet few nineteenth-century entrepreneurs made such a profound impact in so brief a time. Between 1821 and 1825, Ashley rewrote the several-centuries-old playbook for gathering furs from Indians across the North American continent by transforming his industry's business structure. His innovations revived the stagnant American fur industry and made the chronically insolvent Ashley a fortune, while opening up previously unknown regions of the West and whetting interest in future Western settlement and economic development. Biographer Richard M. Clokey described Ashley as a "shrewd and inventive entrepreneur" who revolutionized the fur trade through creative adaptation to the logistical challenges posed by the Rocky Mountains. Ashley, writes Clokey, "rationalized the industry in ways which forecast later American efforts to conquer the distances and exploit the resources of the western third of the North American continent."

William Henry Ashley was born around 1778 into an undistinguished Virginia family. No one knows for certain the exact year or place of his birth. His biographer surmises that "what fragmentary information survives about the Ashleys" suggests that William Henry's father was simple man who left little record behind. Although possessing only a rudimentary formal education, Ashley learned to express himself well in written English, which he combined to advantage with his natural talents in math and bookkeeping, surveying, map making and geology, riding, and shooting—all useful skills for his profession, even if they lacked the polish necessary to join the ranks of Virginia's landed elite. In his teens, Ashley apprenticed as a "mechanic," but, it has been speculated, work as an apprentice craftsman or tradesman may not have offered enough opportunities for advancement for the intelligent, ambitious Virginian. Ashley was hardly the first aspiring young man of his generation to look beyond the Piedmont for new opportunities. In 1798, at the age of twenty, he left Virginia's tobacco economy behind to seek his fortune out west.

Little in Ashley's physical description evoked a sense of destiny. His biographer, Richard Clokey, described him as he would have appeared when he first reached Missouri in 1802: "Now twenty-four years of age, he was of medium height, perhaps five feet nine inches tall, and of slight build, no more than one hundred forty pounds in weight. Only a prominent, aquiline nose and firm chin distinguished his ordinary features." Socially awkward, stiff, reserved, distant, graceless, and self-disciplined, he developed few close relationships, even among lifelong friends. Such characteristics may have hindered him socially, but this same formality made Ashley a natural leader of men. He climbed through the officer's ranks of the Missouri militia, ultimately reaching the rank of brigadier general in 1821. For the rest of his life, he proudly bore the title "General Ashley."

Whatever his future prospects, Ashley initially struggled in the West. Having failed in a farming venture in Kentucky, and lured by promises of free land and mineral rights in Spanish Louisiana, Ashley settled in the lead mining country around Ste. Genevieve, Missouri, in 1802. Source of the first far western mining boom, lead provided important raw material for shot, paint, and building materials. Over the next twenty years, the versatile entrepreneur launched forays into lead mining and trading, surveying, land speculation, and merchandising. Speculation in saltpeter mining and gunpowder manufacturing generated short-term profits during the War of 1812. But it also brought disaster when explosions demolished Ashley's factory on three separate occasions. By 1821, Ashley was in deep financial trouble, with $100,000 (or more than $2 million in 2014 dollars) in debts to show for his nearly twenty years as a Missouri businessman. Yet despite his setbacks, he had built valuable social capital, rising rapidly through frontier Missouri's social and political ranks as a reputable businessman, a good credit risk, a popular militia officer, and, by 1821, lieutenant governor of Missouri.

In 1819, Ashley moved his base of operations from the moribund Ste. Genevieve mining district to St. Louis. He launched his first fur trading venture soon after. Founded as a fur trading depot by partners Pierre Laclède and Auguste Chouteau in 1764, St. Louis still bore strong marks of its French and Spanish Creole founders. Through the efforts of the powerful Chouteau family, supplemented by the enterprise of the swashbuckling merchant Manuel Lisa, St. Louis had blossomed as the gateway to the Rocky Mountain fur and hide trade. Lisa's Missouri Fur Company followed a time-tested fur trading prototype by instituting a trading monopoly with the Hidatsa, Arikara, and Mandan villages of the upper Missouri River and establishing fixed trading posts as far away as the headwaters of the Missouri and Columbia Rivers.

Although the fur trade had languished in the general depression following the War of 1812, the 1820s saw a new surge in fur prices, driven by increased demands for beaver fur hats and fur coats in the East and Europe, and by the closure of the last of the ineffectual "factory" trading posts established by the federal government to regulate prices in 1795. Ashley and his partner, Andrew Henry, consequently entered the business in a time of intense rivalry. No fewer than five St. Louis firms wrestled for control of the Great Plains and Rocky Mountain trade while, from Canada, the Hudson's Bay Company offered stiff competition. The Blackfeet tribe of the Northern Rockies opposed all American incursions into their territory, and other tribes on the mountains and plains alternated between resistance and accommodation to the poaching of their trading prerogatives.

Ashley's success came through innovation in an already crowded marketplace. In 1822 the popular militia general displayed a spark of recruiting genius by advertising in the *Missouri Republican* for "Enterprising Young Men" to join his venture. Ashley personally interviewed the first batch of candidates, securing several untested young men who ultimately developed legendary careers, including Jedediah Smith, brothers William and Milton Sublette, Jim Bridger, Tom Fitzpatrick, Edward Rose, James P. Beckwourth, James Clyman, David Jackson, and Hugh Glass. Ashley's advertisement also revealed another strategic innovation; Ashley and Henry intended to cut out the Indian middlemen by sending non-Indian trappers directly into the field for terms of one, two, or three years in order to reduce the inevitable markup on furs. Instead of hiring *engagés,* salaried employees supplied by the company, Ashley's Rocky Mountain Fur Company outfitted "skin trappers" on credit in exchange for a percentage of their furs, or negotiated directly with "free trappers" who sold their furs to the highest bidder. This arrangement gave Ashley an edge over his competitors by further cutting his company's overhead and reducing payroll.

Ashley and Henry nevertheless fully intended to follow the established model of building fixed trading posts along the tributaries of the Missouri, establishing Fort Henry at the mouth of the Yellowstone River in 1822. But the partners soon realized that their post was an expensive and indefensible liability, unsuitable for trading with mobile

Indian bands and vulnerable to attack by hostile tribes and rival fur companies. As Ashley and Henry absorbed the logistical realities of their initial scheme, they developed a radical change of plans.

A series of disasters during the Rocky Mountain Fur Company's first two years resulted in far more red ink than black. One of the company's supply boats sank to the bottom of the Missouri River, taking down $10,000 worth of trade goods (worth about $204,000 in 2014). Meager returns from Fort Henry and multiple desertions further drained Ashley's credit. Blackfeet Indians attacked several companies of mountain men. And worse, the Arikara Indians of the Missouri River, alarmed at the impact of the American interlopers on their future as fur trade middlemen, killed fourteen members of a resupply expedition on June 1, 1823, closing off the upper Missouri to trade. In response, Ashley sent explorers into the interior West seeking alternate overland routes to the Missouri River highway. The 1824 discovery of South Pass across the Continental Divide by Ashley's new partner Jedediah Smith opened an overland road to the Pacific and allowed Ashley to move the heart of his operations from the Great Plains to the Rocky Mountains.

One final innovation further revealed Ashley's improvisational genius. Unwilling to carry the logistical costs of expensive new trading posts beyond the Continental Divide, Ashley arranged for his trapping brigades to gather at a set point in the mountains to exchange their beaver pelts for supplies and luxuries. The rendezvous system, where trappers remained in the mountains year-round, meeting an annual suppliers' caravan at what amounted to a mobile trade fair, revolutionized the fur business. The rendezvous removed the need for expensive fortified posts in the mountains, provided trappers with ready access to supplies, and usually kept them in debt to their suppliers. For a brief time, until beaver prices and populations crashed in the 1830s, the system made fortunes for Ashley and his successors. Ashley claimed that his four years in the Rocky Mountain fur trade netted more than $200,000 (almost $4.8 million in 2014 dollars), although he also claimed that business expenses absorbed two-thirds of the profit.

Although personally lucrative, Ashley's direct supervision over fur gathering operations was relatively brief. In 1826 he sold the Rocky Mountain Fur Company to the partnership of Jedediah Smith, William Sublette, and David Jackson for $16,000 ($389,000 in 2014), paid in beaver pelts. Although he continued to do business as a supplier, Ashley had learned enough about the trade to acquire a more complete understanding of its risks and rewards relative to production and supply. Perhaps, as fur trade historian David J. Wishart has observed, the intuitive Ashley noticed early on the potential long-term "vortex" that loomed when intense competition and overhunting precipitated the collapse of the Rocky Mountain beaver population.

The historian James P. Ronda observed that, as one of America's oldest industries, the fur trade was a significant harbinger of global capitalism. "Long before railroads and extractive industries like agriculture, ranching, and mining made the West part of the international marketplace, the fur business transformed the economic and human geography of the region," introducing people, goods and marketplaces to the North American West on a "vast scale." Consequently, Ashley's innovations properly allow us to remember him as a "giant" in the fur trade. Successfully merging his business and military experience, Ashley recruited, supplied, and organized corps of young men, led them into previously unknown parts of the interior West, and brought commodities out to a global marketplace. As an explorer and pathfinder, Ashley's impact on the settlement of the West far outreached his own direct involvement. His commercial need to understand the geography of the central Rockies in order to better compete against both British and St. Louis rivals transformed Ashley into a first-rate explorer in his own right. Under the command of the versatile Jedediah Smith, Ashley's enterprising young men filled in many of the blank spaces remaining on American maps. Ashley and Smith kept meticulous records and maps on expeditions that led Ashley to the Green River country and Smith across the best transcontinental wagon route in America and later to the Sierra Nevadas, California, and Oregon. Other Rocky Mountain Fur Company employees probed Utah's Great Basin, the Mojave Desert, and the shores of the Great Salt Lake, in the process pioneering thousands of miles of trails reaching from St. Louis across the Great Plains to South Pass and beyond.

The discoveries of Ashley's mountain men signified much more than a mere expansion of geographical knowledge. Their stories and accounts of the exceptional beauty and adventure awaiting Americans in the West inspired generations of artists, writers, and potential settlers to think of western expansion in romantic terms. Mountain men guided government explorers across the high passes that penetrated the Rocky Mountains and established the forts and posts later occupied by the military forces assigned to subdue American Indian resistance to American incursions. And, when the fur trade ended, the same mountain men led the vanguard of settlers to Oregon, California, New Mexico, and Colorado.

For William Henry Ashley, though, the ultimate exploration and settlement of the American West remained a chapter for others to write. Following his sale of the Rocky Mountain Fur Company, Ashley dedicated his energy to pursuing elected office. He lost a campaign for governor of Missouri in 1824 but won three consecutive terms for the Jacksonian Democratic Party as a United States congressman, serving from 1831 until 1837. Following a crushing loss in a race for governor in 1836, Ashley retired to real estate speculation. The toll of his collective campaigns as a politician and seminal mountain man caught up with the hard-driving businessman at last. He died of pneumonia at his country home near Boonville, Missouri, at the age of sixty, in March 1838.

Clokey, Richard M. William H. Ashley: *Enterprise and Politics in the Trans-Mississippi West*. Norman: University of Oklahoma Press, 1980.

Dale, Harrison C. *The Ashley-Smith Explorations and the Discovery of a Central Route to the Pacific, 1822-1829.* Cleveland: The Arthur H. Clark Company, 1918.

Dolin, Eric Jay. *Fur, Fortune, and Empire: The Epic History of the Fur Trade in America.* New York: W.W. Norton & Co., 201).

Wishart, David J. *The Fur Trade of the American West, 1807-1840.* Lincoln: University of Nebraska Press, 1992, 1979.

Dollar conversions are based on Bureau of Labor Statistics Consumer Price Index and information from Robert Sahr, Oregon State University.

JOHN JACOB ASTOR

GLOBAL TRADER PIONEER {1763–1848}

In a later era, John Jacob Astor would have been recognized as America's first "tycoon"—a word Americans derived in the 1850s from the Japanese term *taikun,* or "great lord" (a title for the shogun). In the early 1800s, there was no one else in the Republic quite like him. Astor united breathtaking willpower with global vision. He transcended political factions and nationalities to forge an economic empire linking New York, Missouri, and the interior West—as well as Western Europe, Canada, Russia, the Pacific Coast, and China—all in a time when instant communication, or even telegraphs and railroads, were a distant dream. He eclipsed earlier efforts to tie the early Republic's newborn economy into a transnational marketplace. And all of this because of fur.

Born in 1763 in Walldorf, in today's southwestern Germany, Johann Jakob Astor was three when his mother died. Life as the fifth child and youngest son of a neglectful, stubborn, and hard-drinking butcher offered little in the way of hope or comfort. When Johann's father remarried and began a new family, opportunities constricted even more. Johann rejected his father's entreaties to succeed him in the meat-dressing business. Instead, he followed in the footsteps of two older brothers who had left Walldorf to seek fortunes in the wider world. At the age of sixteen, Astor joined his brother George, a prosperous musical instrument manufacturer in London. Anglicizing his Christian name to John Jacob, the young craftsman set his sights on life in America.

Even as a young man, the canny Astor realized that timing meant everything. The American War for Independence made it inadvisable for émigrés—even German ones—to travel to the United States from England. Astor waited for peace, finally chartering passage to America in November 1783. No sooner had Astor's ship arrived at Baltimore in February 1784 than winter weather locked it in Chesapeake Bay ice. Because the shipping company was obligated to provide room and board to its passengers until the journey ended, the story goes, young J.J. Astor remained aboard for more than a month, until curiosity drove him to gather his belongings and walk ashore over the frozen bay. Astor didn't linger in Baltimore long. His older brother Henry, a former Hessian soldier deployed to America during the Revolution, ran a butchering and meat delivery business in New York City. Although J.J. was a seasoned meat carver, he chose instead to pursue other ventures, selling a consignment of George Astor's flutes, peddling cakes and baked goods, and ultimately scrounging New York's wharves for good bargains on furs. An apprenticeship with New York furrier Robert Brown exposed J.J. to the complexities of the fur trade. He learned to distinguish between different grades of fur and began his own pelt-dealing enterprise.

Astor's furs and his musical instruments, such as pianos and flutes, supplied highly desirable culture to luxury-seeking New Yorkers. He developed connections with overseas agents, including his brother George, to attract venture capital and acquire trade goods. And he traveled through the backwoods of New York and Pennsylvania, trading flutes and other musical novelties along with more utilitarian items to Mohawk and Seneca fur providers, and establishing connections with a wider Euro-American supply network. At first the future multimillionaire scrounged for capital. His brother Henry reportedly refused a loan request, but offered to give J.J. $200 (about $5,000 in 2014) if he pledged to never ask for money again. By 1787, the year the United States adopted the Constitution, Astor had learned enough about the fur trade to understand that America's meager commerce paled in comparison to that of the big Canadian corporations. Eager to learn more, he traveled to Montreal to meet with Alexander Henry, a legendary frontiersman and principal partner of the opulent Northwest Company.

Founded in 1783, the Northwest Company had made immediate inroads into the territory of its older rival, the Hudson's Bay Company. Its far-flung network of traders and oarsmen spanned vast reaches of Canada, the Great Lakes, and the upper Mississippi River valley, filling Montreal warehouses to the bursting point with hides and pelts. To learn more, Astor traveled as far west as the Northwest Company post at Michilimackinac, located on the hinge between Lakes Michigan and Huron. From that remote post, he could gaze west into the immense, virtually untapped hunting grounds of America's mountains and plains.

Astor used his contacts and knowledge to establish a fur exchange reaching from Montreal and New York to London and Rotterdam, where a fur selling for three dollars ($75 in 2014) could buy a musket worth ten beaver skins when traded to an Iroquois hunter. And still, he was only just beginning.

Astor thought enough of his own success to commission a portrait from America's celebrated artist Gilbert Stuart. The image shows a stocky, sharp-featured young man with a face set in good-humored determination. White hair powder hides his straw-blond hair. In time, prosperity would add heft to his frame and the addition of jowls would soften his pointed nose and chin. Young or old, he never lost the lively, liquid intelligence of his large brown eyes. Contemporaries described his intensely competitive nature, his tolerance for risk, and his rigid self-discipline. Speaking with a soft German accent, he exerted a forceful projection of will and vision.

Astor could not be constrained to trans-Atlantic trade; his aspirations were global. Among his remarkable traits were an ability to accept terrific risks and to transcend political factions—Federalist and Republican—in his desire to create transnational economic systems. The Napoleonic Wars of the early 1800s closed European ports and threatened American ships on the high seas. Closer to home, President Thomas Jefferson's 1808 Embargo Act, intended to withhold trade from all belligerents, dried up commerce altogether. Yet Astor forged ahead, diversifying his investments to minimize risk, outfoxing the U.S. government by cloaking trade communications inside official diplomatic correspondence. Astor lost no time in lobbying Jefferson to support an audacious plan to establish a base on the Pacific coast of North America. Astor planned to circumvent the European crisis, facilitate trade with Russian Alaska, and, most importantly, open a potentially lucrative trade route to China.

During the 1790s, Astor had noted the success of Boston ship owners who developed a lucrative triangular trade linking American manufacturers with Pacific Northwest sea otter furs and Chinese luxury goods. By 1810, Astor profited from a small fleet of China ships. Now he planned to build a permanent base at the mouth of the Columbia River to supply sea otter furs to China. As the businessman likely explained to a sympathetic Thomas Jefferson during an 1808 meeting, a permanent commercial center on the Pacific coast had important geopolitical implications. It would anchor American involvement in the China trade and signal to the British that the Pacific Northwest lay firmly in America's sphere of influence. In time, Astor's persuasion won Jefferson over. Writing in 1812, the former president recognized Astor's genius for planting "the germ of a great, free, and independent empire on that side of our continent."

As it turned out, Jefferson's congratulations were premature.

Historians have pointed out Astor's astonishing tolerance of risk and his patience in seeing a plan through over long periods of time. The attempt to lodge an outpost on the western edge of North America in 1810 required both. If a ship's luck held, the outbound trip took six months from New York to the mouth of the Columbia River and involved sailing around the southern tip of South America. After trading their cargo for furs with the sometimes-unpredictable Pacific Northwest Native American tribes, traders hazarded their pelt-laden ships on a trans-Pacific voyage to China, followed by another long trip through the Indian and the Atlantic Oceans to reach home. Success required a careful navigation of the politics, pretensions, and rivalries of England, Russia, Spain, Chile, China, the United States, the Kingdom of Hawai'i, and countless tribes along the Pacific Coast. The alternative overland route offered similar perils, passing up the Missouri River, through the heart of Arikara, Crow, Flathead, Shoshone, and Blackfeet lands, and into the jealously guarded Hudson's Bay and Northwest Company domains of the northern Rockies.

Investors such as Astor had to wait as long as eighteen months, or perhaps two years, before learning the fate of their investment. And in the case of Astoria, Astor's visionary settlement on the Pacific coast, the initial news was almost all bad. Astor sent off two expeditions in 1810, one overland via the Missouri River and a second by sea around Cape Horn. The seaborne leg resulted in virtual catastrophe. Eight sailors from the *Tonquin* perished during an ill-advised attempt to cross the bar of the Columbia River. Then, after offloading Astor's agents and their gear, the *Tonquin* was destroyed, and nearly all if its crew killed, in an avoidable conflict with the native residents of Vancouver's Clayoquat Sound. The remaining Astorians were left stranded on a distant shore.

Astor's overland company fared somewhat better. The overland Astorians struggled through deep mountain snows and down the treacherous Snake River to reach the Columbia. Their arrival at Astoria with the loss of only three men in January 1811 was celebrated as a minor miracle, and the arrival of a supply ship further raised spirits. But, just as it looked as if Astor's immense global gamble was beginning to pay off, war extinguished the Astorians' hopes. Informed of the outbreak of the War of 1812 by agents of the Northwest Company, the managers of Astoria sold the trading fort and its contents at a tremendous discount rather than face eviction by a British warship. A few fur-laden ships made the trek to China, softening Astor's losses. But Astoria's loss to the British deferred American claims to the Pacific Northwest for another generation. Astor's dream of a transcontinental trading empire faded—for a time.

Confronted with the news of the *Tonquin*'s loss, Astor reportedly reacted with characteristic stoicism: "What would you have me do," he asked of a friend who expressed surprise at his lack of emotion. "Would you have me stay at home and weep for what I cannot help?" His ability to absorb setbacks and transform them into long-term gains was a legendary component of his success. This resilience allowed him to rebound for a second act.

The entrepreneur spent the rest of the 1810s consolidating his commercial foothold in the Great Lakes. Even as the war raged on, J.J. smuggled Canadian furs into the States and slipped contraband goods into Europe under the flags of England's allies. Responding to the pleas of his good friend and fellow immigrant, Secretary of the Treasury Albert Gallatin, Astor also underwrote the American war effort, loaning millions from his wartime profits and thumbing his nose at both sides by selling U.S. war bonds in London. Naturally, Astor profited from inside war information obtained through both Gallatin and President James Madison.

As a young immigrant in New York in the 1780s, John Jacob Astor had scrambled to secure enough capital to finance his modest ventures. By the 1820s he had become the richest man in America— the country's first multimillionaire. Following the War of 1812, the financier aggressively consolidated his position in the Great Lakes pelt trade, driving out competitors and establishing a monopoly for his American Fur Company. Secure in the Great Lakes, Astor relaunched his visionary venture in the American West.

Astor's involvement in the far western fur trade was late compared to the efforts of St. Louis's venerable Chouteau family and others. But the New Yorker came on strong, hiring veterans of Canada's Northwest Company to oversee the newly-created western branch of the American Fur Company and negotiating exclusive business agreements with some potential rivals, while competing ruthlessly with others in order to corner the market. In the 1820s and 1830s, J.J.'s *engagés* built scores of new trading posts. They flooded the market with low-priced trade goods carried up the Missouri River aboard another new innovation introduced to the Far West by Astor's men, the steamboat. They wooed free trappers with sweetheart offers for their furs (at least initially) and provided generous doses of alcohol to lubricate relations with Indian clients.

In Astor's American Fur Company, the western fur trade entered an age of imperial corporate enterprise. Like governors of distant provinces, Astor's agents ruled over life and death from St. Louis to the Shining Mountains in the 1820s and 1830s, conducting diplomacy with potential Indian customers and literally making war on rivals. Like a head of state, Astor commissioned peace medals adorned with his likeness for distribution among friendly Indians. The Missouri River, mountain men joked, had become Astor's "private creek."

Mountain men had some cause to feel sour as they experienced the squeeze of the American Fur Company's domination. Having absorbed initial losses to drive their competitors out, once they had the field to themselves Astor's traders increased their prices for supplies and reduced their offers for pelts. Indians complained about their dependency on American Fur's liquor and expensive goods, while free trappers, and even company employees, expected to end their careers in debt to the monopoly. Trapped in a cycle of debt, Indians and mountain men alike sought out the refuges of the dwindling Rocky Mountain beavers with even greater intensity.

Ever sensitive to the changing fortunes of his enterprises, Astor, as usual, led the field in predicting the crash of beaver prices after 1830. Changing European fashions, with silk replacing beaver as the material of choice for stylish hats, and the rise of a furry South American rodent called the nutria as a cheap alternative to beaver were two reasons for the decline. But both conditions were precipitated by the virtual elimination of beavers from western creeks, streams, and ponds. Astor noted the shift as early as 1832, predicting a decline in prices for pelts. By 1833 the canny businessman ended his involvement in the fur business. Beaver pelts, so recently celebrated as "brown gold" that drove the initial economic development of the frontier West, crashed along with beaver populations the same year.

John Jacob Astor died just short of his eighty-fifth birthday, in March 1848. Not all of his considerable wealth—assessed at between $20 million and $30 million dollars (roughly $588 to $882 million in 2014)—came from trading furs. J.J. shrewdly reinvested his peltry profits in Manhattan real estate and other lucrative schemes. In the West, his enterprises provided essential infrastructure for military posts and transportation networks, while his employees retained a wealth of knowledge that would help future explorers and settlers find their own way into the West.

Not all of the American Fur Company's accomplishments were laudable; the fur trade arguably hastened the decline of American Indian tribes in the West by introducing disease, alcoholism, and dependency. Yet Astor and many of his descendants also deployed the proceeds of their fur-bearing fortune to build a formidable philanthropic legacy. John Jacob himself established the Astor Library, the forerunner of today's New York Public Library. Astor's grandson John Jacob III bolstered the library, supported hospitals and a children's aid society, and lavished the Metropolitan Museum of Art with objects and monetary gifts. Brooke Astor, the wife of J.J.'s great-great grandson, Vincent, became known as the "First Lady of Philanthropy" for her prodigious charity over her 105-year life.

Dolin, Eric Jay. *Fur, Fortune and Empire: The Epic History of the Fur Trade in America*. New York: W.W. Norton & Co., 2010.

Madsen, Axel. *John Jacob Astor: America's First Multimillionaire*. New York: John Wiley and Sons, 2001.

Stark, Peter. *Astoria: John Jacob Astor and Thomas Jefferson's Lost Pacific Empire*. New York: HarperCollins, 2014.

THE BENTS AND CERAN ST. VRAIN

COMMERCE ACROSS CULTURES

{1799–1847}   {1809–1869}   {1802–1870}

Charles Bent, William Bent, Ceran St. Vrain (pictured, left to right, above) were more than romantic fur traders and mountain men. They were visionaries who understood the way to open the West was not to make war with the natives but to trade with them. Bent's Fort, their sturdy outpost in the unsettled West, and the links of commerce and friendship that radiated outward from it, opened the region to new ways of life. Charles and William Bent and Ceran St. Vrain blazed trails that became lifelines for overland immigrants. They helped strengthen American claims to the West by breaking down the Native American and Mexican barriers to American expansion. Though their fort flew the Stars and Stripes, they were not primarily agents of the United States government, but of free enterprise. The success of their trading ventures demonstrated that the American capitalist system was destined to extend its influence beyond the borders of the growing nation.

Charles Bent and his younger brother, William Wells Bent, came from hardy stock of patriotic and enterprising Americans. Their great grandfather, John Bent, had loaded a wife and five children aboard the brig *Covenant* to flee England under Charles I, leaving behind oppressive ship-levy taxes. He settled in the colony of Massachusetts in 1638, helping to hew the new town of Sudbury out of the forest west of Boston. John Bent's son Silas was reputed to have been among the parties of "Indians" who dumped English tea into Boston Harbor and fought in the Revolutionary War with the Minutemen. Feeling the call of the frontier, Silas joined 280 other veterans as members of the Ohio Company of Associates, which purchased 1.5 million acres of land on the northern bank of the Ohio River. Silas's share entitled him to 1,173 acres of land.

His son Silas, Jr., moved to Charleston, Virginia (now West Virginia), where he opened a store and married Martha Kerr, ten years his junior. They eventually had eleven children, including Robert and William. In 1805 Silas was appointed to the post of principal deputy surveyor in the Louisiana Territory. He later served as justice of the Court of Common Pleas, a position which brought Bent and family to St. Louis. Bent then ascended to judge of the Supreme Court of the Louisiana Territory. In these prestigious positions he gained favor with the influential French establishment, which generally did not smile on American newcomers. Bent's sons grew up amid the wheeling and dealing and excitement of St. Louis, the gateway to the West. Young Charles got his first taste of frontier commerce when he joined the Missouri Fur Company, where he became a clerk by 1824 at the age of twenty-five years.

Until 1821, the War Department regulated commerce with the western tribes, issuing stringently limited licenses to individuals and then competing with them at government posts called factories. Lobbying from John Jacob Astor's well-capitalized American Fur Company pressured Congress to junk the factory system in 1822, leading to a frenzy of competition by private parties. Astor's company, independent French traders, and others poured into the Rocky Mountain region seeking a share of the lucrative beaver trade, driven by European demand for hats made from the animal's prized pelts. The outmatched Missouri Fur Company was driven into bankruptcy. In 1825 former Missouri Fur Company manager Joshua Pilcher created a new company, Pilcher and Company, to re-enter the fray. Young Charles Bent joined as one of Pilcher's partners, adding his proven ability to raise investment capital from St. Louis connections.

For every successful fur trading outfit, many failed. Expenses were high, and the requirement of extending credit in the form of traps, powder, blankets, tobacco, and alcohol to Native American tribes, who actually procured the pelts, made for a risky investment. An 1831 report on the fur trade made by the War Department to Congress concluded that "the whole operation . . . is laborious and dangerous, full of exposures and privations, and leading to premature exhaustion and disability. Few of those engaged in it reach an advanced stage of life, and fewer still preserve an unbroken constitution. The labor is excessive, subsistence scanty and precarious; and the Indians are ever liable to sudden and violent paroxysms of passion, in which they spare neither friend nor foe." The Bent brothers would prove among the elite few who could rise above the privations and challenges of frontier trade.

Charles Bent soon left Pilcher's crew to work the Santa Fe Trail for himself. In March 1829 Charles and his brother William outfitted a caravan of trade goods bound for New Mexico. After successful commerce in Santa Fe, the brothers returned to St. Louis, their wagons loaded with a lucrative haul of beaver pelts, buffalo hides, blankets, and Mexican silver. On their second foray over the Santa Fe Trail in 1829, they brought $200,000 worth of goods from St. Louis—a capital investment that dwarfed the $7,712.82 raised to launch Pilcher and Company. The Bent brothers' initial success had brought financial backing and a new partner, whom the Bents had met on the trail in the winter of 1827–1828: Ceran St. Vrain.

Ceran St. Vrain was born Ceran de Hault de Lassus de St. Vrain—a name befitting the aristocratic background of his parents, French loyalists who fled the Revolution. As a young man, Ceran heard the intriguing talk of traders and trappers coming and going through his hometown of St. Louis. In 1824 he hired on with an early trading caravan to Santa Fe led by William Becknell, who had first opened trade between New Mexico and Missouri following Mexican independence from Spain in 1821. Between 1824 and 1831, St. Vrain made almost annual trips bankrolled by St. Louis merchants. After their successful 1829 journey together, he became friendly with the Bent brothers. In 1831 they incorporated as Bent, St. Vrain and Company.

By then a momentous decision had already been taken by the youngest member of the company. On the second 1829 caravan, William left the group to head into the mountains, where he trapped and traded with Indians. William realized the key to success in the fur trade lay in developing a more reliable trade with the Indians. Few Euro-Americans had yet developed good relationships with Indians. Yet Native Americans wanted friendship and peace as encroaching American settlements and the increasingly aggressive federal removal policy threatened their way of life. The Cheyenne and Arapaho, who had been pushed west into Colorado around 1800, welcomed William Bent's overtures. He further endeared himself with the Cheyenne by rescuing two of them from Bull Hump's attacking Comanches. This act of good faith gave Bent access to the Cheyenne and their world. He eventually introduced them to St. Louis trade goods, building their interest in trade and their loyalty to him.

William convinced his partners to build a trading fort, which would give them a great advantage on Santa Fe Trail traffic. He consulted their allies, the Cheyenne, about the best location for such a structure. Yellow Wolf, a chief of the Hairy Rope Clan, advised them to put it out on the plains, near the Big Timbers, an area close to the hunting and trading ranges of the Cheyenne, Arapaho, and other Plains tribes. Bent, St. Vrain and Company followed Yellow Wolf's advice and built on the Arkansas River near its confluence with the Purgatoire River. They built their fort of adobe, employing Mexican adobe makers for the purpose, and opened for business in 1834.

As the first permanent Anglo-American settlement in the central plains region, Bent's Fort was formidable. Its front wall, which faced travelers approaching from the east, spanned 137 feet. The northern and southern walls were 178 feet long, and the adobe walls of the fortress were three feet thick. The fortress walls towered fifteen to thirty feet high, creating an intimidating presence. An American flag fluttered proudly overhead.

Bent's Fort saw many storied figures of the West pass through its gates. As a teenager, Christopher "Kit" Carson, later a famous scout and Indian fighter, worked on lumber crews building the fort. Explorers, trappers, and traders such as James Beckwourth and "Uncle" Dick Wootton were frequent visitors.

The famous fort became the center of a western trading empire with no equal in the Southwest, although Astor's American Fur Company dominated the Northwest. Bent's Fort thrived on cross-cultural alliances, cooperation, and interdependence. Changing fashions meant that in October 1833 beaver prices in St. Louis dropped from $6 per pound to $3.50. This made buffalo pelts—and relations with Indian hunters who were expert in their hunting and preparation—all the more important. William Bent understood this, taking as his wife Owl Woman, the daughter of prominent Cheyenne chief White Thunder. William, like other successful fur traders, knew that Indian wives were essential. They help bond traders with their tribes and could do the hard work of preparing animal skins for market. Following Cheyenne custom, Bent would later marry the sister of Owl Woman after her death. Charles Bent married a New Mexican, Maria Ignacia Jaramillo of Taos. This diplomatic move strengthened the Bents' alliance with the New Mexican power elite.

One of William Bent's four children with Owl Woman, George Bent, grew up at the fort. He described the patterns of trade and multicultural tolerance that enabled the Bents and St. Vrain to succeed:

> My father used to send some of his best traders down to New Mexico—to Santa Fe and Taos—with wagonloads of goods. They brought back from New Mexico horses, mules, cattle, Mexican blankets, silver dollars, silver bullion in bars. I remember as a boy seeing the wagons come in with their loads of bright colored blankets. The Indians prized these blankets with their stripes of bright coloring very highly, and a good blanket was traded at the fort for ten buffalo robes. The silver, horses, mules and cattle, were taken to Missouri and sold. One good mule or horse was traded for two broken-down ones; the broken-down animals were then taken to the fort and kept until they were in good shape again, then they were taken up to the Platte and traded again to the emigrants. I remember several of the traders who were employed at the fort in the early days . . . all good men who could speak Spanish and were experts in the Indian sign language, which was most used in trading with the tribes.

Bent, St. Vrain and Company often ignored the finer points of federal law, borders, and military procedure, operating instead like medieval lords, cultivating intricate systems of duty and reciprocity within a global system of markets and capital. They accepted the customs of their native customers and partners. Horse thieving, for example, was accepted; possession conveyed valid title and the operators of the fort did not question where animals brought to them in trade had come from. The Bents brought with them from Missouri the "peculiar institution" of slavery. William and Charles Bent brought three

African American slaves from St. Louis to work in their households: the brothers Andrew and Dick Green, and Dick's wife Charlotte, who served as a cook. She famously declared herself "the only lady in de whole damn Indian country." It is unlikely that the Bents' Indian trading partners found slavery peculiar: they sometimes kept Mexicans or captives from other tribes as virtual slaves.

By the end of 1832, Ceran St. Vrain and Charles Bent had opened a business house in Taos while William Bent supervised trade at the Fort. In 1838 the company expanded its reach to the north with the construction of Fort St. Vrain at the confluence of the South Platte River and what is now called St. Vrain Creek. Ceran St. Vrain, overseeing the Taos end of the company's business, had become enmeshed in Mexican society and accepted Mexican citizenship in 1831. As the Mexican government sought to keep a hold on its sparsely settled territorial claims in northern New Mexico (including parts of present-day Colorado), it assigned land grants to willing citizens, but found few takers due to well-justified fears of Indian attacks. St. Vrain's experience and ties with the tribes left him with no such hesitation, and he received a lucrative land grant in 1844.

The Mexican-American War brought an American coup at Santa Fe in the summer of 1846 by Colonel Stephen Watts Kearny. Southern Colorado and northern New Mexico passed into American hands, and Charles Bent was appointed governor of New Mexico territory on September 22, 1846. A resentful Mexican population revolted on January 19, 1847. A crowd came to the governor's door. Bent tried to reason with the rebels, but they killed him in front of his wife and children. Ceran St. Vrain erased any doubts about his loyalties when he recruited and helped lead a volunteer force that marched from Santa Fe to stop the rebels. St. Vrain claimed to have personally shot and killed rebel leader Pablo Chavez, who was wearing Charles Bent's shirt and coat. St. Vrain focused on New Mexico interests for the remainder of his life, establishing early flour mills and cattle ranches, and increasing the size of his land grant through strategic litigation. He died in Santa Fe on October 28, 1870.

The army granted William Bent the title of colonel for supplying and guiding U.S. troops during the Mexican-American War. Around 1847 his wife Owl Woman died. In 1849 a cholera epidemic swept through the Cheyenne people, cutting the tribe's population in half and decimating Bent's relations through marriage. After the war with Mexico the fur trade fell off so precipitously that maintaining Bent's Fort became unprofitable. The War Department offered to buy it, but Bent found their price unsatisfactory and blew it up in the fall of 1852 instead. Bent continued trading from a new, much smaller outpost he built of stone some thirty-five miles downriver from the old fort. He did a lucrative business as an Indian agent for the government, hauling annuities for tribes at a good price and returning to West-port, Missouri (now Kansas City) with wagons full of buffalo robes and other goods. He sold the newer fort to the government in 1859, but continued to make a profit outfitting gold rush emigrants to the Rocky Mountains and selling products from his prosperous farm at Westport. He died in 1869.

The trade center at Bent's Fort was the zenith of a short-lived culture of economic collaboration between African American, Anglo-American, Mexican, French, and various Native American partners. Children of the community acquired a special set of skills, including familiarity with a range of cultures, languages, hunting, trading, and business practices. This gave them special advantages. This cross-cultural business and social network did not survive the end of the fur trade and the beginning of United States dominance. The non-white kin, employees, and trading partners of Charles Bent, William Bent, and Ceran St. Vrain would not be welcome in the new communities that succeeded the benevolent fiefdom of Bent's Fort. But the men of Bent, St. Vrain and Company had shown free enterprise could transform relations between disparate peoples.

Bent, Charles, 1799-1847. Letters to Manuel Alvarez, 1837 December–1846 June. Denver Public Library Western History and Genealogy Department.

Broadhead, Edward H. *Ceran St. Vrain: 1802-1870.* Pueblo, CO: Pueblo County Historical Society, 1987.

Comer, Douglas C. *Ritual Ground: Bent's Old Fort, World Formation, and the Annexation of the Southwest.* Berkeley: University of California Press, 1996.

Dick, Herbert William. *The Excavation of Bent's Fort, Otero County, Colorado, 1954.* Denver, CO: 1956. Reprint from *The Colorado Magazine,* v. 33, no. 3, July 1956.

Hafen, LeRoy Reuben. *Bent's Fort on the Arkansas.* Denver: Colorado State Historical Society, 1954.

Hyde, Anne. "Transients and Stickers: The Problem of Community in the American West." In *A Companion to the American West,* ed. by William Deverell. Malden, Massachusetts: Blackwell Publishing, 2004, pp. 304-328.

Hyde, George. *Life of George Bent: Written From His Letters.* Norman, Oklahoma: University of Oklahoma Press, 1983.

Lavender, David Sievert. *Bent's Fort.* Garden City, NY: Doubleday, 1954.

Moore, Jackson W., Jr. *Bent's Old Fort: Archaeological Study.* Denver: Colorado Historical Society & Pruett Pub. Co., 1973.

Mumey, Nolie. *Bent's Old Fort and Bent's New Fort on the Arkansas River.* Denver: Artcraft Press, 1956.

St. Vrain, Ceran. Ceran St. Vrain Papers, 1848–1947. Denver Public Library Western History and Genealogy Department.

West, Elliot. *The Contested Plains: Indians, Goldseekers, and the Rush to Colorado.* Lawrence, Kansas: University Press of Kansas, 1998.

AGRICULTURE AND LIVESTOCK

BRIGHAM YOUNG

MAKING THE DESERT BLOOM {1801–1877}

The résumé of Brigham Young reads like the wish list of a great man: founder of Salt Lake City; governor of Utah; and president of America's largest home-grown religion, The Church of Jesus Christ of Latter-day Saints. Young had a knack for combining the corporate with the spiritual and an absolute gift for organization. His planning, together with the enthusiasm of his followers, turned Utah desert land into a booming agricultural center. He was the most successful colonizer in the American West, the spiritual leader of an enduring international religious community, an empire builder who confounded the United States government, and the chief executive officer of a thriving corporate concern.

In his youth, Brigham Young displayed adaptability and independence. Like many of the West's pioneers, Young came from humble beginnings. He was born in 1801 in Vermont, the ninth of eleven children. His father, John Young, was an itinerant laborer and farmer who never found economic success. Brigham chopped, ploughed, and picked on the many farms his father worked in New England and New York. The family could not afford much formal education for their children, but theological learning was widely available. They lived in upstate New York, which in the 1820s was a hotbed of evangeli-cal Protestant fervor. Like many Americans during the Second Great Awakening, the Young family embraced evangelical Protestantism. Several of Brigham's brothers were Methodist preachers, but Brigham explored many denominations without making a commitment. He at last decided to join the Methodist church, but perhaps simply so that people would stop bothering him about choosing. He married his first wife in 1824 and began a life that did not portend greatness.

Young's early career as an artisan was generally unremarkable, although the future religious leader developed many practical phys-ical skills. Even when he reached the peak of his power, he contin-ued to enjoy working with his hands. As an apprentice, Young learned about business by watching others and then doing for himself. Craft apprenticeships were a common path to self-sufficiency for young men in early nineteenth-century America. He trained as a carpenter, painter, and glassmaker. He also learned cabinetmaking, basket mak-ing, masonry, and the crafts of boat and house building. These trades would help him understand the material requirements of the empire he would later administer.

Eventually, Young established a mill on his father's land, near Rochester, New York, that used water power to turn a lathe. His wood staircases and mantelpieces still grace the homes of people in the area. That some of this work yet stands is a testament to his focus on quality. He was also reputed to be an expert gardener. Young displayed both great skill and an interest in learning during his early working years. Despite these attributes he experienced little financial success.

Young revealed hidden managerial talents once he joined the Church of Jesus Christ of Latter-day Saints, better known as the Mor-mon Church, founded by Joseph Smith in 1830. Young converted in 1832 along with many of his family members. The new religion faced scrutiny, and even outright hostility, for its unorthodox views. Smith directed his followers west, first to Ohio, then to Missouri, and finally to Nauvoo, Illinois, to escape persecution. During that period, Young rose to the leadership of the Quorum of Twelve Apostles, a governing body in the church and the group in charge of missionary work. The insular, tightly organized Mormons aroused the ire of their new neighbors at each stop, and an angry mob killed Smith while he awaited trial for treason in Nauvoo. Young emerged as the new leader of the fledgling church after a brief succession crisis in 1844. He prepared the remaining Saints for a quick exodus to what was soon to become Utah Territory, where he would execute Smith's idea of creating a new Zion in the Rocky Mountains.

The migration of more than 15,000 Mormons on the approximately 1,000-mile trek from Illinois to Utah required incredible organizational skills. Young had to overcome several obstacles. First, the migration had to happen quickly. Joseph Smith's murder hardly quelled hostility against the remaining Mormons, and the new threat of federal action against them made it clear that they could not stay long in Illinois. Second, the Mormons needed supplies to support a concentrated mass exodus across the Rockies. Third, they would have to start building a sustainable city from scratch once they arrived. It seems as if Young had a solution for nearly every crisis he confronted.

Before starting, Young appointed a small group of men to sell the Nauvoo church and family properties. Traveling parties then formed in military fashion. Fifty families comprised large units, and those units were separated into companies of ten families with a captain at the head of each. Most traditional migrants going west did not set out until early spring, but Young sensed danger and launched the exodus in February 1846. The early travelers established a winter camp near present-day Omaha, Nebraska, in 1846–1847. Young supervised the construction of a gristmill and coordinated a mail service that connected families over several hundreds of miles. He also organized aid and relief teams to help those on the journey. He ensured order and survival in harsh conditions, and the thousands of Mormons who reached the promised land in Utah felt they owed their lives to their master organizer.

Once the immigrants arrived in the Salt Lake Valley in 1847, Young set them to work building a city. He laid out the streets, chose the place for the temple, planned defenses, and even erected four of the first log houses himself. After seeing that everything was underway, he returned east to escort the other parties.

One of the cleverest decisions Young made at this time was to direct other Mormon leaders to find ways to attract federal government support for the western migration. A non-Mormon, Thomas Kane, suggested asking President James Polk for permission to raise what became known as the "Mormon Battalion." Young convinced 500 young men to enlist in the U.S. Army, which needed soldiers on the western frontier. The U.S.-Mexico War (1846–1848) was a great opportunity to improve relations with the federal government and to earn hard cash for the church by supplying ready recruits. The United States, in a certain sense, partially paid the Latter-day Saints to help settle the West.

After the Mormons settled in Utah, Young continued to direct the growth of the church and its empire, known among the Saints as Deseret. He became the official successor of Smith as both prophet and president. Growth was an important aspect of the church's success. Young enacted several plans to increase membership. Missionaries found willing converts as far away as Europe. Most lacked the money to immigrate, so Young established financing through the Perpetual Emigrating Fund. Immigrants were expected to repay the loan from the fund so that future immigrants could borrow from it. The program favored people with the skills most needed in the new western territory.

Young also established satellite colonies, both inside and outside Utah, that answered to his central authority and helped to sustain the church's growth. He planned four types of colonies, each with a specific purpose. One type aided immigrants on their journey to Utah. Another supplied raw materials such as iron and coal. The third coordinated efforts to proselytize Indians. The fourth consisted of farming communities. Mormon colonies spread into California, Nevada, Idaho, Colorado, and elsewhere.

Young clearly had an instinct for economic opportunity. Although America contracted gold fever not long after the Saints arrived in the Salt Lake Valley, Young discouraged mining. Why scatter when the Mormons had recently established safety in Utah? Why devote resources in what amounted to a high-risk game of chance? Instead, the Mormons grew wealthy from selling supplies to prospectors crossing the Great Basin. Salt Lake City became a commercial capital in the wilderness, offering flour, meat, and fresh beasts of burden in exchange for cash, tools, clothing, worn-out livestock, and heirlooms that emigrants wished to discard. The gold rush provided the Mormons with a great economic boon without the corresponding problems of permanent non-Mormon settlers. When the architects of the transcontinental railroad needed laborers to build through Utah, they came to Young. Eager by the 1860s to secure a rail link to the larger world, the church leader complied. But when the Union Pacific bypassed Salt Lake City for Promontory Point, Young learned another bitter lesson about dealing with non-Mormons.

Railroads posed both an opportunity and a threat to Young's carefully crafted economy. Outside merchants overcharged Mormons, and challenged Young's economic hegemony in Utah. In response, the church leader encouraged LDS merchants to band together in church-supported cooperatives. Young founded the Zion's Cooperative Mercantile Institution, one of America's earliest department stores. The ZCMI sold goods to Mormons at the best possible prices and shared the profits with the LDS community. If his followers only purchased goods from other Mormons, then the outside investors would gain little power within the system, and even stood to fail.

In more recent histories, Young's legend has become somewhat tarnished. His decisions during the Utah War (1857–1858) exposed him as sometimes brash, short-tempered, and overly aggressive. Young had managed to build an autonomous micronation within the United States, in which non-Mormon federal appointees, such as territorial judges, were stripped of their power. The doctrine of plural marriage—revealed publicly in 1852—was badly received by the mainstream Christian community. Young married fifty-five wives over the course of his life, just as he had also married church and state together in his new Zion. It was unacceptable to most Americans. Constituents begged President James Buchanan to fight what some political leaders called "those twin relics of barbarism, polygamy and slavery." Buchanan decided to act against the Mormons, considering them a softer target than slavery. He dispatched several thousand troops to Utah to install new judicial appointees and a new territorial governor. The Mormons believed they were under attack. Young declared martial law and sent out the militia, known as the Nauvoo Legion. LDS forces skirmished with federal troops, harried military supply lines, and destroyed government property. Federal soldiers retaliated by destroying Mormon property. Hysteria peaked in September 1857 when LDS militiamen disguised as Indians besieged and killed approximately 120 members of an Arkansas emigrant train bound for California. Negotiations finally ended the conflict, and Young's actual role in the Mountain Meadows Massacre and its aftermath remains controversial and questionable. However, Young lost the governorship but retained his leadership in the church.

Brigham Young died in August 1877 at the age of seventy-six. This visionary remains an influential, if controversial, figure. Few nineteenth-century leaders matched his leadership skills and business acumen. Demonstrating a steely resolve in the face of virtually insurmountable political, economic, and logistical challenges, he led his people into a desert—and made the desert bloom. As a religious leader, he incubated, organized, and sustained a thriving American-grown church. As a corporate executive, he helped to build railroads, roads, businesses, and farms, supervising prosperous settlement and commercial activity from the Great Salt Lake to southern California, and from Oregon to Mexico. This complex figure was generous to his followers and friends and could be very determined with his enemies. His pragmatism on nearly all occasions was a major asset, one that allowed him to skillfully expand his vision into actual reality.

Arrington, Leonard J. *Brigham Young: American Moses.* New York: Knopf, 1985.

Bagley, Will. *Blood of the Prophets: Brigham Young and the Mountain Meadows Massacre.* Norman: University of Oklahoma Press, 2002.

Bigler, David L. and Will Bagley. *The Mormon Rebellion: America's First Civil War, 1857–1859.* Norman: University of Oklahoma Press, 2011.

Turner, Joseph G. *Brigham Young: Pioneer Prophet.* Cambridge, MA.: Harvard University Press, 2012.

CYRUS H. M^cCORMICK

AND THE "WONDERFUL MACHINE" {1809–1884}

"You Yankees are ingenious fellows. This is a wonderful machine."
Otto von Bismarck, commenting on a McCormick reaper, 1896

Looking west from Monticello in 1803, Thomas Jefferson envisioned a virtuous farming republic. The seemingly boundless North American interior, he predicted, would one day host vast fields of wheat, producing enough food and providing enough land to protect every American from starvation and want. Jefferson himself switched from tobacco to grain farming in the 1790s. By the time of his death in 1836, wheat was Monticello's primary crop. Considering the available technology of the time, Jefferson made a realistic prediction. Wielding a then-state-of-the-art cradle scythe, a skilled farmhand took all day to cut a one half to three quarters of an acre of wheat. At that muscle-powered rate, Jefferson estimated, it would take a thousand years to settle the American West.

As it turned out, a fellow Virginian, Cyrus H. McCormick, perfected and marketed a machine that helped prove Jefferson wrong. Contrary to myth, McCormick's device was not the first to successfully mow large quantities of wheat and other grains. Yet by the late 1800s, Americans and Europeans alike hailed his reaper as the machine that tamed the plains. Walking, then riding, alongside one of McCormick's horse-drawn reapers, two semi-skilled laborers gathered as much wheat in a day as a farmhand had previously harvested in two weeks. And harvesting only became more efficient from there.

Reapers and steam railroads powered the juggernaut of western settlement. By the time of the Civil War, Secretary of State William Seward estimated that reapers pushed back the American frontier at a rate of thirty miles per day.

Jefferson's guess about the rate of western settlement seemed perfectly reasonable in 1803. For more than three millennia, harvesting technology advanced at a caterpillar's pace. Farmers relied on their own muscle power to cut and harvest wheat. A skilled laborer with a scythe mowed just enough to feed himself during harvest season. Since wheat ripened all at once, it required large gangs of workers to cut a moderately-sized field. Medieval farmers sped the process up with two-handed scythes. The only other significant improvement came in 1794, when a Scottish farmer added a toothed cradle to gather grain stalks into bundles.

To be sure, inventors tinkered with mechanical prototypes long before McCormick first introduced his Virginia Reaper in 1831. More than thirty reaping machines chewed up English and Scottish fields prior to that year, and British inventor and divinity student Patrick Bell exported reapers to the United States and Australia by the 1830s. But for persistence and marketing savvy, no one had yet seen the likes of McCormick.

Born in 1809 the son of a Scots-Irish farmer-inventor, Cyrus subscribed to old-time Presbyterianism and the Protestant work ethic. Agriculture historian Craig Canine describes him an "intense, severely sober man." Standing six feet tall, with piercing dark eyes, a prominent nose, a thick beard, and an unruly thatch of dark hair, McCormick impressed people with his gravity. His attorney credited McCormick's "terrible" willpower for his success. The businessman neither smoked nor drank alcohol, and he was not known for his idle chatter. Business matters so occupied him that he delayed marriage into his fifties. His family motto, "Without Fear," Canine writes, "was engraved deep in his bones."

Like many backcountry settlers, McCormick's father Robert dabbled in a little bit of everything, operating flour and sawmills, a distillery, a smelter, and a blacksmith shop. A mechanical reaper of his own design failed to subdue the steep and rocky fields of Virginia's Blue Ridge Mountains. Cyrus unveiled an improved version, a "right smart curious sort of thing" in the words of one eyewitness, in 1831. The horse-drawn device consisted of a canvas-covered platform fronted by a series of teeth and a blade. A flimsy-looking paddle wheel pushed wheat stalks against the blade, severing them onto the platform. A family slave, Joe Anderson, walked alongside raking the cut stalks onto the ground for collection. Witnesses deemed McCormick's initial demonstration somewhat less than successful. The reaper cut six acres of oats in less than a day, which was good. But it left the field looking like a tornado had hit it.

Cyrus might have moved on to other endeavors, like his father, except for the arrival of competition. Providence provided McCormick with a nemesis in the form of Maine-born Obadiah Hussey, a one-eyed former whaler and prolific inventor. Hussey's entry into the reaper business in 1833 brought McCormick racing back from a side project. The southern farmer's son and the seafaring New Englander engaged quite literally in head-to-head competition, purchasing advertisements denouncing each other's product and racing each other through demonstration fields in order to prove whose mower had the cutting edge. Hussey was one of more than 200 competitors who crowded the field (and fields) in the 1840s and 50s. Their cutthroat competition forced McCormick to improve his design. He added a seat, allowing farmers to ride instead of walk and speeding up the harvesting process from a walking pace. McCormick introduced labor-saving components for gathering stalks into sheaves, binding them with wire or twine, drying them, and threshing out the wheat kernels. By 1880, his salesmen claimed that all farmers had to do was sit behind the horses in comfort and arrange for delivery to the miller.

In time, McCormick's reapers became small assembly plants, pioneering the way to industrialized farming.

McCormick further combined farm and factory when he relocated to Chicago in 1847. It was obvious to McCormick, and nearly everyone else, that the wide-open plains, divided into flat, treeless homesteads, were the perfect arena for harvesting machines. Some thought the entrepreneur's selection of the emerging lakeshore city for his new factory was a curious choice—why not Pittsburgh or Cincinnati, which both had stronger manufacturing bases? McCormick's decision was nevertheless inspired, because Chicago was about to boom. Stockyards, canals, a railway line, grain depots, the telegraph, and a board of trade all emerged in the Windy City by 1848. By 1851 McCormick's production had tripled to almost 1,500 units.

High crop yields enticed thousands of Americans to try their luck at farming in the 1850s, and again following the Civil War. Abundant land, strong urban demand for farm products (bolstered by rising immigration rates), and an acute rural labor shortage made conditions nearly perfect for mechanical production. Railroad expansion helped, opening previously inaccessible farmlands. Assisted by railroads and mechanical reapers, total American farm acreage grew by 315 percent between 1850 and 1890, from under 1.5 million acres to more than 4.5 million. Not coincidentally, urban growth increased even faster. McCormick's machines fueled the American industrial dynamo by freeing up agricultural labor and providing grain to feed the former farmhands now taking up urban jobs.

Such a lucrative field attracted eager competition, but McCormick thrived on beating competitors through creativity and persistence. Critics hailed his Chicago factory as a marvel of automation, mass production, and steam technology. He wrote his own aggressive advertising copy, dropping in detailed testimonials from satisfied customers and inserting illustrations showing potential buyers how his contraption would improve their lives. He seized every opportunity to showcase his devices at national and international exhibitions. This strategy reaped rewards when European heads of state hailed his invention as one of the most important in history. The Virginia Reaper even stole Great Britain's industrial thunder, beating out British models to win a Council Medal for outstanding inventions at London's 1851 Crystal Palace Exhibition. Back home, scores of commission agents positioned themselves as farmers' friends, explaining how the new-fangled devices worked, offering demonstrations at county fairs and in town squares, organizing festive (and often rigged) head-to-head competitions with rivals, supplying spare parts and service advice, taking orders, arranging payment plans, and collecting debts.

The latter two services were especially significant. With a ticket price of more than $100 (about $2,700 in 2014 dollars), a reaper represented the largest purchase many western farmers ever made. McCormick devised several innovative strategies to entice buyers to purchase more with less. He introduced revolving credit and gave farmers the option of paying $115 in cash, or $120 in installments. He sweetened the offer by providing the nation's first money-back guarantee. For $30 down, farmers could test a reaper for six months. If they liked it, they paid the remaining amount. If not (and after they had harvested their crops), they sent the reaper back. McCormick also litigated aggressively over patent infringements—no patent controversy was too trivial to receive his full attention.

It's not an exaggeration to call McCormick's reaper transformative. Historians routinely compare it to Eli Whitney's cotton gin, which sped up the separation of cotton fiber and seeds and helped revitalize slavery in the early 1800s. Both the gin and the reaper mechanized labor-intensive tasks, and both drove explosive western expansion. Business historian Henry W. Brands has called the American Civil War a competition between Eli Whitney's slave-based model for agriculture and Cyrus McCormick's world of yeoman farmers. Advocates on both sides believed that their labor-saving technology would free farm workers to fight on the battlefield, and both prayed that their exports—northern grain or southern cotton—would sway European sympathy in their favor. Secretary of War Edwin M. Stanton predicted that wheat would win the war:

> By taking the place of regiments of young men in the western harvest fields, it releases them to do battle for the union at the front and at the same time keeps up the supply of bread for the Nation and the Nation's armies. Thus, without McCormick's invention, I fear the North could not win and the Union would be dismembered.

Indeed, northern grain exports helped keep Europe neutral, while helping fund the Union war effort. It's no small irony that Whitney, the New Englander, despised slavery, while McCormick, a Virginian, favored the Confederacy.

As profound an invention as the reaper was bound to draw controversy for its inventor. Farmers who condemned Gilded Age inequities of capital and debt criticized McCormick's use of commissioned salesmen to hawk his products because it cut farmers out of the savings they would have enjoyed from buying direct from the factory. One might also argue that his stratospheric acceleration of farming technology set the stage for overproduction, leading to the catastrophic collapse of wheat farming during the 1930s. Yet none of that seemed inevitable when Cyrus McCormick died in 1884. Under his son, the McCormick Harvesting Machine Company merged with several smaller companies to form International Harvester (today's Navistar International Corporation) in 1902.

When McCormick was born in 1809, more than nine out of every ten Americans lived on farms. Three out of every four Americans still called rural America home when he demonstrated his first harvester in 1831. In 1900, after a half-century of explosive agricultural expansion, the ratio of rural to urban residents was three to two. By 1920, urban residents outnumbered farmers and ranchers for the first time. The great irony of McCormick's technology was that it unlocked huge reaches of the American West for agricultural development that ultimately supported larger numbers of city dwellers. This integration of farm and factory was one of the unsung achievements of western expansion.

Brands, Henry W. *Masters of Enterprise: Giants of American Business from John Jacob Astor and J. P. Morgan to Bill Gates and Oprah Winfrey*. New York: The Free Press, 1999.

Canine, Craig. *Dream Reaper: The Story of an Old-Fashioned Inventor in the High-Tech, High-Stakes World of Modern Agriculture*. New York: Alfred A. Knopf, 1995.

Casson, Herbert N. *Cyrus Hall McCormick: His Life and Work*. Chicago: A.C. McClurg & Co., 1909.

Cronin, William. *Nature's Metropolis: Chicago and the Great West*. New York: W.W. Norton & Company, 1991.

Hutchinson, William T. *Cyrus Hall McCormick*. 2 volumes. New York: Da Capo Press, 1968; Appleton-Century, 1935; The Century Company, 1930.

McCormick, Jr., Cyrus. *The Century of the Reaper: An Account of Cyrus Hall MacCormick*. Boston: Houghton Mifflin Company, 1931.

Thwaites, Reuben Gold. *Cyrus McCormick and the Reaper*. Madison: State Historical Society of Wisconsin, 1909.

CHARLES GOODNIGHT

CATTLE, FORTUNE, AND HONOR {1 8 3 6 – 1 9 2 9}

"Better [to] lose your fortune than your honor." Charles Goodnight

Part scout, part frontiersman, 100 percent cattleman, Charles Goodnight had no equal among his peers. The gruff, leathery stockman all but invented the open-range cattle industry, blazing trails from Texas to Colorado, Kansas, and Wyoming for millions of cattle, and providing some of the first Texas herds to stock the northern plains. Goodnight opened new western markets and developed innovative cattle breeding and herd management techniques that improved the overall quality of western cattle. He established major ranches in Colorado, New Mexico, and the Texas Panhandle, organized enduring cattle raisers' associations, and introduced more efficient range management techniques. Unable to read or write, he nevertheless thrived as a born entrepreneur with an iron constitution and a pragmatic outlook just as hard and unforgiving as his western Texas homeland. He became one of the most important originators and developers of the West's thriving cattle industry.

Goodnight was born in 1836, the year of Texas Independence, on a family farm in Illinois. Charlie's father died when the boy was five, and his mother married a neighboring farmer. The family went to Texas in 1845, soon after the United States annexed the republic. In Texas, his mother left her abusive second husband for a minister.

Charlie consequently absorbed a more-or-less religious upbringing. He avoided drinking and carousing, even as he picked up the gritty vocabulary of his trade. Those who knew him praised his integrity. A child of Texas, he possessed the racial prejudices of his region and generation. Yet he was scrupulously honest, he despised hypocrites, liars, and religious bigots, and he learned to value individual African American and Mexican cowhands for their character and expertise. He was a merciless enemy to Comanches, Kiowas, and cattle rustlers who threatened his herds. In later years, he became sentimental toward vanquished foes, and he always respected his opponents even as he drove them into the ground. Most of all, Goodnight subscribed to a rigid code of honor. He stood on his principles, and he was ready to fight any man, at any time, to defend them.

At the age of eleven, Goodnight hired his labor out to nearby farms. Small and lithe, he took to the saddle, becoming a natural roper and rider. He worked briefly as a professional jockey when a teenager, although that avocation's connection to liquor, vice, and gambling soon turned him against the profession. Charlie received only a few months of formal schooling. Of more value were the lessons of an elderly Caddo Indian who taught him to hunt and track. He rounded out his teenage years driving freight wagons and occasionally supervising plantation slave gangs.

In 1857 Goodnight started west with his stepbrother, John W. Sheek, to try his luck in California. The pair turned back after receiving an offer to raise cattle on shares in the Cross Timbers, a wooded area near the Brazos River dividing the eastern Texas prairie from the western plains. Goodnight and Sheek signed a ten-year contract to tend 400 head of cattle. In exchange they received permission to brand one quarter of each year's calves as their own.

Taking up stock raising, the twenty-one-year-old cowboy ventured into a business as old as the first European settlement of the Americas. The first English cattle arrived in Jamestown in 1611. Over the centuries, drovers moved their herds westward across the Appalachians. Southern cattle raisers blended English techniques with the knowledge of their experienced African slaves and the skills of Spanish *vaqueros* they encountered on Louisiana's coast. Spanish ranchers, proficient with the horse and lariat, first trailed cattle north from Mexico in 1598. The Anglos readily adopted Spanish terms and practices, adding words such as "rodeo," "lariat," "lasso," "cinch," "corral," and "buckaroo" (a corruption of *vaquero*) to their vocabulary. They also crossbred English longhorns with Spanish cattle to create the Texas longhorn breed. Tough, wiry, and stringy, the longhorns survived in a nearly wild state on the Texas prairies and plains. Ranchers favored them for their hardiness, even if consumers found their beef a little tough to chew.

In the Cross Timbers, Goodnight also met his most important future partner, Oliver Loving. Born in 1812, the forty-five-year-old Loving operated a store, owned a few slaves, and ran more than a few head of cattle. The experienced, enterprising former Kentuckian made a good living driving herds east to New Orleans and Missouri. In 1860 Loving hired Charlie to help deliver a thousand head of cattle to the Colorado gold mining towns. Goodnight's own herd also continued to expand. By 1860 his first calves had matured enough to ship to market.

A long period of frontier unrest in the late 1850s and early 1860s temporarily derailed Goodnight's progress. Comanche and Kiowa warriors increased their efforts to push back the leading fringe of Texas settlement, sowing devastation among the unfortunate settlers who pushed too far onto the western plains. Charlie joined the Texas Rangers as a scout and guide to fight back against the Indians' depredations. When the Civil War erupted in 1861, his company was absorbed into the Texas Frontier Regiment.

Goodnight never fought Yankees directly. He spent the war crossing and re-crossing the arid Llano Estacado, the infamous "Staked

Plains" of western Texas, in pursuit of rustlers, outlaws, and Indian war parties.

Goodnight's term of enlistment expired in 1864. The cattleman went home to assess the losses accrued during his long absence. Four years of war had left the Texas cattle industry in shambles, while former markets in New Orleans and Missouri lay in ruins. Corrupt government officials, dishonest neighbors, and starving Indians drained stock away from everyone's ranches. Neglected cattle overran the open range, and no one really knew which new yearlings belonged to whom. Yet in the postwar chaos enterprising ranchers such as Goodnight recognized new opportunities. If he could round up a herd from the overcrowded range and bring it to market, the Texas steers would provide a ready food supply for his former Yankee foes. A steer selling for less than ten dollars in Texas could bring twenty-five dollars or more in Chicago or Kansas City. After 1865, the advancing Kansas Pacific and Atchison, Topeka, & Santa Fe rails brought these markets closer to the western range every day. But to get cattle to buyers, cattlemen had to drive their herds along established trails through country populated with bandits and hostile Indian tribes. Besides, Goodnight figured, "all of Texas would head north" to market cattle at the conclusion of the war.

The unconventional rancher instead looked west. Gold and silver miners in Colorado provided a ready market, and the grasslands of Colorado and Wyoming, recently emptied of bison, beckoned as prime cattle raising country. In theory, herds could reach these promised lands over a westerly route along the base of the Rocky Mountains through New Mexico. But no one had yet probed such a risky path. Goodnight nevertheless assembled a thousand longhorns for a staged journey to Colorado. The first leg consisted of a seven-hundred-mile odyssey from Fort Belknap, on the western edge of the Cross Timbers, to Fort Sumner, New Mexico. The route touched Comanche homelands and included a demanding stretch across the Llano Estacado that required a three-day forced march between watering holes. Charlie expected to lose a fair portion of his herd, but the rewards for success were also potentially great. In addition to hosting a U.S. Army garrison, Fort Sumner was the involuntary home of the Navajo Tribe, which had been forcibly removed from its western homelands. The meager farmlands assigned to feed the reservation Indians hardly met their needs. Goodnight intended to sell cattle to both the starving Navajos and to the soldiers who guarded them.

Goodnight pursued this goal with a determination born of necessity and nerve. Perhaps no one was better equipped for the task. Muscular, compact, and only thirty years old in 1866, Charlie had more scouting and trail experience than many seasoned frontiersmen. He knew the Llano Estacado intimately from his time as a Texas Ranger and prided himself on his excellent eyesight and superb trail sense. "I've never had a compass in my life," he stated to a biographer. "But I was never lost."

Still, Charlie couldn't do it alone. Recognizing the need for another experienced trail boss, he invited Oliver Loving into a partnership. Loving added a thousand head from his own herd and provided several veteran cowboys. Goodnight recruited other expert trailhands, including Bose Ikard, a well-respected African American cowboy, to bring his crew up to eighteen. To enhance logistical support, Goodnight reconditioned an old government wagon with seasoned hardwood and iron axles. He designed a cargo box with multiple drawers and shelves and attached a hinged lid that swung down to form a worktable. He stocked the wagon with sugar, salt, flour, a water barrel, plenty of coffee, salted beef and pork, beans, spices, and a jar of sourdough starter he acquired from his mother, and hired a cook to manage his rolling kitchen. It was the first chuck wagon.

Despite intense hardships and the loss of over three hundred cattle, the trek was more than worth the effort. Goodnight and Loving netted $12,000 in gold ($118,200 in 2014), more money than either had ever seen. Loving continued north with eight hundred range cattle, selling them to the prominent Colorado rancher John Wesley Iliff. Goodnight headed south with the gold, intent on purchasing another herd for a return trip. Business grew enough for Goodnight to open a ranch on Colorado's Apishipa River. From this swing station, Goodnight introduced thousands of Texas cattle to the Colorado and Wyoming rangelands, often selling the breeding stock to his sometime-partner Iliff. Irritated by tollgate keeper Richens "Uncle Dick" Wootton's ten-cent-per-head charge to cross Raton Pass, Goodnight found an alternate route across Trinchera Pass to the east. The cattleman suffered a blow when Oliver Loving died from wounds inflicted in a Comanche fight during an 1867 cattle drive. Making good on a deathbed promise to his friend, Charlie honored the partnership for two additional years, sending Oliver's share of the profits to his family and returning the remains of his deceased partner from New Mexico to Texas for burial. Author Larry McMurtry popularized the Goodnight-Loving partnership in his 1985 Pulitzer Prize-winning novel *Lonesome Dove*. The protagonist, a former Texas Ranger named Captain Woodrow Call, is patterned after Charles Goodnight, and many of the novel's incidents are based on actual events.

In 1869 Goodnight partnered with another legendary cattleman, John Chisum, to open the PAT Ranch, near Pueblo, Colorado. Success with the PAT, where he earned a reported 37 percent annual return, allowed the rancher to settle down. Partnering with John Wesley Iliff, as well as Pueblo's banking clan of John and Mahlon Thatcher, Charlie invested in banking, a ditch company, a meatpacking firm, an opera house, and town lots. He became a director of Pueblo's Stock Grower's Bank, serving more effectively on his reputation as an astute businessman than through his minimal reading, writing, and ciphering abilities. He improved his ranch, importing Durham bulls, planting an orchard, and sowing crops. And he somehow found time away from his driving business concerns to marry an aristocratic Kentucky woman named Mary Ann Dyer, known affectionately as Molly. People began referring to the prosperous rancher as "Colonel" Goodnight.

Cattlemen such as Goodnight benefited from public resources by grazing their cattle on gigantic swaths of government rangeland. The free government grass was a huge boon, but the cattlemen still faced several common problems. So in 1871, Goodnight helped found the Colorado Stock Raisers' Association to meet their mutual needs. The association drafted bylaws and a code of ethics, arranged for brand registration and communal roundups, and restricted inferior bulls. More ominously, they warned sheep raisers and homesteaders away from pre-existing cattle ranges and organized vigilante groups to punish cattle thieves. The Colorado Cattlemen's Association, as it is known today, remains a prominent economic and political institution in the state.

The good years in Colorado proved fleeting. In 1873 overstocking on the range, a harsh winter, and a financial panic annihilated herds and investments. Practically broke, Goodnight rounded up his remaining herd of about sixteen hundred head, and he and Molly headed south to start over. Goodnight had his eye on the Texas Panhandle, recently cleared of his old enemies the Comanches and Kiowas. After a layover in New Mexico, he probed the Panhandle for new ranch site. Relying on geographical knowledge he had acquired as a Texas Ranger and following a former Comanchero guide, he selected a promising spot in Texas's Palo Duro Canyon. In 1876 Goodnight built a dwelling complex, "the Home Ranch." Palo Duro Canyon boasted good grass, protection from foul weather, and reliable watering holes. But it was also situated in a remote and virtually unpopulated part of Texas, where bandits, rustlers, and occasional Comanche hunting and raiding parties still prowled. The state legislature had only just organized the area into counties, and Molly Goodnight complained that she had to travel eighty miles to visit her nearest neighbor.

Goodnight's ranch was the first cattle outfit established in the

Panhandle. Yet in Charlie's view, the Texas Panhandle was still not big enough to accommodate both cattlemen and sheepherders. Cattlemen inherently loathed sheep as the "locusts of the plains." Sheep, cowboys claimed, ate grass down to the roots, destroying rangeland, while their sharp hooves caused further damage. Goodnight's cowboys retaliated against these alleged injuries by driving a herd of sheep into a bog, where they drowned. Goodnight paid for the sheep and negotiated an agreement with the neighboring New Mexican sheep raiser, Casimero Romero, in order to avert a war. Romero agreed to confine his operations to the Canadian River drainage, while Goodnight received exclusive use of the upper Red River and its tributaries. Similarly, Goodnight parlayed with the outlaw gang of "Dutch" Henry Born, convincing the bandit to confine his criminal activities north of the Red. He also forged an agreement with the famous Comanche chief Quanah Parker, providing the Comanches two steers a day in exchange for Parker's promise that his warriors would not molest Goodnight's herds. Equipped with the resources, the determination, and the diplomatic skill necessary to enforce his will in the wild Panhandle country, Charles Goodnight was practically a law unto himself.

But even rugged individuals such as Goodnight relied on outside financial assistance. He found a backer in John G. Adair, an Anglo-Irish financier headquartered in Denver. Adair was typical of the English and Scots investors whose venture capital fueled the open range cattle industry in the 1870s and 1880s—by 1886, British investors risked more than $25 million (about $608 million in 2014) on western cattle. A graduate of Trinity College trained for the British diplomatic corps, Adair was known for his explosive temper and undiplomatic manners. He made enemies among Ireland's peasantry by evicting forty-seven families from his County Donegal estate to enhance the view around his private castle. Goodnight and Adair first met on a Colorado bison hunt. Adair shot no buffalo, but he did kill his own horse and badly injured himself when his firearm discharged by mistake. He also entertained Goodnight's pitch about the promising cattle country in Panhandle country. The rancher and the investor entered into a five-year partnership. Adair fronted two thirds of the capital and loaned Goodnight his one-third stake at 10 percent interest. Goodnight received a $2,500 annual salary ($52,687 in 2014) to manage Adair's JA Ranch.

The partnership prospered enough for Goodnight to swallow his misgivings about Adair's character and sign a second five-year agreement in the early 1880s. At its 1885 peak, the JA Ranch covered 1,325,000 acres and contained 100,000 cattle. And as its manager, Goodnight continued innovating. He enforced strict rules against gambling, drinking, and fighting among his cowhands, and he blazed new trails, linking his remote spread to rail lines in Dodge City, Kansas, and Granada, Colorado. He pioneered breeding techniques, improving his already excellent herd through the careful selection and cultivation of Hereford breeding stock. His outfit trained a new generation of cattle industry leaders, and Charlie led them as co-founder and first president of the Panhandle Stock Association. He was reportedly the first rancher to fence in rangeland with barbed wire.

When Goodnight first arrived at Palo Duro Canyon, he discovered a small herd of bison living on his spread, a remnant of the immense Southern Herd—estimated at more than 3 million in 1871—that had once carpeted the Great Plains. Bison had been nearly wiped to extinction in Texas by the 1850s. During the 1870s, commercial hunters launched one of the greatest wild game massacres in history, slaughtering millions of bison to make way for railroads and ranchers. A confirmed cattleman, Charlie had little use for the beasts. But Molly Goodnight realized that without their protection, the bison would soon go extinct. Molly prodded her husband to rope two calves for her to raise. They acquired a few more, building a private herd from seven to 250. Ever the practical rancher, Charlie crossed bison with Angus cattle to create "cattalo"—hardy crossbreeds that withstood winter storms better than cattle and produced more beef than bison. The Goodnights also sponsored early forms of cultural preservation. They hosted buffalo hunts for Goodnight's friend Quanah Parker and his former Comanche enemies. They donated one herd to the Taos Pueblo tribe, supplied others to New York City zoos, and still others to Yellowstone National Park.

Goodnight's success as a corporate rancher carried him far from his humble beginnings. Complicated land development schemes, lawsuits, and fights over leasing rights occupied more of his time than trail drives by the mid-1880s, even as falling beef prices and competition reduced his profits. Drought and blizzards, combined with overstocking and industry-wide financial mismanagement, devastated the open range cattle industry in 1887, forcing him to reduce his holdings.

In that year, Charles Goodnight sold his interest in JA Ranch and went into semi-retirement. He spent his remaining days with Molly in a beautiful two-story ranch house near the town of Goodnight, Texas. The old rancher continued to experiment, suffering losses in Mexican gold and silver mining speculation during the 1890s and testing the commercial possibilities of buffalo, elk, antelope, and other wild herd animals. Along with his wife, he opened Goodnight College in 1898, boarding students at his home and giving them free cowboy lessons to go with their book learning. By now a frontier legend, Charlie opened his home and freely shared his reminiscences about the bygone frontier days with inquiring historians. He died on December 12, 1929 in Tucson, Arizona, having become the most famous and influential cattleman in history, at the age ninety-three.

Dobbs, Emanuel. *Pioneer Days in the Southwest from 1850 to 1879*. Guthrie: Oklahoma State Capitol, 1909.

Flanagan, Sue. "Charles Goodnight in Colorado." *Colorado Magazine* 43:1 (1966), 1-21.

Hagan, William T. *Charles Goodnight: Father of the Texas Panhandle*. Norman: University of Oklahoma Press, 2007.

Haley, J. Evetts. *Charles Goodnight: Cowman and Plainsman*. Boston: Houghton Mifflin Co., 1936.

Rosen, Richard Dean. *A Buffalo in the House: The True Story of a Man, an Animal, and the American West*. New York: New Press, 2007.

JOHN WESLEY ILIFF

WESTERN CATTLE KING {1831–1878}

Most fortune seekers viewed the High Plains as a treeless wasteland to be hurried through on the way to Rocky Mountain gold and silver. Few saw that the prairies could become productive. One pioneer, however, realized that millions of buffalo had thrived there for hundreds of years. He saw the possibilities and ultimately built up one of the West's great ranches, occupying much of northeastern Colorado and part of southeastern Wyoming.

Iliff pioneered large-scale ranching in the West. By providing quantities of inexpensive, wholesome beef, he helped to change the American diet. Whereas only wealthy people could afford beef before the Civil War, Iliff's transformation of the cattle industry and use of refrigerated railroad cars helped turn the United States into a nation of beef eaters. Iliff transformed not only the way Americans eat but also the western landscape, replacing once vast buffalo herds with herds of cattle.

John Wesley Iliff was born December 18, 1831 on a farm in McLuney, Ohio, near Zanesville. His parents, both devout Methodists, named him for that sect's founder. They later sent John, their third child and first son of ten children, to nearby Ohio Wesleyan College, hoping he would become a minister. John focused on science courses instead and dropped out after three years. His father offered him a $7,500 interest in the family farm, which raised cattle, if he would stay. Eighteen-year-old John Wesley replied, "No, just give me $500 and let me go west."

Young Iliff joined a group of migrants headed to Kansas. Along the Oregon Trail they founded Ohio City (now Princeton) thirty miles south of Lawrence. There Iliff established the first store. When news of the gold strikes in what was then western Kansas began flooding the Midwest, Iliff sold out and struck for Denver. Traveling across the vast grassy prairie made an impression on Iliff, especially when he saw fat buffalo grazing.

"July 1, 1859. Arrived Denver City 6 o'clock evening, found much more of a city than expected" wrote the young John Wesley in his diary. Rather than mining, he decided to mine the miners by offering goods they needed. The big Ohioan and two Ohio City friends, Alfred Fenton and David Auld, opened a Larimer Street store near 15th Street. According to the 1859 guide to Denver City and Auraria, *The Commercial Emporium of the Pike's Peak Gold Regions*, they sold "Groceries, Provisions and Clothing." With proceeds from sales, in 1861 John Wesley began buying land along the South Platte in northeastern Colorado. There he started a cattle ranch near the present-day town of Iliff. To stock his ranch, he purchased travel-worn and foot-sore cows for a song from emigrants hurrying to Denver and the diggings.

He turned the weary cattle out to pasture to fatten on the short-grass prairie in the fall and then took a calculated risk. Could the cattle survive the winter eating native grasses that dried and turned into a natural hay? Unsure what he would find the next spring out on the open range, Iliff was delighted to discover most of the cattle fat and healthy, ready for market.

Cattle, as Iliff liked to say, literally raised themselves. And the natural increase in his herds ranged from 70 to 80 per cent. Winter losses to blizzards were usually small and reduced somewhat by Iliff's cow camps and large adobe corrals, where cattle could be sheltered and fed if necessary.

In 1868 Iliff contracted to supply beef to the Union Pacific Railroad construction crews laying track through Nebraska, Wyoming, and Utah territories. Jack Casement's construction gangs consumed huge amounts of meat. To fulfill the UP order, Iliff offered Charles Goodnight forty thousand dollars to deliver ten thousand Texas cattle to his cow camps. Goodnight drove the longhorns up from Texas along the Goodnight-Loving Trail. Roughly paralleling today's I-25, this was the westernmost of the great cattle trails.

Soon Iliff was supplying not only the Union Pacific crews but also Indian reservations and the new railroad boomtown of Cheyenne. Iliff also contracted with former Colorado territorial governor and railroad promoter John Evans to feed the Denver Pacific construction crew building a line from Cheyenne to Denver. Evans paid Iliff $6.90 per hundred pounds of beef delivered. Iliff likewise provided beef for crews building the Colorado Central Railroad from Golden up Clear Creek to the mining towns of Black Hawk, Central City, and Georgetown as well as Union Pacific crews building a line from Julesburg to Denver along the South Platte River route.

To nourish all his cattle, Iliff shrewdly began acquiring land and water rights in northeastern Colorado. Sometimes he bought the land, sometimes he had his cowboys file "dummy" or "hobo" homesteads, which he then bought from his cowhands. The majority of homesteaders failed to stick it out for the required five years and build the required habitation to "prove up" under the 1862 Homestead Act. When they failed or had their homesteads foreclosed upon, Iliff was there to buy up their repossessed or abandoned 160 acres.

By 1878 he owned a ranching empire of 15,558 acres. For as long as homesteaders did not move in with their barbed wire fences, Iliff grazed his cattle on the public domain at no charge. Iliff amassed

herds of as many as 35,000 head. He told the *Rocky Mountain News,*
October 8, 1870:

> I have been engaged in the stock business in Colorado and Wyoming
> for the past eight years. I consider the summer cured grass superior
> to hay. My cattle have not only kept in good order on this grass
> through all eight winters, but many of them left out on the range
> during the winter have become fine beef in the spring. The percent
> of loss in wintering here is much less than in the states where cattle
> are fed on hay and corn. . . . I am confident, from my experience,
> that this trans-Mississippi country can defy all competition in the
> production of wool, mutton, beef and horses.

With his spectacularly successful ranching, Iliff promoted the
American West as a haven for the livestock business. As his beef
empire grew, he expanded and began shipping cattle to the Chicago
Union Stockyards, in which he bought a financial interest. While he
had originally driven live cattle to market, Iliff took advantage of new
technology—refrigerated rail cars—to ship butchered, dressed beef to
distant markets such as Chicago.

Iliff became well acquainted with Colorado water law, which followed the Doctrine of Prior Appropriation. That meant that whoever
first claimed and used any flowing water gained perpetual legal rights
to it. By acquiring water rights and land along the South Platte and its
tributaries, such as Crow and Lodgepole Creeks, Iliff came to dominate northeast Colorado between Greeley and Julesburg. Owning the
flow of the South Platte River and its tributaries gave him virtual control of the drylands beyond. For land without access to water would
not serve well for grazing purposes. The cattle king's strategic holdings
along waterways also gave him grazing access to an estimated 650,000
acres of public domain lands.

Unlike many cowboys, Iliff made it a point to get along with the

Native Americans. Seeing their starving and pitiable condition, he told them to take whatever cattle they needed to feed their families. Although Indians raided a few of Iliff's cow camps, they never molested his main ranch headquarters, Riverside, located in a cottonwood grove at today's town of Iliff. According to many accounts, Iliff smoked peace pipes with native peoples who once reigned over his vast domain and presumably also shared with the tribes his heavy black cigars.

Iliff's system was impeccable. He bought Texas longhorn cattle weighing six hundred to eight hundred pounds for $10 to $15 dollars a head. He fattened them for two years on his vast grasslands, turning them into thousand-pound cattle that sold for $30 to $35 a head. He paid nothing for the grass. His cowhands—thirty-five to forty men during the summer months—got the going rate for cowboys of $25 to $30 a month.

Later Iliff began replacing the scrawny Texas longhorn bulls with improved breeding stock such as beefy Herefords. As an early student of cattle breeding, he also purchased Angus, Durham, and Shorthorn bulls to improve his herd, becoming one of the first to experiment successfully with crossbreed cattle.

Unlike many absentee ranch owners, Iliff personally rode and inspected his empire, checking his herds and getting to know his cowhands. He joined them on cattle roundups, gathering for meals around the chuck wagon and sleeping under the stars. He treated his men well and they repaid him with loyalty—unless they were drinkers. Iliff never touched liquor and forbade his employees to do so, claiming that "cows and whiskey do not mix."

Out among his herds, Iliff recognized that rustlers were becoming a growing problem and fought back by becoming one of the first to brand his cattle and hold annual roundups to count his herds. Iliff also became active in both the Wyoming and Colorado Cattlemen's Associations, organized to deal with rustlers and other industry problems. By the time of his death, Iliff's herd had grown to 45,000. Like other business giants, Iliff strove to control much of the region where he competed. By operating on a huge scale, he could offer his product cheaper and more dependably than most competitors.

John Wesley Iliff, a handsome, respected and successful cattleman, stood over six feet tall, had a muscular build, wavy brown hair, and deep blue-black eyes. His first wife, Sarah (Sadie) Elizabeth Smith, died in 1865, two years after their marriage. Three years later Iliff was attracted to Elizabeth Sarah Fraser, who had come to Denver from Chicago as the Singer Sewing Machine's manager for the western region. He was impressed with her high energy and spunk. She had a storefront in Denver and also peddled sewing machines out of a buckboard. The young woman married Colorado's most affluent and eligible widower in Chicago in 1870, but she herself was widowed only eight years later when the forty-seven-year-old cattle king died of gall bladder complications. Fellow cattlemen eulogized him as "the squarest man who ever rode over these plains."

All over the West, cattle have become a fixture of the landscape. Cowboys have become American heroes and a persistent symbol of America for the rest of the world. Cheap mass-market beef first produced by Iliff and other ranchers revolutionized the American diet. Americans, once eating mostly fish, pork, and chicken, became beef eaters favoring hamburgers for lunch and steak for dinner. Thanks to pioneers such as Iliff, refrigerated cars, and cheap beef, the livestock industry has become a financial mainstay of many western states.

Milligan, Edward W. "John Wesley Iliff." In *The Denver Westerners Brand Book,* 1950. Denver: Denver Posse of Westerners, 1950, pp. 43-60.

Noel, Thomas J. *Riding High: Colorado Ranchers & The First 100 Years of the National Western Stock Show.* Golden: Fulcrum Publishing Co, 2005.

Peake, Ora Brooks. *The Colorado Range Cattle Industry.* Glendale, CA: The Arthur H. Clark Company, 1937.

Spring, Alice Wright, "A Genius for Handling Cattle: John Wesley Iliff." In Frink, Maurice, W. Turrentine Jackson & Agnes Wright Spring. *When Grass Was King: Contributions to the Western Range Cattle Industry Study.* Boulder: University of Colorado Press, 1956.

Templin, J. Alton, "John Wesley Iliff and Theological Education in the West." In *Methodist History,* January, 1986, pp. 67-81.

CHARLES BOETTCHER

"HARD GOODS. HARD WARE. HARD CASH."

{1852–1948}

Among western business leaders, Charles Boettcher vividly demonstrates the advantages of diversifying economic interests. While Horace Tabor and other mining moguls sank with mining busts, Boettcher rose higher with each economic wave. He foresaw economic fluctuations and educated himself on new and different enterprises. This industrious German immigrant endures as a vivid example of how to navigate a full spectrum of economic opportunities—and of how to pay back with a major, model charitable foundation.

Born April 8, 1852 in Kolleda in Prussia, Charles grew up the youngest of six children. All worked in their father Frederick's hardware store, a family business started by Frederick's father. Young Charles came to the United States at the age of seventeen in 1869, probably for the same reason that Adolph Coors and many of about fifty thousand others annually left Germany—to avoid the Prussian Army and its continual wars.

The youngster stepped off a Union Pacific Railroad car in Cheyenne, Wyoming Territory, in 1871 as a poor immigrant searching for his older brother, Herman. Herman had immigrated to Wyoming earlier, following the transcontinental railroad construction boom, to set up a hardware business. Herman put his younger brother to work as a tinner, cutting, shaping, and seaming tin cups, plates, and coffee pots, even making and installing tin ceilings. He paid Charles a dollar or two a day and allowed him to sleep in the store. Young Charlie managed to get ahead by making loans to fellow employees and friends going out on weekend sprees. Charles collected the loans—plus interest—on paydays.

After the Denver Pacific Railroad reached Cheyenne in 1870, Herman opened a hardware store along that line in a promising new settlement called Greeley. He left Charles in charge in Cheyenne. In both stores the Boettchers' slogan was "Hard Goods. Hard Ware. Hard Cash."

In 1872 the Boettcher brothers opened a third hardware store in Fort Collins. This was not a wise move; Fort Collins stagnated without railroads and with grasshopper infestations. Boettcher learned that key lesson of any successful businessperson—when to cut your losses and get out. During his brief stay in Fort Collins, he found a wife, Fannie Augusta Cowan, the daughter of a Kansas farmer.

In 1874 Charles closed the Fort Collins store and moved his business and new bride to Boulder. Later, he would call his four years in Boulder the happiest of his life. Boulder saw steady growth and Charles built a fine two-story brick store at the main intersection of Pearl Street and Broadway. It stands to this day with a carved stone inscription over the corner entrance reading "C. Boettcher A.D. 1878." Charles also built a small one-story cottage nearby at 925 Pearl Street.

R.G. Dun, the credit rating entrepreneur who later became half of Dun & Bradstreet, first appraised Boettcher in 1875 as "a tinner by trade. Is industrious and economical and we think his prospects fair."

In 1879, a year after opening his new Boulder store, Charles turned it over to an assistant and set out for Colorado's most lucrative new boomtown—Leadville. In the two-mile-high "Cloud City," Boettcher avoided the silver mining fever that had reached epidemic proportions. When asked why he ran a hardware store in a city of mining millionaires, Boettcher replied, "Axes and hammers, picks and shovels don't go out of style." Leadville, Boettcher recalled later, was

> so crowded that you could scarcely wedge your way through. There were any number of reckless people there, so many lounging around doing nothing, just living on excitement . . . . Men would sleep on chairs and be glad of one. People were living right on the streets. Many had tents, log cabins, or shelter covered with brush.

Overnight Leadville became the second largest city in Colorado. Boettcher bought two lots on the main street, Harrison Avenue, and by April 1879 had erected a hardware store. He invested very little in mining, but acquired a one-sixth interest in the Little Johnny Mine and other Ibex Mining Company operations from his associate John F. Campion. Boettcher put far more money into non-mining investments such as the Carbonate Bank of Leadville and the Leadville Electric Light Company, which he helped found. (Hanging onto investments paid big dividends. When Public Service Company acquired the Leadville Electric Light Company in 1923, Charles still owned it, and he, his son Claude, and his grandson Charles II became major stockholders and directors of Public Service, now Xcel Energy). In Leadville, Boettcher became one of a dozen millionaires created by that city's boom. Others included John F. Campion, the Guggenheim brothers, David May of department store fame, and silver king and future U.S. senator Horace Tabor.

In 1884, to supply his growing hardware store empire, Boettcher bought a large wholesale company in Denver and began wholesaling mining, milling, railroad, construction, and agricultural supplies. He established the Big Horn Ranch in North Park, where he raised cattle and horses to haul his hardware and other goods.

In 1890, Boettcher moved to Denver, as had fellow Leadvillites such as J.J. and Molly Brown, John F. Campion, Horace Tabor, and Dennis Sheedy. There he built a relatively modest $26,000 home at 1201 Grant Street, then Denver's Millionaire's Row. In the Denver city directory, Charles stated his occupation as "loans and investments" rather than listing his multiple businesses. His Denver "investments" included Boettcher & Company Investments, long one of Colorado's largest stock brokerages, and the Denver U.S. Bank (now Wells Fargo Bank).

Boettcher's philosophy surfaced in a letter he wrote prodding the Denver Chamber of Commerce: "Big Things must be done in a Big Way." He followed that policy in his own endeavors, expanding his Denver-based companies into statewide and sometimes regional or even national players.

Fannie finally persuaded her workaholic husband to take a vacation in 1900 to Germany. To Fannie's dismay, the trip turned into a tour of the German sugar beet industry. Her husband inspected the fields where the beets grew and the plants where each was reduced to several teaspoons of pure white sugar. According to legend, Boettcher insisted that Fannie empty some of her suitcases so that the couple could take home sugar beet seeds. In 1900 Charles, his son Claude, John F. Campion, Chester S. Morey, and several others set up the Great Western Sugar Company with Denver headquarters. As Charles was well aware, the U.S. in 1901 passed the Dingley Tariff, taxing imports, including sugar, to protect and encourage U.S. production. Charles, "The Father of the Colorado Sugar Beet Industry," built the Sugar Building (elegantly restored in 2000) at 16th and Wazee Streets as a headquarters for Great Western. As Charles had foreseen, sugar beets became a leading Colorado industry by the 1920s.

Waste and inefficiency always annoyed Charles Boettcher—especially when he was paying. During construction of Great Western's first sugar beet plant in Loveland, he noted that the cement was imported from Germany at extremely high cost. He was told that Germans made much more reliable cement than anyone in the U.S. So Charles began investigating. He found that cement's ingredients—limestone and silica—could be found in Colorado. In 1901 he founded the Colorado Portland Cement Company (later Ideal Basic Cement, then Ideal Basic Industries) to mass produce high-quality cement. He built large plants at Concrete, Colorado, on the Arkansas River near Florence, and at Boettcher, near Fort Collins. He also began buying up cement companies in Colorado, Utah, Montana, and surrounding states. By 1903 Boettcher's cement company was worth $1 million, and he began building a headquarters building in downtown Denver, at 17th and Champa Streets. Denverites watched his eight-story Ideal Building rise as one of Colorado's first steel skeleton reinforced concrete buildings. One day, when the cement had dried, Charles had the wooden forms set afire. Everyone in town, including all the local press, rushed to 17th and Champa to see the new building burn down. After the wooden forms burned, all were amazed to see the concrete building still standing, undamaged. Boettcher had dramatically made his point about steel and concrete construction being fire resistant. From that day forward, most large downtown buildings would be made of cement and steel instead of wood and masonry.

Charles moved into the fifth floor corner office of the Ideal Building to direct his empire. He stayed there for almost forty years, presiding over Ideal Cement, Great Western Sugar, extensive real estate, and myriad other interests. Boettcher hated to buy anything he might make himself. Tired of buying dynamite from the DuPonts and others for his mining supply business, he formed the National Fuse and Powder Company in Denver in 1901.

David Moffat died of an apparent suicide in 1911, after financial crises affected his railroad, the Denver, Northwestern & Pacific, and the bank where he was president, First National of Denver. Boettcher took over as president of the railway line. In 1928 Boettcher and his son

Claude helped complete the Moffat Tunnel, which Moffat had begun, at last providing Denver with a direct, all-weather route beneath the Continental Divide.

To process his own cattle and those of other Coloradans, Boettcher and some partners set up the Western Packing Company in Denver in 1901, which sold out to Swift & Company in 1912. Instead of buying insurance from someone else, Boettcher formed Denver's Capitol Life Insurance Company in 1905. It became Denver's biggest hometown insurance company, with an impressive building complex still standing on East 16th Avenue between Grant and Logan Streets. Boettcher also joined William G. Evans and other friends as a major stockholder in the Denver Tramway Company (forerunner of today's Regional Transportation District), which monopolized Denver's streetcar service.

Charles's devotion to hard work and innumerable business interests left him little time for family life. Over the years he and his wife Fannie grew increasingly independent of each other. She traveled around the world spending money, but not as fast as he made it. Charles left her in their Grant Street home in 1920 and moved into the Brown Palace Hotel, where he lived for the rest of his life. Two years later, he bought the hotel in partnership with Horace W. Bennett. Charles's son Claude —known as "C.K."—also fell in love with the elegant old hotel. C.K. persuaded his father that the Brown could be a good investment. In 1931 the Boettchers bought out Bennett's share of the business. Major changes to the hotel during subsequent decades still reflect C.K.'s taste and times. Like his father, C.K. also moved into the hotel, bringing with him his model ship collection. He had the hotel's Ship Tavern built to celebrate the 1933 repeal of Prohibition and to house his model ships. Charles also had a terrific collection of European arms, armor, and military trophies, with which he decorated the hotel's Palace Arms Dining Room.

Into his eighties and nineties, Charles continued to walk daily from the Brown Palace six blocks down 17th Street to his Ideal Building office. His son Claude made the trip to the Boettcher Investment Company just across 17th Street in the Boston Building. Claude, however, went to work in an enormous chauffeured Packard, attired in fashionable and conservative suits. Asked why he didn't ride and dress like that, Charles replied, "Unlike myself, Claude has a rich father."

In 1948 *Time* magazine profiled the ninety-four-year-old tycoon who was still actively involved in his businesses as "a quiet, hard working German." Charles said, "I like work. I've worked hard all my life and I suppose I'll keep working as long as I can raise a hand. Clubs and social life don't interest me."

Stories of his frugality delighted Denverites. At night he left his suite in the Brown and walked across 17th Street to a pop machine. When clerks asked him why he didn't use room service, the millionaire replied, "And pay the price we ask for a Coke here at the Brown?" He died in his sleep on July 2, 1948 at ninety-six and was buried in a large stone mausoleum bearing his name at the Fairmount Cemetery.

Boettcher left an estate of $16 million. Like Rockefeller and Ford, he set up a foundation to duck President Franklin D. Roosevelt's "soak-the-rich taxes." He and his son established the Boettcher Foundation in 1937 with the provision that all its proceeds be given to Colorado causes. Charles had made his money in Colorado and wanted to enrich the state in gratitude. Claude took a great interest in setting up and running the foundation, helping to make it the state's fifth largest foundation giver.

Claude Boettcher did not squander his father's fortune but greatly increased it. At his death in 1957, he left millions to the Boettcher Foundation. Boettcher was Colorado's "one over-riding magnate," according to John Gunther in his 1945 book *Inside USA*. "This margrave of the sugar beets, this padishah of cement, potash, mining, and what not," Gunther wrote, was "one of the richest men in America and one of the least known."

Claude Boettcher ran the city, according to Mayor Quigg Newton, by having key players on any issue come to the Boettcher Mansion for cocktails and conversation. In 1958 the Boettcher Foundation donated the family mansion to the state for use as the governor's residence.

The Boettcher Foundation has given more than $300 million to Colorado civic and cultural programs, community and social services, education and health care. Between 1940, when the foundation made $22,369 in grants, and today, when it gives away more than $10 million a year, it has benefited Coloradans in many ways. Its gifts include Boettcher Scholarships to keep bright students in state by giving them full four-year funding to attend any Colorado college or university they choose; Boettcher Hall at the Denver Center for the Performing Arts, which houses the Colorado Symphony Orchestra; the Boettcher Wing at the Denver Museum of Nature and Science, with its life-size animal dioramas, a very popular attraction; Boettcher Conservatory at the Denver Botanic Gardens, a tropical paradise for plants and visitors; The Georgetown Loop Narrow Gauge Railroad, a $1 million 1976 reconstruction that has become a popular attraction of History Colorado; Boettcher Seminar Building, part of the Aspen Institute for the Humanities; the Denver Art Museum; the Charles Boettcher Mansion atop Colorow Peak on Lookout Mountain, a splendid 1917 10,000-square-foot Arts and Crafts–style house designed by leading Denver architects William and Arthur Fisher and built of native rock and logs harvested from the site. Three generations of Boettchers entertained Colorado's movers and shakers in the structure. Donated to Jefferson County in the 1970s, it is now a premier historic event venue.

Among notable western business leaders, Charles Boettcher stands out as a study in economic diversity and targeted philanthropy. Ahead of his time in many enterprises, he is especially remarkable for being a multi-discipline, multi-industry investor in the American West.

Boettcher Foundation Annual Reports

Bean, Geraldine. *Charles Boettcher: A Study in Pioneer Western Enterprise.* Boulder: Westview Press, 1976.

Charles Boettcher Collection, Hart Library, History Colorado Center, Denver

R.G. Dun & Co. Credit Ratings, Dun Collection, Baker Business School Library, Harvard University

Interviews with Louisa Ward Arps, Chris Dobbins and James Quigg Newton.

HENRY MILLER

THE "INDUSTRIAL COWBOY" {1827-1916}

Arguably, the Miller and Lux cattle company is one of the most influential western outfits that no one has ever heard of. The historian David Igler, who studied the corporation closely in his book *Industrial Cowboys,* called it "one of the largest and most innovative industrial enterprises in the Far West." Between the California gold rush and the 1910s, German immigrants Henry Miller and Charles Lux owned more land and cattle, and controlled more water rights, than anyone else in California. The entrepreneurs succeeded in developing a complex, integrated industrial ranching system by continually acquiring and expanding their land holdings and by re-engineering the physical landscape of California's Central Valley, as well as parts of Nevada and Oregon, to serve their own economic ends. A company that measured its domain in square miles rather than acres, it employed more than a thousand laborers and cowboys to raise and move hundreds of thousands of cattle, irrigate desert land, grow alfalfa, and butcher and process beef to feed the growing Golden State. Their extensive canal system accelerated land development and formed the basis for modern agriculture in California's Central Valley, while their legal battles with rivals influenced water allocation policies throughout the West.

Born Heinrich Alfred Krieser in Wurtemberg, Germany, in 1827, Henry Miller learned the skill of animal dressing from his father, a master butcher. The restless young apprentice felt alienated from his staid countrymen and became impatient with prospects for advancement under his father's strict supervision. He left Germany for Holland and England in 1842. Upon reaching America five years later, he found employment in the disassembly lines of New York City's "hog shops." Unhappy with his occupation's filth, confinement, and stress, he jumped at the chance to claim a friend's steamship ticket to California. Since the ticket was non-transferable, Heinrich assumed his friend's name and, as "Henry Miller," began a new life on the West Coast.

Four years older than Miller, Charles Lux was born in a small town called Hatten in southwestern Germany. Lux also chafed under a dominating father, running away from home and traveling to America at the age of seventeen. He worked as a delivery boy and apprentice New York City butcher and advanced to become his shop's manager. In 1849 he invested his savings in a boat ticket to California.

By the early 1850s, both German immigrants had progressed beyond wage labor to become butcher-shop owners in San Francisco. They joined forces in 1858—Miller reinforcing their relationship by marrying Lux's sister-in-law. After she died in childbirth, he married her niece.

Beyond their shared ethnicity and occupation, however, the business partners had little in common. The sociable and refined Lux was a natural conversationalist, comfortable in the salons and political halls of pioneer California power brokers. The taciturn and tough-minded Miller preferred cattle to people and was more at home on the range than in stuffy drawing rooms. Each partner's strengths covered the other's weaknesses. Lux tended the company's urban contacts and contracts, while Miller managed the rural cattle operations. Together, they created an unbeatable team.

Cattle ranching arrived in California with the first Spanish settlers and missionaries. Hide and tallow exports fueled the region's economy during the Spanish and Mexican eras of the 1700s and early 1800s, and the 1849 California gold rush set off a skyrocketing demand for beef, pork, and mutton. As business partners, Miller and Lux saw an opportunity to dominate the state's urban markets by integrating the beef production process in San Francisco and its northern California hinterlands. In order to do so, they expanded beyond butchering, opening new San Francisco slaughterhouses and meat packing facilities and purchasing all the cattle they could fatten on rented rangeland. Then they expanded horizontally, aggressively acquiring and consolidating former Mexican ranchos and large tracts of public land near San Francisco, in the San Joaquin Valley, and beyond. The partners became the state's largest land speculators, purchasing a large section of the public domain with second-hand military, college land grant, and internal improvement scrip, and directing employees to file hundreds of proxy homestead claims. By the end of the 1860s, Miller and Lux controlled more than 300,000 acres of rangeland. And they were just getting started.

Part of the drive to consolidate and expand sprang from a need to mitigate the environmental extremes of central California. The San Joaquin Valley, by turns, was a desert and a swamp, a dry wasteland in arid years and a huge inland sea in wet ones. Large private holdings allowed Miller and Lux to hedge against climactic extremes by taking advantage of geographic variations. The partners worked to weatherproof their ranches by aggressively claiming "worthless" swampland, then draining it to create rich pastures. They also developed irrigated land to grow alfalfa to feed their herds during lean years and to help put a final finish on their cattle before slaughter at the Miller and Lux feedlots outside San Francisco. Summing up his philosophy that unused water was wasted water, Miller ordered a superintendent to "use every bit of water you can possibly get."

Aggressive appropriation of water rights consequently became the second component in Miller's and Lux's business strategy. The partners' public land claims strategically enclosed watersheds in the San Joaquin Valley and elsewhere. They also invested heavily in one of the West's first corporate irrigation companies, the San Joaquin and King's River Canal and Irrigation Company, acquiring complete control of this major Central Valley irrigation artery by 1878. To shore up their political fences against rival land developers, large and small, who complained that Miller and Lux were squeezing them out, Charles Lux and his agents cultivated friendly relations and accumulated political capital with officials from the local sheriff's office to the United States Senate.

Tensions between the cattle corporation and rival water claimants came to a head in the landmark *Lux v. Haggin* lawsuit, initiated by the business partners in 1879. James Ben Ali Haggin, a prominent California businessman, partner of mining magnate George Hearst, and rival land developer, had a somewhat different view of irrigation than did Miller and Lux. Whereas the cattlemen viewed water as their hedge against environmental insecurity on the range, Haggin saw it as the key to intensive settlement and agricultural development. The San Francisco mining man began buying up canals and water rights along the Kern River, promising settlers to make the arid San Joaquin Valley bloom. His diversions reduced the flow in the Buena Vista Slough bordering Miller and Lux rangelands; when Miller and Lux cattle died in a drought during the 1870s, Charles Lux brought suit.

The case raised the issue of which system of water appropriation best applied to California. As landholders along the Buena Vista Slough, Miller and Lux defended the traditional system of riparian rights, defined as nontransferable rights enjoyed by all users whose property borders a given stream. Haggin appealed to the right of appropriation—that water users have the right to divert water away from a watercourse. In 1886 the California Supreme Court ruled that appropriation rights were subsidiary to riparian rights. The case was considered a landmark in California water use policy—despite the inflow of millions of non-river dwelling emigrants over the following 130 years, its finding is still the basis of California water law today.

Miller and Lux's rapid expansion and massive irrigation projects soon told on the environment. The drainage of swamps and diversion of watercourses into flood irrigation networks to grow alfalfa for cattle feed raised the water table and increased the salinity of valley groundwater, degrading valley pastures. Yet the partners also did what they could to encourage sustainable irrigation and ranching practices. They opposed efforts by San Joaquin irrigation companies to expand unsustainably. They rotated cattle to allow rangeland to recover, eventually expanding into Nevada and Oregon to rest California pastures. And they worked to restore some wild spaces for the valley's nearly-extinct tule elk population, threatened by the partners' intensive swamp reclamation. In time, the demands that Miller and Lux, as well as other large land developers, placed on the valley would cause considerable environmental problems. But by treating the landscape with a measure of respect, the company was able to extend central California's usefulness to livestock raisers for several decades.

By 1900, the Miller and Lux corporation employed more than 1,200 hands to transform central California, as well as parts of Oregon and Nevada, into a vast industrial system for moving and processing cattle into beef for hungry Americans. Hundreds of immigrant and itinerant workers, including many from Germany, China, Portugal, Italy, and Mexico, kept the ranches, feedlots, and rendering plants humming. Mexican and Anglo vaqueros moved cattle from range to range and drove them to cattle cars for transfer to slaughterhouses in the noxious San Francisco wharf area known as "Butchertown." Mexican and Italian laborers dug and repaired irrigation canals and harvested and stacked fifty-foot-tall mounds of alfalfa. Workers killed, carved, and dismembered beef, converting it into salable parts. As a hedge against vandalism and to maintain a reserve labor pool, the partners offered free meals to transients on what became known as the "Dirty Plate Route," so called because drifters took their handout dinners on unwashed plates used first by Miller and Lux employees. Between the 1850s and 1900, Miller and Lux transformed central California, as well as parts of Oregon and Nevada, into a vast belt of industrial agriculture dedicated to the purpose of raising, butchering, packaging, and transporting beef. Their distinctive HH brand was synonymous with large-scale cattle ranching from Oregon's Columbia Plateau to the Kern River, and east across the Sierras into Nevada.

Charles Lux died suddenly of pneumonia in 1887, leaving behind an estate of $20 million (about $500 million in 2014 dollars). Henry Miller assumed greater responsibility for operations, eventually buying out Lux's heirs and carrying on alone. As successful as it became, the Miller and Lux Cattle Company was unable to fend off the forces of economic, regulatory, and environmental change. Long-term salination and flooding wreaked havoc in Miller's carefully-ordered San Joaquin rangeland, and years of intensive grazing began to degrade the company's best pastures. By century's end, California truck farmers outperformed big cattle companies in crop diversity and productivity. Government regulators reacted to shifting public opinion and tightened regulatory oversight in ways that favored smaller, more nimble operations over large, monolithic landowners and water users such as Miller and Lux. Yet the aging Henry Miller seemed unwilling, or unable, to turn away from his expensive, cattle-based economic model to adopt more cost-effective options.

Worse, large midwestern meatpackers, led by Chicago's "Big Five" meatpacking firms, began making inroads into the Pacific Coast beef market. Henry Miller fought back vigorously, forming a trust of California meatpackers and ranchers and launching a public relations smear campaign that accused Chicago packers of endangering consumers by chemically tainting their "embalmed" beef. Still, by controlling access to immense midwestern herds and operating on an economy of scale undreamed of by the butchers of San Francisco, the midwestern meatpackers undercut Pacific Coast producers and slowly began to inch locals out. Perhaps the final straw came in the San Francisco earthquake of 1906, which obliterated Miller and Lux's Butchertown slaughterhouses but left most of the Chicago-based facilities relatively undamaged. The HH cattle operation, formerly California's largest, declined along with the health of its surviving partner. By 1910, the eighty-three-year-old Miller retired from the range for San Francisco. He toured all his ranches a final time in 1911, leaving detailed instructions with each of his managers. Cattleman Henry Miller died in 1916 at the age of eighty-nine.

In the end, times had passed Henry Miller by. His heirs slowly sold off his immense holdings to pay his debts—the hated Swift meatpacking company purchased his HH brand in 1930. Yet the work of Miller and his partner Charles Lux transformed the California landscape and set the table for future agricultural projects. Irrigated by waterworks first laid out by Miller and Lux, the San Joaquin Valley is still a major agricultural producer; farmers still allocate water based on rules that the cattle ranchers pioneered. The innovative achievements of Miller and Lux demonstrated the promise of industrial agriculture. Their system became a model for large ranches and farms for generations to come.

Bancroft, Hubert H. *Chronicles of the Builders of the Commonwealth*. San Francisco: History Company, 1891-92.

Igler, David. *Industrial Cowboys: Miller & Lux and the Transformation of the Far West, 1850-1920*. Berkeley: University of California Press, 2001

Sawyer, Charles, Ralph L. Milliken, and David Lawrence. *One Man Show: Henry Miller in the San Joaquin*. Los Banos: Loose Change Publications, 2003.

FREDERICK WEYERHAEUSER

SUPPLYING LUMBER TO A NEW LAND {1834–1914}

By the time of his death in 1914, Frederick Weyerhaeuser had quietly become one of America's wealthiest men. Through soft-spoken influence, a penchant for risk, and a keen sense of timing, Weyerhaeuser and his associates dominated the nation's timber industry. The companies he owned and invested in controlled the supply, production, and distribution of lumber supplies in the Midwest and Pacific Northwest that were crucial to America's western expansion. Weyerhaeuser was an organizer, not a tinkerer. He was happy to let others innovate in techniques and technology; once competitors or associates proved the worth of new ways to fell trees or cut boards, Weyerhaeuser eagerly adopted their methods. What he could do that few others could, however, was to consolidate the lumber industry into an integrated whole. Through strategic partnerships, sensible investments, and a talent for persuasion, he brought order and planning to an industry dominated by small-scale loggers, mill operators, and lumber dealers.

Friedrich Weyerhäuser (the German form of the future timber magnate's name) was born in 1834 in Niedersaulheim, an agricultural village in the German Rhineland. He was the only surviving son of prosperous Lutheran farmers Johann and Margareta Weyerhäuser.

Friedrich plunged into adulthood early. Johann died when he was only twelve, leaving him to manage the family's sizable farm and vineyards. The boy left school to support his mother and sisters. He did well, and would have followed in his father's footsteps as a farmer and winemaker, if the family hadn't decided to sail for America. The Weyerhaeusers were part of a massive wave of German immigration to the United States in the 1840s. In ten years, nearly a million people from German-speaking states arrived there, seeking opportunity and fleeing political instability in central Europe. Frederick's immediate family was financially comfortable, but extended relatives were burdened with debt. Letters home from his sister Katharina, who had emigrated earlier, painted America in a glowing light. The entire family sold its land, divided the profits equally (Frederick, still young, received his share later), and moved across the Atlantic.

The family settled in Pennsylvania, where Frederick dabbled in various occupations. He apprenticed to a brewer—a common profession for a young German immigrant—but decided to seek other opportunities. According to family legend, Weyerhaeuser "saw that a brewer was often his own best customer." After four more years of vocational experimentation, he finally collected his share of the family money and moved west to Illinois, hoping to buy a farm of his own. He landed in the town of Rock Springs, home to a distant cousin and a thriving community of German immigrants. Rock Springs was a river city located on a bend in the Mississippi. But it was also a railroad town and lay close to Illinois's nascent industrial centers. Fortunately for Frederick's future, the town was also a transportation hub between the forests and the prairie, connecting people who desperately needed timber with parts of the country where trees grew abundantly.

Of all the cargo floating up and down the Mississippi River in the mid-nineteenth century, few products were more important to economic growth than lumber. America consumed wood for homes, fences, stores, railroad tracks, and more. The demand for lumber rose

as the nation expanded west, especially once Americans began to settle the largely treeless plains. As the trade journal *Northwestern Lum-
berman* explained in 1880,

> Every new settler upon the fertile prairies means one more added to
> the vast army of lumber consumers, one more house to be built, one
> more barn, one more 40 acres to be fenced, one more or perhaps a
> dozen corn cribs needed. But it means more; it means an extension
> of railroad lines . . . it means new channels of enterprise constantly
> opening which add to the yearly increasing demand for lumber.

In 1856, Weyerhaeuser found employment at the Mead, Smith, and
Marsh sawmill, established a year earlier. He proved to be a capable
salesman and soon managed the firm's lumberyard. Pleased with the
skill and industriousness of their new hire, his employers relocated
him to the nearby town of Coal Valley to supervise the firm's lumberyard there. Frederick brought his new wife, fellow immigrant Elisabeth Blodel, with him. Their growing family—there would eventually
be seven Weyerhaeuser children—flourished. A recession and a bad
lumber deal caused Mead, Smith, and Marsh to go bankrupt. Weyerhaeuser, aided by his brother-in-law F.C.A. Denkmann, bought the
company's assets, including its sawmill, in 1860. Denkmann ran and
maintained the sawmill while Weyerhaeuser bought logs and sought
customers for the mill's finished lumber. The two partners prospered,
making $3,000 their first month in business (roughly $76,000 in 2014
dollars) and $5,000 ($128,000 today) the next.

The company's future relied on dependable sources of timber.
Weyerhaeuser initially bought logs locally, but soon sought a better
supply. He began spending much of his time in Wisconsin and
Minnesota seeking logs that could be obtained more cheaply upriver.
He acquired stumpage—rights to fell trees on land others owned—
along Wisconsin rivers and, everywhere, gathered a deep knowledge

of how local timber and lumber markets worked. He also spent considerable time deep in the northern forests, learning the business of timber harvesting and tracing his lumber back to its source. Lumbering was a harsh business. Lumberjacks felled trees in the winter, when deep snow smoothed the rocky forest floors and made it easier for log-laden sleds to carry cargo to the banks of frozen streams. Spring thaws flooded rivers, allowing lumber crews to float their timber downstream to sawmills and dealers. Each cut log would be marked with the name or symbol of the lumber mill or company that owned it. Harvesting and transporting timber was hazardous work: logs were heavy, and streams easily got jammed with floating timber. But Weyerhaeuser loved working in the forests. He traveled between Illinois and the forests of Wisconsin and Minnesota for fifteen years, spending months at a time away from Elisabeth and his children. A friend once asked him how he put up with so many snowy winters in distant logging camps, and Weyerhaeuser replied, "I love the woods life."

The lumber industry in Minnesota and Wisconsin was full of small millers and dealers similar to Weyerhaeuser and Denkmann. There was plenty of room for rivalry, as Weyerhaeuser quickly found when he began focusing his efforts on Wisconsin's Chippewa River basin. The region was home to both high-quality timber and high-intensity conflicts between local lumber men and outsiders. Area lumberjacks and land owners didn't care who they sold their logs to, as long as they were paid well. But local mills and timber dealers wanted to keep timber from floating downstream to competitors, especially since the end of the Civil War meant more demand for wood.

Weyerhaeuser began creating partnerships with other Mississippi River lumber companies, aided by his strategy of investing profits from his own mill into shares of his competitors. In 1870 Weyerhaeuser and Denkmann, along with fifteen other lumber companies, formed a coalition named the Mississippi River Logging Company (MRLC).

Each member received a fixed percentage of that year's timber harvest, rather than competing with one another for logs. Weyerhaeuser's alliance—he was elected president of the MRLC—helped quell the conflicts between locals and outsiders, especially after a disastrous flood in 1880 threw havoc into Wisconsin's timber industry. Frederick offered his competitors generous terms for their ruined timber, using his warm personality and reputation to soothe decades of conflict.

In time, Weyerhaeuser owned, forged alliances with, or bought shares in, many timber firms, including Weyerhaeuser and Denkmann, the MRLC, and the Chippewa Lumber Company, which he formed with his former Wisconsin competitors. He kept expanding, buying up sizeable tracts of timberlands around the Great Lakes, forming new lumber companies around the region, and building the largest timber mill in the world along the Chippewa River. Weyerhaeuser eventually controlled nearly every log milled into lumber on the upper Mississippi River. He did so by bringing order, influence, and corporate organization to a once-scattered industry.

Weyerhaeuser found success in the forests around the Great Lakes, but trees replenished too slowly to rely on just one region. He moved his family to St. Paul in 1891 and began focusing on Minnesota timber once Wisconsin's wood supply became depleted. When Minnesota's formerly vast forests were gone, Weyerhaeuser faced a dilemma. Where could he go next? He briefly investigated the promising yellow pine and cypress forests of the South, making a few small investments in lumber companies and mills. Yet Weyerhaeuser worried that southern heat and malaria might endanger his northern staff, and he disapproved of any of his family living so far from St. Paul. He also held a grudge against the region from the Civil War, when young men from Coal Valley, including the one he hired as his substitute, went off to fight and never returned. For both business and personal reasons, Weyerhaeuser charted his future elsewhere.

The forests of the Pacific Northwest are among the lushest and most productive on earth, but they were peripheral to America's timber industry for most of the nineteenth century. Oregon and Washington had small-scale lumber industries, but their lumber mainly went to San Francisco or other ports on the West Coast. Shipping forest products to the East Coast or Midwest by rail or sea was still too difficult and expensive. Americans preferred to buy boards made from white and yellow pine, rather than the Douglas fir and other woods prevalent in northwestern forests. No one knew how much timber grew in the Pacific Northwest—the area had never been fully surveyed by experts. The steep slopes of the Cascades were harsh terrain for lumber harvesting, and logging conditions there were primitive. It would take different techniques and improved technologies to tap the area's timber potential. Still, area boosters promoted timber's promise, and the Northern Pacific Railroad connected the region with national markets when it completed its transcontinental route in 1883. Lumber barons, many from the increasingly deforested Great Lakes region, began to look at the Northwest with new eyes.

The federal government granted James J. Hill's Northern Pacific Railroad generous portions of timberlands in Washington, and the railroad took advantage of them, routing its tracks through some of the state's most promising stands of timber. In 1883 the Northern Pacific owned 7.7 million acres in Washington—nearly 18 percent of the state's entire land area. But Hill needed capital, not trees, to reinforce the Northern Pacific's shaky finances, and he knew just where to find it. Hill and Weyerhaeuser were friends, living in the same exclusive St. Paul neighborhood. They frequently dined together and shared drinks well into the night, even though Weyerhaeuser, an early riser, often dozed off as Hill talked.

Weyerhaeuser had shown interest in Washington land before, and now agreed to buy 900,000 acres of Northern Pacific land for $5.4 million (now roughly $1.4 billion), or $6 an acre. At the time, it was the largest private land purchase in American history. Hill needed $3 million right away. Weyerhaeuser and Denkmann put up $1.3 million of their own and raised the rest through the network of associates they had built up over decades in the Mississippi River timber business. Weyerhaeuser's reputation for honesty and fairness meant investors were willing to trust him with what seemed like a risky deal. The associates of the new Weyerhaeuser Timber Company, formed in 1901 and named such over Frederick's protests, soon realized they had invested well.

Through the Northern Pacific deal and other purchases, Weyerhaeuser Timber Company, headquartered in Tacoma, Washington, eventually owned 26 percent of all the timber acreage in the state. By the early 1900s, Washington became the top lumber-producing state in America, as Weyerhaeuser and other midwestern lumber interests took their business westward. Local timber interests suffered as the prices of once-cheap timberland soared. Weyerhaeuser chose trusted associate George Long to manage and expand his Pacific Northwest empire. Long had never been in Washington before, but he quickly went to work consolidating the company's land holdings and purchasing more, and building friendly relationships with local producers, much as Frederick once had.

Purchasing land from the Northern Pacific brought the reclusive Weyerhaeuser into the public eye. Who was this man who could raise $3 million in just a few weeks? Journalists began inquiring into the German immigrant's background and business practices. One writer, penning a piece for *Cosmopolitan* magazine in 1907, called him "richer than John D. Rockefeller." At a time when some Americans were questioning the seemingly infinite power of big business, the ability of one man to purchase an immense acreage of timberland once in the public domain seemed suspicious. Timber baron Weyerhaeuser took a beating in the court of public opinion. But it wasn't just the press. Since the late nineteenth century, both conservationists and scientists trained in the new discipline of forestry worried about the future of America's shrinking forests, arguing that timberlands needed to be better protected or managed. Near the end of his life, Weyerhaeuser advocated for a limited amount of state management or preservation of forest land. He helped call attention to the problems of forest fires and set aside former timberlands in Wisconsin to be used as state parks.

As Weyerhaeuser aged, his sons managed more of his timber assets. Frederick and Sarah traveled back to Germany frequently, and they began spending more time in Pasadena, California, far away from the brutal Minnesota winters. When Weyerhaeuser died in Pasadena in April 1914, he headed more than fifteen different lumber companies and was a major investor in dozens more. His combined timber assets were worth more than $150 million. Weyerhaeuser was an understated builder of the West. His numerous companies helped supply millions with the lumber they needed to establish roots in a new land and drew thousands more to work in the timber industry. He modernized a disorganized industry and helped open up one of America's richest timber regions to national and international markets.

Cronon, William. *Nature's Metropolis: Chicago and the Great West.* New York: W.W. Norton, 1991.

Ficken, Robert E. "Weyerhaeuser and the Pacific Northwest Timber Industry, 1899-1903." In *Experiences in a Promised Land: Essays in Pacific Northwest History,* eds. G. Thomas Edwards and Carlos Schwantes. Seattle: University of Washington Press, 1986, 139-152.

Forester, Jeff. *The Forest for the Trees: How Humans Shaped the North Woods.* St. Paul: Minnesota Historical Society Press, 2004.

Healey, Judith Koll. *Frederick Weyerhaeuser and the American West.* St. Paul: Minnesota Historical Society Press, 2013.

Twining, Charles, and George S. Long. *Timber Statesman.* Seattle: University of Washington Press, 1994.

HENRY WELLS AND WILLIAM FARGO

WESTERN EXPRESSMEN

{ 1 8 0 5 – 1 8 7 8 }

{ 1 8 1 8 – 1 8 8 1 }

Neither Henry Wells nor William Fargo, pictured above, left and right, spent much time in the West. The two New Yorkers and their families were too established in their East Coast lives and enterprises to venture westward when gold was discovered in California in 1848. Yet, mining meant opportunity, and the two longtime business partners established a corporate presence in booming San Francisco, against the advice of their associates. Their express firm, Wells, Fargo & Co., transported gold, mail, and people throughout California and from west to east, carrying the riches of the West Coast into the larger American economy. Wells Fargo grew as the West expanded and prospered. It diversified its services to meet the needs of western customers and successfully adapted to the dizzying rate of technological change in mid-nineteenth-century America. Wells and Fargo largely managed their namesake company from afar, but they built one of the most important—and most trustworthy—businesses in the West.

Henry Wells was born in Vermont in 1805. His father, a Presbyterian minister, moved the family to New York, where Henry began his working life as a farmhand and then apprenticed to a shoemaker. Over six feet tall, the adult Wells was physically imposing and ambitious. He devoted nearly a decade to education, establishing a series of schools for people with speech disorders. Wells stuttered, and although he never cured his own speech problems, his schools helped others. In his thirties, he began working in the freight industry, securing employment as a ticket agent on the Erie Canal. In 1840 he took a job with William Harnden and Company, a fledgling express company transporting packages and goods to cities along the East Coast.

Stagecoach lines had long been a staple of American commerce, but express companies—private companies that specialized in the speedy delivery of letters, freight, and parcels—first blossomed along the East Coast in the 1830s. These companies became the information networks of the early and mid-nineteenth–century United States. Their services helped knit the expanding country together. They transported currency, goods, and information to growing towns and expanding markets, often more cheaply and reliably than the federal government or other businesses could. Bankers relied heavily on the express services. After President Andrew Jackson closed the Second Bank of the United States in 1836, the federal government no longer transported cash, gold, and securities between banks. Express services offered banks a safe, reliable alternative to transporting specie themselves. Express companies extended services to a wide range of businesses other than banks. They carried finished goods and supplies from storefront to customer, allowing business owners to expand their markets. They handled fragile and perishable items as well. Most importantly, they secured federal contracts to carry mail, allowing Americans to share news and keep in touch with one another over long distances.

Wells's tenure at Harnden and Company was short. Although Wells wanted to expand the company's delivery services west of Albany, the firm's principal, William Harnden, disagreed. Wells replied by joining with two other partners and several other investors in starting his own express firm, Pomeroy and Company, in 1841. Pomeroy and Company began express services between Albany and Buffalo, taking advantage of the rapid population growth and industrial expansion of central and western New York wrought by the Erie Canal. Wells executed much of the firm's messenger service himself, traveling extensively throughout the developing region by rail or stagecoach. The travel was dangerous and tiring, but people were always happy to see Wells. At each stop, he reported, people were "anxious to see . . . whether our trunks seemed well fed by packages."

Dependable mail delivery helped Pomeroy and Company prosper and made Henry Wells into a household name in New York. Sending letters and packages was an expensive gamble for many customers. Postal rates were high and delivery often slow and untrustworthy. Federal postmasters were frequently selected for their political connections rather than their ability or interest in delivering mail. Wells offered a solution, and he earned a reputation for reliable delivery at competitive rates. No matter that the government considered his mail services illegal. After all, the federal government was supposed to enjoy a Constitutional monopoly over postal delivery, and federal postal agents pursued Wells's messengers as they carried letters across western New York. To counter this, Wells sought the fastest horses, the most skilled riders, and the quickest routes. Other delivery services soon followed Wells's lead, and the war between the U.S. Post Office and the express companies deepened. Wells even proposed to take over the entire American mail system and deliver letters for only five cents. The federal government rejected his offer, but Wells's initiative forced the postal service to lower rates for mail delivery.

One of Wells's most reliable messengers during this battle was William George Fargo. He was a native New Yorker, born in 1818 in

Onodaga County. The eldest child of William and Tacy Fargo, he left home early to seek employment. At thirteen, Fargo delivered mail and clerked for a Syracuse grocer. Like Wells, he was drawn to the growing freight and express industry and took a job as an agent for the Albany and Syracuse Railroad. In 1842 Wells hired him away and made him his main agent for the city of Buffalo. Fargo soon became Wells's business partner and an investor in his growing express empire.

Wells sought to continuously expand his business to the west, seeking new markets for delivery services. Eventually, Wells's companies —the names of these firms and the investors behind them continually shifted in the 1840s—offered express services as far west as Detroit, Cincinnati, and Chicago. In 1850 Wells, Fargo, former competitor John Butterfield, and other rivals consolidated their express companies into the American Express Company.

American Express dominated freight and delivery in New York, but neither Wells nor Fargo could ignore the fact that the geography of opportunity was shifting westward. Gold was discovered in northern California in 1848, and other express firms—including Adams and Company, a main competitor—quickly established a presence on the West Coast. Shouldn't American Express follow? Wells and Fargo argued in favor of expansion, but Butterfield and the rest of the American Express board believed venturing to California was too risky. Wells and Fargo formed yet another express company in response.

Wells, Fargo & Co. was born in 1851. Company representatives established headquarters in San Francisco the following year. From the start, Wells Fargo aggressively promoted its banking and express services and expanded quickly in order to stand out in an already crowded field. Wells Fargo shipped freight more cheaply than its competitors, offered generous rates for gold dust and bullion, and delivered newspapers by messenger or coach for free, in exchange for good local press. Rather than purchasing its own coaches or hiring messengers, Wells Fargo contracted with existing express companies, which allowed the company to expand its geographical reach quickly. Within a year, Wells Fargo had established more than twelve branches, acquired smaller competitors, expanded eastward to Sacramento, and shipped more than $300,000 worth of gold (about $9 million in 2014 dollars) to New York.

But the fledgling firm faced problems. Adams and Company still outweighed the newcomers in the northern California market, shipping gold worth $5 million (roughly $150.5 million today) to New York during Wells Fargo's first year in business. An even bigger problem was the company's remote management. Henry Wells and William Fargo remained in New York when their namesake company moved west, and Wells Fargo's western managers felt the two easterners insufficiently understood the needs of California customers. At their request, Wells made the long journey to California by sea in 1853 for a three-week tour of the gold camps.

Wells learned how miners lacked secure, easily accessible places to stash their gold. A gold-laden prospector was in danger of being robbed or killed. He decreed that no one would lose money entrusting their gold or other possessions to Wells Fargo. The company would only accept what it could afford to lose. If a Wells Fargo bank or coach was robbed, its customers would be paid back in full, and the company would help bring the culprits to justice. Wells's conservative nature kept Wells Fargo smaller than its competitors, but it also protected company assets and gave the firm a reputation for honesty. When a panic swept the California gold markets in 1855, Wells Fargo was one of the few express companies to survive with its assets intact. It bought up many of its former competitors; by the end of the 1850s, Wells Fargo was the dominant express company in the coastal West.

Miners also needed reliable, affordable mail service. Many letters from the East bearing news from home piled up in San Francisco, and postal workers made little effort to match letters to recipients, especially since many letters were addressed with only "California" as the recipient's location. Express companies took up the slack, much as they had when Henry Wells was expanding his business back in New York. The postmaster-general objected, but Wells Fargo officials came up with an ingenious solution. The company began attaching its own postage to government-issued three-cent envelopes, charging senders nine cents extra for the promise of speed and reliability. The Post Office got its share, and so did Wells Fargo. Green-colored Wells Fargo postboxes began dotting the streets of Sacramento and San Francisco, as many people chose to pay more to ensure that their letters and packages would arrive safely. Carrying the mail was expensive, but Wells Fargo officials believed they would be rewarded with loyalty and future business. The company remained in the postal business until 1895.

In the decade and a half between the 1855 crash and the completion of the first transcontinental railroad in 1869, Wells and Fargo built a stagecoaching empire, transporting goods and people across the interior West. The company began running its own stagecoach lines in California, rather than using contractors. It also became financially entangled in the business of transporting mail across the United States by land. Fargo and Butterfield founded the Overland Mail Company in 1857 to send mail from St. Louis to California, winning a government contract to do so. Wells Fargo invested heavily in its co-founder's new venture, but Butterfield's poor management and unreliable government payments doomed Overland Mail, and Wells Fargo took the company over. It also acquired the Pony Express, one of Overland's main competitors. In 1866 Wells Fargo purchased Ben Holladay's stagecoaching company, its main rival in the field. It briefly controlled the transport of goods and people throughout the West, until the expansion of the railroad made transcontinental stagecoaches obsolete. Wells and Fargo remained afloat by adjusting to the changing times. As California transitioned from mining to an agricultural state after the Civil War, Wells Fargo also transformed its business. Still in the cargo business, it began shipping more goods via rail, even transporting out-of-season California produce east via refrigerator car. The company aggressively expanded from west to east. By 1904, its banking and express network boasted over 4,000 offices, and it transported goods across the country and around the world.

Confirmed easterners Henry Wells and William Fargo struck gold in California express services, but they also recognized that their western business affairs required the attentions of younger, more dynamic managers. Wells, during his visit to the West Coast, remarked, "I am called sanguine at home, but I am an old fogey here and considered entirely too slow for this market." The partners spent much of their energy managing American Express and often left matters of Wells Fargo governance to its California staff.

Wells retired from Wells Fargo in 1867 and spent much of his later life at his estate in Aurora, New York. He founded Wells College, a women's seminary, in 1868, and died a decade later. Fargo directed American Express, as well as guiding the finances of the Northern Pacific Railroad, for nearly two more decades. He died in 1881. While neither man could truly be called a westerner, both believed in the promise of California and together built an empire that was crucial to the region's economic success. Their banks, stagecoaches, and messengers made the western economy more reliable and secure, and tied the region into national networks of information and capital.

Chandler, Robert J. "Integrity Amid Tumult: Wells, Fargo & Co.'s Gold Rush Banking," *California History 70*, no. 3 (Fall 1991), 258-77.

Fradkin, Philip. *Stagecoach: Wells Fargo and the American West*. New York: Free Press, 2003.

Grossman, Peter Z. *American Express: The People Who Built the Great Financial Empire*, New York: Beard Books, 1987.

Moody, Ralph. *Wells Fargo*. Lawrence, Kan.: Bison Books, 2005.

Teisler, Ruth, and Catherine Harroun. "Origin of Wells, Fargo & Company, 1841–1852," *Bulletin of the Business Historical Society* 22, no. 3 (June 1948), 70-83.

JOHN EVANS

PHYSICIAN, CITY BUILDER, CITIZEN {1814–1897}

John Evans's grave is marked by a tombstone in Denver's Riverside Cemetery. Visible from his grave is a much larger memorial—Mount Evans, a 14,264-foot-high natural monument named for the tireless builder and dominating Denver's western horizon. Evans the man dominated nineteenth-century Colorado with contributions not only to business, but also to government and cultural life. Few business leaders have left such a permanent legacy in shaping their community and their state.

When John Evans came to Denver as territorial governor in May 1862, he had already made contributions that would mark him as one of America's success stories. But he did not come to Colorado to rest on his laurels.

Born in 1814 to a Quaker farming family in Ohio, he graduated from the Cincinnati College of Medicine. Dr. Evans practiced in Indiana, where he established one of the first and most successful state hospitals for the insane. In 1845 Dr. Evans moved to Chicago to join the faculty of Rush Medical College. Besides teaching, Professor Evans conducted pathbreaking research on cholera epidemics, edited the *Medical and Surgical Journal,* helped organize the Chicago Medical Society, and invented an instrument for obstetric surgery.

Evans also began investing in Chicago real estate and railroads and developed the fashionable northside suburb of Evanston, where he served as a principal founder of Northwestern University. With his Chicago real estate profits, Evans co-founded the Fort Wayne and Chicago Railroad in 1852 and acquired land along its projected route knowing it would greatly increase in value. Few understood as well as Evans how railroads rearranged cities—and affected property values. When his railroad suffered the usual financial ups and downs, Evans, unlike many others, held onto the stock and stuck out the tough times. "Every man," he noted afterward, "got his money back if he held onto his stock long enough, and most of them with liberal interest."

Elected to Chicago's city council in 1852, Evans championed public schools and a juvenile justice center and supported an up-and-coming politician by the name of Abraham Lincoln. Lincoln, after being elected president in 1860, rewarded Evans by offering him the governorship of Washington Territory, but Evans preferred Colorado because it was closer to his Chicago interests.

His wife, Margaret Gray Evans, and many Chicago friends and associates wondered why he would leave Chicago for primitive, dangerous and remote Colorado Territory. Why leave one of the most exciting, vibrant, and booming cities in America for a little crossroads in the middle of nowhere? In Chicago, Dr. Evans had an Evanston mansion on Lake Michigan, a prestigious medical career, lucrative business interests, and considerable political clout. Evans's own writings suggest the he came west for idealistic reasons—to build a prosperous, civilized state out of a wild, raw territory inhabited by only a smattering of native and Hispanic settlers.

Evans and his family built an elegant house at 14th and Arapahoe Streets in Denver, which he called "really the only tolerable place" in Colorado Territory. There he and his wife entertained with Colorado's first piano and finest library. Margaret immersed herself in charitable causes, her husband in civic, cultural, and business affairs.

Evans strove mightily to turn dusty little Denver into the Queen City of the Mountains and Plains. He gave at least $100 to any congregation that would start a church in the godless territory cursed by gunfire and drunken brawls. He also started a seminary and a university, but his greatest achievement consisted of a network of rails to rescue a town whose isolation nearly doomed it to disappear.

Denver stagnated after the 1859 gold rush. Between 1860 and 1870, the federal census taker found a net gain of only ten residents, from 4,749 to 4,759. Many had abandoned Denver for Cheyenne when the transcontinental railroad went through Wyoming instead of Colorado. President Lincoln had appointed Evans to the board of the Union Pacific, and he was among the crowd at Promontory Summit, Utah Territory, on May 10, 1869, to see the wedding of the Union Pacific and the Central Pacific. Now Evans vowed to save Denver from becoming just another of Colorado's many ghost towns. He became the prime mover as well as president of Denver's first railroad, the Denver Pacific, and the driving force behind the Denver, South Park & Pacific, the Denver & New Orleans, and other early Colorado railroads. He promised that Denver would tie into the transcontinental, a promise fulfilled in June of the following year when he presided over completion of the Denver Pacific, a 106-mile rail lifeline connecting Denver to Cheyenne and the main transcontinental line.

When the overextended Union Pacific failed to come through with promised capital and equipment to complete the Denver Pacific, construction lurched to a stop in spring of 1869. That June, Evans undertook to raise the necessary cash by stock and bond sales and negotiated for the support of the Kansas Pacific. He managed to raise the funds and to save his city with an essential rail artery.

When numerous Colorado railroads failed to reach the Pacific Ocean goal in their names, Evans came up with another idea for how to give Denver access to a saltwater seaport. He began planning this railroad in 1870 even while preoccupied with the DP and the DSP&P,

he turned his full attention to construction of the Denver & New Orleans (D&NO), of which he was the president and driving force. Evans knew that much had to be done besides just building his most visionary railroad. He negotiated with the federal government to designate Denver a port of entry for goods arriving by rail from the Gulf of Mexico.

The D&NO ultimately reached the Gulf of Mexico at both Galveston and New Orleans. At an 1887 banquet, the Denver Chamber of Commerce honored Evans for securing Denver's rail link to the sea "all largely the result of his indefatigable energy and skill . . . which have made our city . . . the commercial metropolis of the Rocky Mountain Region."

Evans invested much of his personal fortune in the D&NO and lost much of it. He likewise lost financially when others mismanaged his Denver, South Park & Pacific Railroad. Like other bold businessmen, Evans did not always succeed in his business ventures. Yet, as he wrote to his wife Margaret after the DSP&P faltered, "my honor is at stake in many of the debts and I must raise the money and put them right." Although he lost personally, his city and the American West gained profitable rail connections.

For all the good he did, John Evans should be remembered. Yet his role as territorial governor (who also served as acting head of Indian affairs) became tarnished by the Sand Creek Massacre. Although Governor Evans was not in the territory at the time the Cheyenne and Arapaho women, children, and old men were slaughtered, he was forced to resign in 1865 as the highest ranking official involved. Despite the step down, Evans continued to be the city's greatest builder. Even during the stagnating 1860s the six-foot-tall citizen, with a thick patriarchal beard and hawklike eyes, foresaw a great city. Others admired his business leadership. R.G. Dun & Company's confidential, impartial Denver credit agent wrote of Evans in 1874: "Excellent character, habits and business ability . . . said to have $200,000 worth of property in Chicago and his estimated worth is three quarters to 1 million dollars." Evans shrewdly invested in real estate in both Chicago and Denver, relying on his conviction that "to buy only when property is low, and sell only when it is high is the rule that makes individual fortunes . . . It is a fair estimate that the value of the real estate of a city is doubled every one hundred per cent increase in its population."

Evans had seen, indeed had been a player, in Chicago's amazing rise to America's second largest city. Despite many ups and downs in Colorado, he never doubted that Denver too would become a great city. To that end, he devoted his remarkable vision and energy not only to commerce but also to funding churches and schools. The University of Denver was a favorite object of his philanthropy. In an 1874 speech to the Denver Board of Trade (predecessor of the Chamber of Commerce) he said, "A well founded University's significance runs through all time . . . there is nothing in all a man's lifetime that he can do that will be so permanent in its beneficial results." Simultaneously Evans remained on the board of trustees of his earlier creation, Northwestern University in Chicago, placing his Chicago experience in the service of the University of Denver.

A man who looked far into the future, Evans saw beyond railroads to street railways, which allowed cities to spread out into streetcar suburbs where homes and retail stores quickly sprouted along their tracks. Evans spearheaded founding of the Denver Tramway Company, which came to monopolize streetcar service. That public transit network has evolved into today's Regional Transportation District.

Evans's commitment to railroads was epitomized by his Railroad Building at 1515 Larimer Street. This eight-story, stone faced building became the tallest—and one of the handsomest —in town when Evans erected it in 1888. Beyond rails, however, his business interests were encyclopedic. While promoting railroads, commerce and industry, he did not forget agriculture. He invented a plough designed to break Colorado's tough soil. He co-founded the Colorado Agricultural

Society to promote farming and ranching and helped establish an agricultural fair. He imported highland cattle to his mountain ranch on upper Bear Creek to demonstrate that livestock could prosper at higher elevations. He helped found the Colorado Historical Society in 1879 and in 1887 the Charity Organization Society (forerunner of today's United Way).

As a businessman who also served in politics, Evans knew government could partner effectively with business. He proposed Denver's first park and parkway plan in 1894. A decade before Mayor Robert W. Speer implemented his city beautiful plan of parks and parkways, Evans planned 23rd Avenue or Park Avenue as a landscaped scenic drive from downtown to City Park. Ahead of Speer, Evans championed creating parks in all parts of the city.

Evans brought a sense of aesthetics to his many creations. He worked with architects on designing churches and University of Denver buildings. He also saw beauty in industrial development and frequently said that the most handsome objects in Denver were the towering smelter stacks that crowned the city's skyline. As long as those smelters were humming and smoking, Evans knew Denver's basic industry, and largest employer, thrived by extracting the riches of the earth.

Evans never moved from his original modest house at 14th and Arapahoe Streets, unlike most of the power elite who upgraded to Capitol Hill. He died in that house in 1897. Two years earlier the Colorado legislature renamed Mt. Rosalie. They called it Mount Evans so that it would become a snowcapped tribute to the man who had put Denver on the big-city map.

The character and motives of John Evans have been scrutinized by numerous historians. Some call him a robber baron and point out that he was the state's first millionaire. His own words, however, indicate that Evans was motivated by the idealistic Christianizing and civilizing mission dear to many nineteenth-century Americans. "It is the imperative of the Almighty," Evans wrote shortly before his death, "that we shall do all the good we can."

There is little reason to question his sincerity or that John Evans failed to practice what he preached. Although primarily a successful businessman and railroad builder, he also excelled as a physician, philanthropist, educator, and civic leader. No other Coloradan did more good or built so well and so permanently as John Evans.

Evans emerged as a national model of how westerners could use eastern capital, resources, and contacts to build the American West. He used connections with President Lincoln in Washington, with Chicago capital and culture, and Union Pacific connections in Omaha to provide multi-dimensional leadership needed out west. Great visionary city builders were needed as well as farsighted entrepreneurs.

John Evans Collection, Stephen Hart Library, History Colorado, Denver.

Kelsey, Henry E., Jr. *Frontier Capitalist: The Life of John Evans.* Boulder: Pruett Press & the Colorado Historical Society, 1969.

McMechan Edgar Carlisle. *Life of Governor Evans: Second Territorial Governor of Colorado.* Denver, CO: The Wahlgreen Publishing Co., 1924.

Scott, Walter Dill. *John Evans: An Appreciation.* Evanston, IL: Privately Printed, 1939.

Overton, Richard C. *Gulf to Rockies: The Heritage of the Fort Worth and Denver-Colorado and Southern Railways, 1861-1898.* Austin: University of Texas Press, 1953.

Poor, Meredith "Mac" D. *The Denver, South Park, and Pacific.* Denver: Rocky Mountain Railroad Club, 1949, 1976.

BENJAMIN HOLLADAY

STAGECOACH KING {1819–1887}

According to the American wit Mark Twain, the feats of stage-coach impresario Ben Holladay outshone those of Moses himself. It took forty years for the great patriarch to lead his followers across three hundred miles of Sinai Desert. "Humph!" a character retorts in Twain's love letter to the American West, *Roughing It,* "Ben Holladay would have fetched them through in thirty-six hours."

Before railroads rolled through the West, Americans hailed Benjamin Holladay as their "Stagecoach King." Holladay earned the title by creating legendary transportation and communication networks across the West. His extensive and reliable system revolutionized the stagecoach industry in the 1850s. Holladay scattered stage lines and stations across a five-thousand-mile frontier reaching from Kansas to Utah, Montana to California. The Holladay Overland Mail and Express Company, worth an estimated $1.5 million in 1866, delivered freight, mail, and passengers to the most remote corners of the West.

A restless, ambitious, and zealous competitor, Holladay beat out rivals by any means necessary, and had fun doing it. Always an ardent advertiser and showman, he raced his topnotch coaches crosscountry, smashing speed records and announcing his stages' arrival with shotgun blasts. During the Civil War, the nation relied on Holladay to keep East and West connected with mail, newspapers, and official documents. Ben Holladay was described by *Harper's Weekly* as the "greatest organizer of transportation that the West ever produced."

Remembered as an iconic westerner, the multifaceted Holladay bridged East and West. Tall, well-built, with unruly hair and a long, dark beard, he thrived in polished eastern salons, and equally enjoyed the thrills of life on the trail. Out west, he drank (moderately) with his drivers, defended his property from American Indian raids, and slept under the stars. Back east, he hobnobbed with politicians and charmed high society with vintage wines and costly jewels at his luxurious New York homes. He wore buckskin pants from Utah and tailor-made suits from Paris. Holladay was both a formidable foe and generous family man. He invested in mining camps and dabbled in the New York stock market with equal self-assurance. At times, he was endearing and sociable; at others, shrewd and rude. He was equally capable of exploding in laughter or fierce fits of temper. One trait remained consistent: Cigar in hand, he was constantly on the move towards the next competitive endeavor.

People either loved Ben Holladay or hated him, but no one denied his commanding presence. German investor Henry Villard considered Holladay "illiterate, coarse, boastful, false and cunning;" others called him "clever," "untiring," and a born leader. He took energy from criticism, collecting negative newspaper articles in a scrapbook on his desk. An avid gambler, Holladay risked his fortunes on various enterprises, including freight wagons, steamships, and railroads. He reportedly won a stake in the prosperous Ophir Mine, located in Nevada's Comstock Lode, during a card game. Holladay demanded the highest quality, the best coaches, the best livestock, and the best drivers, paying the price no matter the expense. With his outlandish personality and astute business methods, it's no wonder the influential clergyman Henry Ward Beecher called Holladay a "magnificent barbarian."

Benjamin "Ben" Holladay's early life fit America's "rags to riches" model. He was born in a Kentucky log cabin on October 14, 1819 to poor, hard-working parents. As one of five brothers, Holladay developed his competitive edge early, especially during sharpshooting contests. He learned the skills that bolstered his future success by handling livestock and absorbing the mechanics of farm wagons, axles, and spokes. Disdainful of manual labor, but with little formal education, Holladay vowed never to be a farmer like his father. In 1836 Ben took off for St. Louis, Missouri, looking for opportunity.

Shortly after his arrival in the "Gateway to the West," Holladay signed on as a stock tender for an eight-hundred-mile trek to Santa Fe on an ox-drawn Conestoga freight wagon. The young laborer spent much of his time pushing the wagon's large rear wheels out of ruts and mud holes. Along the way, he determined that wider iron wheels would provide more stable footing than Conestoga wheels, which were four to six inches wide. He also concluded that pack mules and horses would be more efficient than the burly, troublesome oxen. In 1837 Holladay moved to Weston, Missouri, a critical transportation junction on the Missouri River. He opened a general store, saloon, and small hotel, and served as postmaster for a stint. All the while, Holladay worked behind his store perfecting iron wagon rims that were ten to twelve inches wide. When the leading western freight company, Russell, Majors and Waddell, rejected his ideas, he decided to go into business for himself. Although still only nineteen, he mortgaged his store and bought fourteen freight wagons, sixty mules, and twenty horses.

With his small fleet, Holladay landed small army contracts to deliver freight from Fort Leavenworth to Fort Laramie and Santa Fe. His five-ton wagons, carrying army supplies and trade items, made three round trips a season and cut the usual travel time by several days. He earned handsome profits and doubled the size of his caravans. Holladay's success led to freighting contracts for General Stephen Kearny's Army of the West during the Mexican-American War. Holladay's freight wagons traveled 3,500 miles with General Kearney's army and netted a 200 percent profit. After the war ended, Holladay expanded his fleet by purchasing cheap military surplus wagons, supplies, and livestock.

The freighting business was anything but easy. Wagon teams wrestled with impassable terrain, unpredictable weather, and exhausted livestock. Drivers got drunk or lost, equipment malfunctioned, and both bandits and Indian war bands created added dangers. The greatest challenge of all, however, came from rival companies. Competitors resorted to sabotage and subterfuge to sideline rival wagons and interfere with opponents' schedules. Holladay thrived in this competitive arena, organizing his own fake "Indian" raiding parties to disrupt challengers' lines, according to biographer Ellis Lucia.

Such trickery aside, Holladay's real breakthrough came when he developed commercial connections with the Mormon Church of Utah. Holladay had earned a good reputation with the Mormons for his service in the so-called Missouri "Mormon War" of 1838. Serving under Brigadier General Alexander Doniphan, Holladay delivered messages between the volunteer militia and the Mormons. Doniphan indignantly defied the wishes of Missouri's Governor Lilburn Boggs, who had issued an "Extermination Order" to kill all Mormons in his state. A decade later, Holladay presented a letter of introduction from Doniphan to Latter-day Saints leader Brigham Young. Young and Holladay struck up a mutually beneficial friendship. Holladay dispersed $2,500 in trade goods ($70,000 in 2014 dollars) among the Mormons, and received a contract to drive Mormon cattle to the California gold camps. As one of the few LDS-approved non-Mormon merchants in Utah, Holladay established a steady trade in hardware, lumber, jeans, flannel, glass, paper, furniture, and tea.

With a near-monopoly in Mormon trade, money began to build up in Holladay's pockets. But it didn't stay there long. An ambitious, venturesome risk-taker, Holladay explored other opportunities. He bought a thousand steers for $4 to $6 each and drove them across the Nevada desert, selling them for $60 each in Virginia City and other mining districts. He continued to haul Mormon cattle to the California mining towns, supplying settlers and developing a monopoly in western army contracts. According to biographer James V. Frederick, western army posts depended on Holladay's freight business for their very existence. From 1851 to 1853, Holladay shipped a total of 65,911 pounds of army supplies, clearing $4,036 ($119,000 in 2014 dollars) in profits. Holladay launched a line of riverboats on the Sacramento River, furnished goods for the Pacific Mail Steamship Company, and opened a slaughter- and meatpacking house to supply beef for the army at Benicia, California. He purchased large tracts of land in the Midwest and opened a distillery in Weston, Missouri. With all of his enterprises, Holladay could have retired to a life of ease, but his restless, ambitious spirit pushed him on.

Throughout the 1850s, the firm of Russell, Majors and Waddell had dominated western freighting. As Holladay's fortunes rose, those of Russell, Majors and Waddell declined. Holladay advanced loans to his competitors, receiving as collateral $600,000 ($15.5 million in 2014 dollars) in government vouchers. According to biographer Ellis Lucia, Holladay deliberately "lost" the vouchers, leaving the Russell firm in deeper straits. Bankrupt, Russell, Majors and Waddell went up for auction in March 1861. Holladay purchased the firm and reorganized his company as the Holladay Overland Mail and Express, capitalizing the new enterprise with $3 million ($77.5 million in 2014 dollars) in stock. Holladay quickly began surveying passenger routes and established a 1,200-mile stagecoach line between Atchison, Kansas and Salt Lake City.

Holladay's extensive stage system required hundreds of employees. The businessman hired two superintendents to oversee an eastern (Atchison to Denver) and a western (Denver to Salt Lake City) division. Each division was split into three 200-mile sections, overseen by division agents. The agents hired drivers, stock tenders, harness makers, carpenters, and blacksmiths. Holladay built a home station every fifty miles along the 1,200-mile route, often complete with repair shops, overnight accommodations, dining rooms, lounges, and a telegraph office. Women were hired to help run some of the home stations. Travelers found the finest ones decorated with brightly colored flowers, tablecloths, pictures, and curtains.

Holladay knew that motivated drivers were the key to success. He employed seventy-five drivers to travel fifty to sixty miles a day, paying each between $75 and $100 per month. When American Indian resistance escalated, Holladay offered his drivers higher wages to keep the coaches rolling on schedule. Priding himself on ostentatious appearances, Holladay clad his drivers in flashy outfits, including broad-brimmed sombreros, corduroys trimmed with velvet, high-heeled boots, leather gloves, and nine-foot rawhide whips with ornately decorated handles. Holladay provided warm underwear and wool socks at no cost to the drivers, demanding only their best behavior in return. Holladay prohibited on-the-job profanity and drunkenness, although division agents were known to look the other way if drivers over-indulged while attempting to stay warm on frigid nights. His tactics proved efficient as drivers remained loyal to Holladay and consistently shattered travel records.

Equipped with his innovative wide wheels, Holladay's stagecoaches set his company apart. His coaches were the finest in the country, bought at $1,500 each (about $40,000 in 2014 dollars) and fitted with the best harnesses from New Hampshire. Weighing a ton each, the coaches were painted fiery red with yellow and black trim and emblazoned with the legend "Overland Stage Company" in a fancy font. Good draft animals were hard to come by during the Civil War, but Holladay insisted on quality, spending as much as $250 (about $6,500 in 2014 dollars) for each horse or mule. With an annual $1 million spent on livestock, Holladay reportedly had $1,500 to $2,000 ($40,000 to $50,000 in 2014 dollars) invested in a single hitch of six horses. While other stagecoach companies worried simply about the health of their livestock, Holladay also concerned himself with the finest looking animals, arranging the animals by color combinations. With the meticulously-dressed drivers and elaborate stagecoaches, Holladay's Overland Stage Company coasted ahead of the competition.

In addition to passenger traffic, Holladay pursued every mail contract the government offered in the West. In order to prove his line's superiority (and to draw headline news), Holladay raced from Salt Lake City to Atchison, Kansas, in eight days and six hours, then made a dizzying dash from Salt Lake City to Carson City, Nevada, in three days and twenty-three hours. Holladay spent $2,425,000 (almost $63 million 2014 dollars) equipping and repairing the original Overland route, bought local feeder lines, and acquired toll bridges and ferry concessions. Local settlements and mining camps also needed supplies, so Holladay swept in with one thousand miles of branch lines to smaller towns. Two years after acquiring the Russell, Majors, and Waddell, Holladay had built the world's largest stage company. Overland stages and wagons transported more than 100 million pounds of supplies on 20,000 wagons, supported by 15,000 employees and 150,000 animals. Holladay's seven mail contracts earned $1,896,023 (nearly $50 million in 2014 dollars) over four years. By 1865, Holladay's stagecoaches roamed over 5,000 miles of roads, earning $31 million in freight costs from the Missouri River to the Rockies and $13 million in Nevada and Utah.

As successful as his stagecoach and freighting services became, Holladay recognized dark clouds on the horizon. Resistance by Plains Indian tribes provided setbacks. Native raiding parties stole livestock, burned stations, and damaged equipment. Following the Sand Creek Massacre, Cheyenne, Arapaho, and Lakota warriors destroyed every stage station between Denver and Julesburg. Holladay claimed an estimated $151, 543 ($4 million in 2014 dollars) in losses from the raids, and sought reimbursement from Congress. The oncoming railroad construction posed an even greater threat of competition. By 1866, Holladay foresaw the end of his industry. He merged his line with the Butterfield Stagecoach Company, acquiring every federal mail contract in the West in the process. In November 1866, Holladay sold his combined company to Wells Fargo. As a final hurrah, Holladay staged a record-breaking twelve-day crosscountry stagecoach ride that made him an international hero.

The versatile Holladay branched out into new transportation ventures. He moved to San Francisco to focus on the steamship business in 1869. His steamship company established routes throughout the Northwest, carrying prospectors swiftly to the Fraser River goldfields in Canada. Holladay then organized the California, Oregon, and Mexico Steamship Company, established a regular service to Hawaii, and earned the South Seas and Australia mail subsidy. The restless Holladay next poured millions into Oregon's development, enticing new settlers with land promotions and real-estate companies. He financed Portland's first streetcar, built the finest wharf and bridges, and organized the Oregon Transfer Company in 1871. He made the jump from stagecoaches to railroads as well, organizing the Puget Sound and Columbia River Railroad Company.

Initially a success, the Puget Sound Railroad brought about Holladay's financial downfall. As did many other attempted railway ventures, the line defaulted on bond payments during the Panic of 1873. German investor Henry Villard began investigating Holladay's business practices, uncovering several shady transactions. In May 1876, Holladay agreed to sign away all of his interests and stock to the foreign investors. Stripped of his power and prestige, Holladay was left with a mere $5,000 annual income from a resort in Nevada. In the decade before his death, Holladay pleaded for Congress to reimburse the losses from the 1860s Indian raids and fought a lengthy and heated legal battle with his brother. Stress, along with chronic kidney issues, rheumatism, and a heart condition, proved too great a burden. Nearing the end of his life, he reportedly remarked, "Strange how time at last makes all things even." Benjamin Holladay passed away on July 8, 1887. His estate of $125,000, while respectable, was a shadow of his former wealth.

In the West before railroads, Benjamin Holladay was the undisputed transportation king. By supplying affordable, reliable, and reasonably rapid transportation, his freight wagons and stagecoaches provided a lifeline to remote mining camps, frontier settlements, and growing towns. He provided an essential segment of the required infrastructure needed to drive the expansion of the American West. Active, restless, and indomitable, Holladay never shied away from a gamble, yet he was also flexible enough to adapt to the West's fluid economic conditions. His lines created a stable conduit for trade, commerce, and settlement, and prepared the way for subsequent rail lines, roads, and highways, and, even later, air routes, while his colorful style contributed to our romantic conceptions of the West.

Frederick, James Vincent. *Ben Holladay, The Stagecoach King.* Glendale, CA: Arthur H. Company, 1940.

Lucia, Ellis. *The Saga of Ben Holladay: Giant of the Old West.* New York: Hastings House, 1959.

THE BIG FOUR

"One man works hard all his life and ends up a pauper.
Another man, no smarter, makes twenty million dollars.
Luck has a hell of a lot to do with it." Charles Crocker

{1821–1900}   {1824–1893}   {1822–1888}   {1813–1878}

Collis P. Huntington, Leland Stanford, Charles C. Crocker, and Mark Hopkins. The four men, pictured above left to right, called themselves "the Associates." When their Central Pacific and Southern Pacific Railroads became famous, the press deemed them the "Big Four." Farmers, workingmen, and journalists sometimes called their network of railroads, real estate, and financial institutions the "Octopus" for its apparent stranglehold on California's political and economic life. Californians hailed the Big Four as saviors, or damned them as unscrupulous profiteers, or both at once. To a certain extent, it was all true.

The four businessmen assembled in 1860, meeting in a cramped room above a hardware store to hear Theodore Judah's pitch for a transcontinental railroad. Agreeing to risk their entire fortunes on Judah's dream, they became the richest, most powerful men in

California—authors, really, of the Golden State's glorious ascent. They eventually controlled more than 11,000 miles of railroad line. Their Central Pacific Railroad pierced the fastness of the Sierra Nevada mountain range, linking San Francisco, Sacramento, Nevada, and the Pacific with the rest of the nation. A separate route, the Southern Pacific, connected southern California and Arizona to the Mississippi Valley and the Gulf Coast, completing the long-sought southern transcontinental line. The Big Four diversified into real estate, civic development, timber, mining, shipbuilding, steamship lines, and ocean freight, allowing them to weather financial downturns that wiped out many of their rivals. One of their members, Leland Stanford, became California's governor, then a U.S. senator. The others made or broke governors and senators whenever they saw fit. Significant portions of their wealth helped underwrite major libraries, churches, the arts, and, most famously, a university. All in all, this wasn't a bad showing for four Sacramento shopkeepers whose greatest previous ambition was to corner the local market on shovels. As Charles Crocker once observed, "One man works hard all his life and ends up a pauper. Another man, no smarter, makes twenty million dollars. Luck has a hell of a lot to do with it."

Luck may have had something to do with the Associates' rise, but hard work, aggressive business tactics, and the pursuit of an audacious dream also contributed. The partners pursued their dream to build a railroad linking California with the rest of the nation tenaciously, often ruthlessly, and it made them rich. Empire builders in the truest sense, they did far more than merely secure the Union in a network of steel; they opened up new markets and new possibilities beyond each of their wildest hopes.

The four partners shared much in common. Each spent his childhood in upstate New York. Each experienced hardscrabble times as a young man. Each supported the nascent Republican Party. Each recognized the potential for wealth in California. And each understood that the most reliable path to mining riches came not from wielding the business end of a shovel, but in selling shovels to the miners. In other ways, their clearly differentiated skills and responsibilities gave them a definite advantage over potential rivals. Collis Huntington thrived as the group's strategist, lobbying political and financial decision makers; procuring rails, ties, and rolling stock; and issuing telegraphic directives to his partners from his spare New York City office. As the Central Pacific's first president, Leland Stanford was the ideal front man, shaping the company's public image with carefully prepared statements and tending to local political fires. The florid, energetic Charles Crocker oversaw construction, hustling up and down the line and supervising the largest workforce America had ever seen in some of the most challenging conditions. The cautious, affable Mark Hopkins directed the Central Pacific's finances, keeping (and sometimes cooking) the Central Pacific's books, and bringing his partners' wilder flights of fancy back down to earth.

Of the four, Collis Huntington was universally hailed as the smartest and most crafty. Born in 1821, the gifted, abrasive businessman grew up in a poor family. He considered hard work and thrift a privilege, boasting in later life of clocking twelve-hour days, seven days per week. Long hours chopping wood and tramping the countryside as an itinerant peddler gave him an ox's strength and endurance, if little sentiment. One contemporary described him as "a hard and cheery old man, with no more soul than a shark," although such barbs usually bounced harmlessly off his sharkskin hide. He refrained from drinking and smoking and expected no less from his employees. He was also famously pragmatic. He offended Parisians on an 1889 excursion by calling the Eiffel Tower impractical, then asserted that American engineers could build one a mile high if they chose. He was a bulldog in defense of his railroad though, sparring with tough customers such as Thomas Durant, Oakes Ames, and Jay Gould, and usually winning. He was a champion grudge holder. When Leland

Stanford ran for senate against a Huntington protégé, Huntington waited five cool years before forcing Stanford out as Central Pacific president and taking his place. At his inauguration, he took a moment to publicly gloat over Stanford's exile. The coup gave life to Stanford's assertion that no one should trust Huntington farther than they could throw a church up the side of California's Mount Shasta.

Various members of the Big Four took credit for first recognizing the potential in Theodore Judah's proposal to build a railroad across the Sierras. In all likelihood it was the canny Huntington who made the deal. But no sooner had the Big Four organized the Central Pacific Railroad than Huntington virtually left California behind, venturing east to open a New York office from which he could work in the background to procure rails and equipment and protect the railroad's political interests. Stanford, by contrast, assumed the railroad's public mantle. Slow of speech and thoughtful in approach, unwilling to stray from his meticulously prepared public comments, Stanford was never Huntington's mental equal. Yet he remained far more comfortable in the public spotlight, and his dignified demeanor drew favorable comparisons to that of Augustus Caesar and Napolean Bonaparte. Born into a large New York family in 1824, he saw emerging railroads slowly strangle the local stagecoach trade, and his father's innkeeping livelihood along with it. In 1852 he joined his older brother's California merchandising business, eventually assuming control of the family's Sacramento store. Always happy to stand in the limelight, Stanford steered into politics, serving on Sacramento's board of aldermen and, in 1861, winning a two-year term as California's governor.

Stanford's gubernatorial term helped the Central Pacific by equating the good of the railroad with the good of the governor and, logically, the good of California. Audiences saw Stanford at his best when he played the ceremonial role of Central Pacific president. (Leland's only material contributions to the Central Pacific, Huntington sneered, were to turn the first shovelful of earth and to drive the final spike). Generally less recognized was Stanford's advocacy for technological innovation. Leland stuffed his mansion with technological wonders, including an automatic music machine, known as an orchestrion, and mechanical birds who whistled tunes to startled guests. When the pace of blasting tunnels in the Sierras slowed to an earthworm's crawl, Leland forcefully pushed for the adoption of compressed air drills, nearly causing a rupture in the partnership. Much later, he hired photographer Eadweard Muybridge to capture images of a galloping horse with a series of cameras to learn if all four of its feet ever left the ground at once. The overlapping shots not only proved that horses could briefly fly, but laid the groundwork for the development of motion pictures.

Vain and a touch insecure, Stanford construed the world as a grand stage and cast himself in the role of Railroad King. He spent extravagantly on mansions, paintings, jewelry, and on his namesake university. He plunged an immense amount into breeding and training thoroughbred racehorses, and he was an early adopter of California's wine industry. Stanford's lavish lifestyle embarrassed his other partners, who affected the appearances of poverty whenever government inspectors happened by.

The good-natured Mark Hopkins could not have presented a greater contrast. The oldest partner by nearly a decade, and the thinnest, Hopkins stood out among Gilded Age businessmen who equated a generous waistline with opulence. The spare merchandiser possessed, in a biographer's words, a "long thin nose set in a long thin face and surmounting a long thin beard." Cautious and unostentatious, Hopkins shunned complications. Like Huntington, he abstained from alcohol and tobacco, savored thrift, and loathed waste. Unlike Collis and the others, Mark had an unusually petite appetite.

The cautious Hopkins loathed risk. He voted against speculation that drained resources away from the Central Pacific's main line. Success and failure both seemed to make him queasy. He acted, a contemporary observed, "as if he wanted to apologize for his millions." Instead, he preferred simple, orderly things. He abhorred messiness and savored small details—a meal, a friendship, or a nicely balanced set of account books—and he preferred to live in a simple rented cottage. At least, that is, until his wife Mary persuaded him to build the grandest of all the Nob Hill mansions. Almost unique among pioneer Californians, Hopkins embraced vegetarianism. Almost nothing pleased him more than coaxing carrots and potatoes out of the soil behind his house.

Almost nothing pleased him more, that is, except keeping accounts. As the Central Pacific's treasurer, the publicity-shy Hopkins thrived as the Big Four's most silent partner. He preferred honest dealing and labored mightily to steer his partners away from shadier deals. But he also helped mislead state and federal officials about the true state of the railroad's finances once the deals were done. Congressional investigators became curious about the CP's billing records and whether the Big Four had accepted any unreported revenues, and it was Hopkins who carried the construction company's fifteen immaculately kept leatherbound account books down to furnaces in the basement of the Central Pacific's offices. And it was Hopkins who shoved them all in—reportedly coining the phrase "cooking the books."

While the other members of the Big Four took credit for financial development of the railroad, Crocker proudly said, "I built the Central Pacific." Large—he tipped the scales in excess of 250 pounds—and mercurial, Crocker swung between spells of demonic energy and long periods of lethargic depression. When active, he was a dynamo, just the sort of man to ride in and take charge of a difficult construction project. He was also, biographer Oscar Lewis reports, "boastful, stubborn, tactless, vain," as well as guileless and sometimes a little lazy. Far more comfortable in the field, Crocker disdained deskwork. A visiting San Francisco newspaper editor who visited him at his office noted that his feet were "more often on his desk than under it."

Crocker got his start at the age of twelve as a newspaper agent in his hometown of Troy, New York. Selling out for a profit, he tried farming, blacksmithing, and operating a primitive foundry. Soon, California fever struck, and the young blacksmith made his way west to work in a family store near Sacramento. By 1856 he was serving as town alderman along with fellow merchants Mark Hopkins and Leland Stanford.

The initial division of labor for the Big Four seemed clear enough. The affable Stanford would assume the role of front man. Huntington went east to procure supplies, lay the partners' political foundation, and develop a growth strategy for the railroad. Hopkins remained at home tending to financial matters. That left Crocker in charge of the actual construction, even though he still had everything to learn about building railroads. He formed a construction company, Crocker & Company, with the other three as silent partners. He signed a contract for $400,000 (about $9 million in 2014), and got to work.

The first flat stretch from Sacramento to the Sierras was easy. But even with Judah's excellent survey, the ascent into the mountains nevertheless required the steepest ascent to the highest summit yet reached by a railroad. Construction crews had to blast miles of tunnels through some of the hardest granite on earth. Pecking away at the stubborn stone ramparts, the workers sometimes logged only two or three inches per day. Worse, record-breaking snow fell. Forty-four major storms and unbearable cold blasted the crews out of the mountains for three consecutive winters. Oscar Lewis vividly described the "curious mole-like lives" of the Central Pacific's winter army, "passing from work to living quarters in dim passages far beneath the snow's surface."

That Crocker was able to marshal 3,000 laborers by 1865 was a logistical miracle. As late as 1864, the company employed only 600 men on work that really required 5,000. American laborers preferred homesteading or digging for gold to chipping railroad grades through the Sierras; three out of five white workers employed by the company quit immediately to work in the mines. Crocker noticed that small groups of Chinese laborers had worked well on other local lines. But when he suggested hiring them, the other directors balked. Since their arrival along with the first gold seekers in 1849, the Chinese had been consistently excluded from white society. The Irish and other laborers scoffed at their unfamiliar customs, food, and clothing. Governor Stanford had called for their exclusion, and Crocker's superintendent declared them unfit for building railroads.

To such critics, Crocker pointed out that the Chinese had built the Great Wall. As a business strategy, hiring Chinese was the only viable option, and Crocker suspected that detractors were mistaken about Chinese capabilities. So he arranged a working trial for fifty Chinese laborers. Their discipline, frugality, and cleanliness, aversion to off-duty carousing, and willingness to give the project their all converted the Central Pacific directors. Organized into tidy gangs, the Chinese workers scaled precipices and lowered themselves on ropes down cliffs to eke out ledges for the right-of-way, sometimes carrying vials of explosive nitroglycerine. They built lasting rock fills and buttresses, blasted away the Sierra granite, and spun track across the Nevada wastelands. They gave their lives by the scores, too. More than 1,500 died in accidents and avalanches.

The efficiency and endurance of the Chinese brought Stanford around. He admitted that "without them it would be impossible to complete the western portion of this great national enterprise." Crocker agreed, "If we were in a hurry for a job of work, it was better to put Chinese on it at once." Before long, the partners were sending recruiting agents directly to China—by 1869, the Central Pacific employed more than 15,000 Chinese.

"Crocker's Pets," as the Chinese workers became known, were part of the largest single force of workmen assembled in American history up to that time. And they were the type of workforce Crocker enjoyed driving forward, in the most challenging of conditions. "Wrapped in furs like an Eskimo," writes Oscar Lewis, the big construction boss constantly patrolled the line, exhorting snow shovelers, encouraging a gang pulling locomotives over the high passes on sleds, or finding fault with a stretch of thirty-seven miles of snowsheds designed to protect passing trains. As Durant did on the eastern section, Crocker often sacrificed quality for speed. The Sierra Nevada line nevertheless cost $280,000 (about $6.3 million in 2014) per mile—a dead loss on the government's $48,000-per-square-mile subsidy that would have to be made up somewhere. But he worked his crews to a peak of efficiency. Working over flatter terrain than the Central Pacific, Union Pacific crews sometimes laid six or even seven miles of track per day. When the Union Pacific crews reached seven and a half, Crocker speculated that his Chinese workers could lay ten. Union Pacific General Manager Durant wagered $10,000 (about $226,000 in 2014) that it couldn't be done. Crocker carefully selected his time. On April 28, 1869, his handpicked work gang of 850 tracklayers, backed by a supporting crew of 5,000, started off. Twelve hours later, the last of the exhausted crew collapsed, but they had laid ten miles and fifty-six feet of track—a record that has never been surpassed in the age of muscle labor.

Crocker unaccountably absented himself from the Golden Spike ceremony at Promontory Point, Utah, in early May 1869, and he was the first to seriously consider retiring from the company. After briefly selling out and recuperating in Europe in 1871, he returned to the fold. Before long, the former storekeeper built his own plush early Renaissance mansion on Nob Hill, where he nurtured a magnificent art collection. Like his colleagues, Crocker diversified his investments into coal mining, real estate, and banking. He lavished particular attention on his beloved hotel, the Del Monte beside Monterey Bay, and he died there on August 14, 1888.

By linking the Golden State to the rest of the nation, the Associates forged modern California. But their achievement meant far more to the nation, and to the political and economic dynamics of the nineteenth century. Powered by steam locomotives, businessmen such as the Associates opened new avenues of political and economic power. The decision to build a line to a certain point meant prosperity to the targeted settlements; bypassing a town almost certainly signaled its failure. The age of steam opened new avenues of wealth and made those who controlled these avenues the masters of America's economic destiny. Within only a few years, it was clear to the Big Four that their rewards would more than repay their audacious risks. By 1900, when Edward H. Harriman's Union Pacific began to absorb the Central Pacific and Southern Pacific, the Big Four's tracks reached from Oregon to Louisiana—and for a spell their ships provided the most direct route to Asia—and the heirs of Huntington, Stanford, Hopkins, and Crocker oversaw a national empire of shipping, manufacturing, mining, and real estate concerns.

With large fortunes came an obligation for largesse, and here, the Big Four left an uneven legacy. Crocker eluded philanthropic pressures; his entry in the *American National Biography* reports he "gave nothing to charity [and] nothing to public institutions of any kind" (although his brother, Central Pacific general counsel Edwin B. Crocker, left behind a world-class art collection that became the core of Sacramento's Crocker Art Gallery). Before the Civil War, Mark Hopkins made modest gifts to support abolition. Fifteen years after his 1878 death, Mary remembered her first husband by creating the Mark Hopkins Institute of Art. In public, Collis P. Huntington bragged about his aversion to philanthropy. In private, he gave several lasting gifts to his community, including a technical school for African Americans in Virginia and Huntington Falls in Golden Gate Park.

Arguably, the Big Four's greatest charitable legacy sprang from tragedy. Leland and Jane Stanford doted on their son, Leland, Jr. The bright, curious boy enjoyed collecting old coins, medals, and ancient pottery and sculpture fragments. When he received an acceptance letter to Harvard at the age of fifteen, his proud parents sponsored a family tour of Europe. In Greece, Leland, Jr., developed flu-like symptoms. The Stanfords traveled to Italy, and young Leland's condition grew worse. Hastily summoned doctors from Paris and Rome diagnosed typhoid, a bacterial disease caused by drinking contaminated water. As Leland lingered, his parents paid people to layer the streets below his hotel room with straw to deaden the noise. Leland passed away on March 13, 1884. Gathering themselves from their devastating loss, Leland, Sr., and Jane Stanford dedicated themselves to providing the educational opportunity to others that had been denied their son. Together, they founded Leland Stanford, Jr., University. Stanford characteristically spared no expense. As much as the creation of the Central Pacific, his university became the crowning achievement of his career.

Historians, both in the early 1900s and today, write a lot about the corruption, manipulation, and waste inherent in the race to build a transcontinental line. But it's also important to remember the profound economic transformation ushered in by the railways. The Central Pacific and Union Pacific, and their successors, jump-started western economic development. The steel rails extended the reach of eastern capital, provided access to remote natural resources, carried a flood of immigrants, Civil War veterans, tourists, and settlers into the West, and transported farm products, livestock, gold, silver, and timber back to the East. Steam engines into the West gave political leaders direct contact with their national audiences, and powered the industrial revolution. Critics condemned railroad monopolies as conduits of grasping opportunism, while boosters praised the iron horse as a vehicle of opportunity and economic mobility. In the end, both were correct.

Bancroft, Hubert Howe. *History of the Life of Leland Stanford: A Character Study.* Oakland, CA: Biobooks, 1952.

Chen, Jack. *The Chinese of America: From the Beginning to the Present.* New York: HarperCollins Publishers, 1980.

Gordon, Sarah H. *Passage to Union: How the Railroads Transformed American Life, 1829-1929.* Chicago: Ivan R. Dee, 1966.

Lavender, David. *The Great Persuader: A Biography of Collis P. Huntington.* Garden City, NY: Doubleday, 1970.

Lewis, Oscar. *The Big Four: The Story of Huntington, Stanford, Hopkins, and Crocker, and the Building of the Central Pacific.* New York: A.A. Knopf, 1938.

Rayer, Richard. *The Associates: Four Capitalists who Created California.* New York: W.W. Norton, 2008.

Tutorow, Norman E. and Evie LaNora. *The Governor: The Life and Legacy of Leland Stanford.* Two volumes. Spokane, WA: Arthur H. Clark Co., 2004.

THOMAS C. DURANT

PUSHING FROM OMAHA TO PROMONTORY POINT

{ 1 8 2 0 – 1 8 8 5 }

"What is the chief end of man?—to get rich.
In what way?—Dishonestly if we can; honestly if we must."

Mark Twain, "The Revised Catechism," 1871

Mark Twain, a leading liberal journalist of his time, probably had Thomas C. Durant in mind when he penned these words for a satirical *New York Herald Tribune* essay. Durant, the leading genius behind the eastern portion of the transcontinental railroad, took his fortune however he could get it. He was one of the nation's most flamboyant and restless promoters and an accomplished manipulator of people and capital. He nearly ruined the Union Pacific Railroad with his unabashed plundering, his tenure as vice-president and general manager of the line ended in charges of corruption, fraud, and bribery, and his manipulation of the infamous Crédit Mobilier of America construction company made his name the byword for Gilded Age scandal. And still, the erratic and unscrupulous promoter managed to complete the near impossible. In a time of immense national upheaval, Durant organized, promoted, and supervised the construction of the inaugural 1,085 miles of rail from Omaha, Nebraska, to Promontory Point, Utah—an accomplishment in expense and technological innovation equal to a trip to the moon a century later. Whatever his critics might say of his ways, Durant provided the skill, the means, and the will to complete a vital national project.

Born in Lee, Massachusetts, in 1820, Durant graduated with a medical degree at the age of twenty. After a brief career as an opthamology professor, he took over his family's New York City grain exporting firm.

He also became interested in railroad speculation. Fortunately for Durant, the 1850s were a profitable era for young railroad entrepreneurs. Spurred along by the first federal railroad land grants, developers tied together a handful of disconnected eastern lines into a national system. By 1860, four major railroads linked the Atlantic to the Mississippi River Valley, and pioneer lines probed the Iowa and Missouri frontiers. In the meantime, the federal government sponsored four major surveys of the western territories, seeking the best route for a transcontinental line. Anxious to join the action, in 1851 Durant formed a partnership with respected engineer Henry Farnam to complete the Chicago & Rock Island Railroad. Under Durant, the Rock Island was the first line to span a railroad bridge across the Mississippi River. The partners also founded the Missouri & Mississippi (M&M) Railroad to bind Iowa in a network of steel. Much to Farnam's dismay, Durant used company paper to back his own private speculations, a manipulation that only became clear when the Panic of 1857 exposed the M&M's liabilities. Farnum became the first—but not the last—to suffer from Durant's avarice.

Durant's apprenticeship on the Rock Island and M&M lines exposed him to the gifted engineer Grenville M. Dodge who, in turn, surveyed potential rights-of-way west of Omaha. Dodge's surveys gave Durant an enviable head start in the race to begin a transcontinental line. Durant also hired an accomplished Illinois corporate lawyer, Abraham Lincoln, to defend the bridge spanning the Mississippi River from litigation by steamboat owners. His railroad work inspired the future president to embrace the potential of a Pacific railway. President Lincoln no doubt recollected his time as Durant's corporate lawyer when he signed the Pacific Railroad Act into law in 1862.

The transcontinental challenge stoked Durant's ambition, and the generous government subsidies appealed to his acquisitiveness. The new Railroad Act offered railway builders generous grants of cash and land, payable by the mile of line constructed. Yet great obstacles lay ahead. The Civil War continued to absorb the government's resources, and venture capital remained scarce. Potential investors balked at a provision in the Pacific Railroad Act granting the government the first lien on defaulting bonds. The president delayed his decision about whether the eastern terminus would be located in Omaha or across the Missouri River at nearby Council Bluffs. And in St. Louis, the famous western explorer John C. Frémont emerged as a serious rival. The 1862 Pacific Railroad Act specified that the first railway to reach the 100th meridian would become eligible to win the Pacific railroad contract. Well capitalized by Frémont's California gold mines, his Union Pacific-Eastern Division (UPED, later renamed the Kansas Pacific) represented a significant threat.

As the self-appointed lead promoter of the federally chartered Union Pacific Railroad, Durant raced to catch up. Liquidating his assets—mostly earned through dealing contraband southern cotton—and tapping every possible source of credit, he offered friends and acquaintances an irresistible bargain. Durant personally fronted each investor's 10 percent down payment for Union Pacific stocks, and guaranteed to take or buy back any share at any time. The risk-free gamble for investors paid great dividends for Durant. He now influenced a large voting bloc, and he had opened an avenue to control far more stock than allowed by law.

Armed with control of nearly half the company's shares, Durant dominated the first stockholders' meeting in October 1863. He quickly appointed malleable cronies into executive positions. Durant selected General John A. Dix as the Union Pacific's first president. Dix was Durant's ideal front man. He enjoyed a reputation as an honest, respectable military officer with strong political connections. Even better, his military responsibilities as Union commander of the Department of the East kept him conveniently away. The doctor saved for himself the positions of vice president and general manager, two behind-the-scenes spots from which he could direct the Union Pacific's future.

Having secured control of the Union Pacific's directorate, Durant contrived a new expedient to divert funds into his private coffers. He acquired a construction company, the Crédit Mobilier, to manage the railway's construction contract. Since the government issued payments by the mile, it was a small step to maneuver the Union Pacific's protesting engineers into surveying a meandering route that added more mileage, costing more taxpayer dollars than was necessary. And, just to be safe, Durant exorbitantly padded the company's construction invoices, diverting funds into bank accounts for himself and his associates. Any overly inquisitive congressman who threatened to expose Durant's manipulations quickly received a piece of the action.

Durant missed few tricks when it came to lining his own pockets. When President Lincoln ordered the eastern terminus to be located at Council Bluffs, Iowa, Durant ignored him, starting construction in Omaha, where he owned substantial real estate, instead. When congressmen were needed to make friendly amendments to the Railroad Act, a smiling Durant arrived in Washington ready to wine and dine, freely distributing Union Pacific cash and stock certificates. When stock prices for Durant's Missouri & Mississippi Railroad were beginning to droop, the Union Pacific general manager awarded the M&M the franchise to link up with transcontinental railhead. Then, after selling off his premium M&M stock at premium prices, he granted the link to the rival instead. Since Durant secretly controlled the rival as well, he again cashed in from elevated stock sales of that company. And, always and in between, he siphoned off any loose cash that came his way.

To his credit, Durant hired extremely talented professionals to survey and build the road. After his initial surveyor quit in protest over the doctor's financial shenanigans, Durant persuaded Grenville Dodge to take the job. Since the government paid railroad subsidies by the mile, speed counted for everything. So Durant hired the hard-nosed Casement brothers, Jack and Daniel, to oversee construction. Although constantly pressured to design a more circuitous route, Dodge surveyed a line that needed very little subsequent straightening. Meanwhile, the Casements forged a huge army of surveyors, graders, tracklayers, blasters, teamsters, lumbermen, and drovers, driving them forward with military discipline. The brothers recruited discharged Union and Confederate veterans, Irish immigrants, and newly freed African Americans. Brigham Young, a major stockholder, contributed Mormon laborers for the Utah segment. Under "General Jack" Casement's command, the diverse workforce operated together like the pistons of a finely-tuned locomotive.

Durant pushed his employees hard. After all, each mile constructed by the Union Pacific was money taken from the rival Central Pacific. No one could accuse him of not spending lavishly on occasion. He poured money into newly-invented steam shovels to speed up grading. Casement's laborers reached such a peak of efficiency that it was not unusual for the railhead to advance two, three, or more miles a day over open country. (Competition became so fierce between the UP and CP crews that after the lines met, each crew continued building past each other for another 100 miles.) Still, the constant drive for speed, combined with Durant's obsession with inflating his profit margin, compromised the line's quality. The doctor cut corners by purchasing substandard rails and ties. He insisted crews anchor tracks with sand ballast when his engineers called for more reliable (and expensive) stone. Ironically, Durant nearly missed the golden spike ceremony at Promontory Point on May 10, 1869, when one of his shoddy Union Pacific bridges gave out, stranding his special train on the wrong side of the gorge. That same year, government inspectors estimated that the UP needed an additional $7,000,000 (or about $118,000,000 in 2014 dollars) in upgrades and repairs to become a first-class road. Railroad managers scrambled to replace hundreds of miles of crumbling bridges, bedding, and track almost from the moment Dodge drove the last ceremonial spike home.

Durant's elusive bookkeeping, along with constant clashes with Dodge, President-elect Grant, and some of the more honest members of the Union Pacific's board, eventually spelled the end of his tenure as UP general manager. Anticipating ouster, he resigned on May 24, 1869, just two weeks after the golden spike ceremony. He left behind a hopeless tangle of debts, obligations, inflated invoices, murky accounts, along with a strong odor of political scandal and corruption that would long taint the Union Pacific.

When Durant's machinations of the Union Pacific and Crédit Mobilier became public in 1873, his name became synonymous with scandal. Yet he certainly wasn't the only post-Civil War businessman who used personal profit as a motivation to build great things. In his defense, the Union Pacific generated robust operating revenues almost from the start. In many ways, the transcontinental line was just a throughway; feeder track still needed to be laid to link the two major western cities of Denver and Salt Lake City, as well as settlements in Nevada and California. Yet the line immediately overshadowed slower, less reliable wagon freight, and it allowed the rapid settlement of the vast reaches between the Missouri River and the Pacific. Nebraska, for example, had been virtually unsettled in 1864. In 1867 it entered the Union with a thriving population of 122,000. Of course, Durant's line at times caused as much "unsettlement" as settlement. Cheyenne, Arapaho, Sioux, and Crow warriors fought fiercely to prevent the railroad from invading their domains—ambushing construction crews, tearing up track, derailing locomotives, and cutting telegraph wires. Durant never hesitated to call on the military to crush resisting tribes, and his advancing line made it all the easier for the U.S. Army to transport troops and supplies for that very purpose.

When Thomas Durant died in 1885, the trans-Mississippi West was a far different place than it had been in 1862. Railroad lines girded the West, tying the region closely to the national economy. Farmers and ranchers poured onto the plains and deserts, sending back bounties of grain, livestock, and produce. Travel from St. Louis to California was no longer a grueling, months-long ordeal, and the Native American tribes of the greater West were losing their freedom and entering the long twilight of the reservation system. While one could easily argue that the Union Pacific line could have been completed more efficiently and less expensively, it had been completed. In the long run, Durant's vision outshone his plundering ways.

Athearn, Robert G. *Union Pacific Country.* Chicago: Rand McNally & Co., 1971.

Bain, David H. *Empire Express: Building the First Transcontinental Railroad.* New York: Viking Penguin, 1997.

Klein, Maury. *Union Pacific: The Birth of a Railroad, 1862–1893.* Garden City: Doubleday & Co., 1987.

Williams, John Hoyt. *A Great and Shining Road: The Epic Story of the Transcontinental Railroad.* Lincoln: University of Nebraska Press, 1988.

CYRUS K. HOLLIDAY

THE ATCHISON, TOPEKA AND SANTA FE

{ 1 8 2 6 - 1 9 0 0 }

Railroad developer Cyrus K. Holliday was notable enough to merit a supporting role in the 1940 Warner Brothers western, *Santa Fe Trail,* starring Errol Flynn, Ronald Reagan, and Olivia de Havilland. In an early scene, Holliday, portrayed by American character actor Henry O'Neill, introduces the two male leads to the unsettled political situation in Kansas. He also shares his vision for a rail line into the unpopulated wastes west of Leavenworth. When an eavesdropping railroad conductor scoffs at his plan, Holliday promises: "There's half a nation out there, Cap. And someday I'll build a real railroad to open it up, clear to Santa Fe."

The cinematic Holliday mirrored some of the exuberance of the historical one. In impromptu stump speeches, the real-life Colonel Cyrus K. Holliday spun rhetorical fantasies about railroad lines reaching from his adopted home in Kansas to the "Halls of Montezuma" in Mexico City, and across the Pacific to China and beyond. According to railroad historian Keith L. Bryant, Jr., audiences sometimes responded with the cry, "Oh kind Lord, give us a rest!" Holliday, the founder, first president, and longtime director of the Atchison, Topeka, and Santa Fe Railway, may have been a dreamer. But he represented a kind of dreamer who was fairly successful in the American West in the mid-1800s. A town booster and relentless promoter of Kansas and its railroad potential, Holliday spun his dreams into reality. He linked national aspirations for western expansion and commerce with the means to expand, creating one of the most important—and enduring —western railroads.

C. K. Holliday was born in Carlisle, Pennsylvania, in 1826, the last of seven children. He received a public school education and earned bachelor's and master's degrees at the Methodist-run Allegheny College in western Pennsylvania. He also picked up a solid legal education. Good fortune fueled his trek to Kansas. Upon graduation, he found work with a railroad contracting firm called the George Howard Company. When the company dissolved, Holliday received $20,000 in county bonds (equivalent to more than $500,000 today) as compensation. Armed with a respectable amount of venture capital, he circulated through the Midwest and West, trying his luck in Cleveland, Chicago, and St. Louis. By 1854 he arrived in the frontier town of Lawrence, Kansas.

For an enterprising promoter such as Holliday, Kansas in 1854 was a boon. Frontier settlers boiled into the newly-created territory, seeking to break the rich prairie sod and ready to fight over the future of slavery in the United States. Holliday found the political and economic ferment in Kansas irresistible. He dove right in, buying a share of the Lawrence Town Company and traveling west to co-found the new settlement of Topeka. He wrote copy praising Topeka's charms for publication in eastern newspapers and became a recruiting agent for the New England Emigrant Aid Company, a prominent antislavery organization. The increasingly influential businessman helped organize Kansas's Free Soil party and served as a colonel in the territory's antislavery militia. He lobbied to make Topeka the territorial capital. He even took up arms against proslavery forces when Kansas erupted into civil war over slavery in 1855 and 1856. As Bleeding Kansas simmered down, the entrepreneur began looking for new ways to develop his adopted home. In 1857 he became director of the St. Joseph and Topeka Railroad, one of several competing companies vying to build railway lines through Kansas. In 1859 he wrote a charter for the Atchison & Topeka Railroad Company, proposing to build a line linking the former proslavery and antislavery strongholds, then continuing, as long as capital held out, in the general direction of Santa Fe.

Open for business almost forty years by 1859, Santa Fe was no longer a new or exotic destination to Kansas and Missouri businessmen. But it still stood out as the shining hub for commerce with the West and Southwest. Writing in the 1930s, Santa Fe Trail historian Walker Wyman reported that goods worth $10 million (about $275 million in 2014 dollars) annually traveled up and down the trail in 1859. Between the beginning of March and the end of July, the *Missouri Republican* counted 2,300 men, 1,970 wagons, 840 horses, 4,000 mules, 15,000 oxen, 73 carriages, and over 1,900 tons of freight departing for New Mexico, in addition to Pikes Peak and Nevada gold seekers, who were "too numerous to count." Holliday hoped to profit from this movement by linking Kansas by rail with the Rocky Mountains and the Southwest.

Drought and impending civil war delayed progress on the new railway line as the 1860s began, but Holliday continued to recruit subscribers and organize the company's directors. He was elected the company's first president, and he worked to organize rivals into a consortium to lobby Congress for railroad land grants. The outbreak of the Civil War dramatically improved the Atchison & Topeka's fortunes. Looking to consolidate America's western territories, Congress admitted Kansas to the Union, and passed the 1862 Pacific Railroad Act to authorize land grants to promising railway companies. Holliday submitted a handwritten bill to one of Kansas's first two United States senators, Samuel C. Pomeroy, authorizing a land grant for the Atchison & Topeka. Pomeroy, an A&T director, shepherded the bill through Congress and, in 1864, the newly renamed Atchison, Topeka,

& Santa Fe (AT&SF) Railway received enough federal land to build a line from the Missouri River to the Colorado border. Since much of the right-of-way passed through lands that had already been settled, Holliday and the other directors had to innovate to get the most from their grants. Holliday successfully lobbied the state legislature to grant additional lands within twenty miles of the line to replace lands already occupied by settlers, and he pushed through a law allowing counties to float bond issues to finance the line. In spite of his efforts on both the state and federal level, Holliday never convinced Congress to issue national bonds. He relied instead on local and county bonds, and sales from the railroad's land grant, for initial construction.

Despite Holliday's relentless optimism, the absence of reliable funding delayed construction on the line until 1868. In the meantime, the railroad director shuttled between Kansas, New York, Boston, Philadelphia, and Washington to drum up additional resources to cover the estimated $11,794-per-mile construction costs. Closer to home, he literally went door to door convincing reluctant Kansas voters to approve the railroad's county bonds. A big break came when a rival line failed to exercise its option to purchase a section of valuable potential farmland from the Potawatomie Indian Reservation in 1868. Holliday and the other AT&SF officers negotiated an agreement to purchase 338,766 acres of the Potawatomie reserve for an average price of $4.41 per acre (about $72 in 2014 dollars). Some tracts went for as little as $1 per acre. The sale of the fertile reservation land enriched Pomeroy and provided a sound financial basis from which to construct the Santa Fe line. Work finally began in the fall of 1868. Construction crews bridged the Kansas River to connect with Kansas Pacific track north of Topeka, and others began grading a roadbed to nearby coal deposits in Carbondale. Ironically turning their backs on the line's namesake town of Atchison, which was already served by the Kansas Pacific, laborers headed south and west, driving the first iron spikes home in March 1869. Two months later, the first Santa Fe locomotive, named the *Cyrus K. Holliday,* crossed the Kansas River into Topeka.

Settlers in southern and western Kansas had been wary when Holliday first made his pitch to fund the line with county bonds. The approaching Santa Fe tracks converted them into true believers. Historian Keith L. Bryant, Jr., reported the words of a Burlingame, Kansas, newspaper editor who wrote: "The 'Colonel Holliday's' whistle can be heard distinctly when the wind is favorable, and the music thereof accelerates one's spirits and sends the blood tingling to the end of the toes." Long before it reached its namesake destination, the Santa Fe increased land values and accelerated settlement by lowering transportation time and costs. It connected Kansas and Colorado railway towns such as Abilene, Wichita, Granada, and Dodge City with meat-processing centers in the Midwest, and cattle trails reaching deep into Texas. The AT&SF and other railroads, in the words of historian Richard White, compressed time and space, consumed local raw materials such as wood, iron, and coal, and rapidly transformed the West by injecting large numbers of new animals, crops, and people.

Stimulated by Texas cattle and Kansas wheat, the AT&SF barreled across the Great Plains towards the Rocky Mountains in the 1870s. Although Holliday remained a director, control of the railway had passed into the hands of a consortium of Boston investors in the mid 1860s. The line continued west through southern Colorado, looking to reach Santa Fe via the coal-rich Raton Pass region. Plans to build track up the Arkansas River to Trinidad and Pueblo, and possibly on to the Leadville silver bonanza, put the railroad directly in the path of William Jackson Palmer's Denver & Rio Grande. Like the directors of the Santa Fe, Palmer planned to build one line into New Mexico and another to the silvery mountain boomtowns. Both routes crossed narrow choke points that only allowed one railway to build through. In 1878, AT&SF engineers seized the Raton Pass route into New Mexico, purchasing the good will of Colorado toll road builder Richens "Uncle

Dick" Wootton, who claimed the pass, with a promise of free groceries and train travel for life. Denver & Rio Grande engineers arrived a half hour too late, only to find their way blocked by a small, well-armed force of men laying a new AT&SF line through the pass.

Farther north, the D&RG and the Santa Fe raced to be the first to Leadville. Both sides needed access to a bottleneck in the Royal Gorge, west of Cañon City. To enforce their claim, the AT&SF superintendent sent 300 hired guns to Cañon City. The D&RG struck back by offering some of them better pay. The AT&SF sent reinforcements from Dodge City, led by the western lawman Bat Masterson and supported by the legendary gunman John H. "Doc" Holliday. The rival crews built fortifications and prepared for an armed face-off. Realizing that their escalation threatened to end in bloodshed, the directors of the rival railways turned to the courts. As tensions continued to rise in the Royal Gorge construction camps, the case made its way through the legal system. In April 1879, the United States Supreme Court ruled that the Denver & Rio Grande's claim had precedent. AT&SF gunmen made a last, symbolic stand at a fortified D&RG roundhouse in Pueblo before Santa Fe directors signed an agreement to lease traffic on Palmer's line to Leadville, in exchange for a promise that the Denver & Rio Grande would abandon its New Mexico ambitions.

The Atchsion, Topeka, and Santa Fe line finally reached the ancient New Mexican capital after nearly two decades of planning, fundraising, and construction, but it didn't stop there. Tracklayers arrived in Albuquerque in 1880 and in 1881 connected with the Southern Pacific line in Deming, New Mexico. The southern connection created the nation's second transcontinental rail line. The company continued on to Arizona, finally linking with a Mexican subsidiary, the Sonora Railway, to reach the Gulf of Mexico. Over the next few decades, the line expanded until it connected the Midwest to the Southwest, the Rocky Mountains, and California.

Cyrus K. Holliday died in 1900, after nearly forty years of service to the Santa Fe Railway. By then, his line served Barstow, Los Angeles, and San Diego, California; Galveston and Fort Worth, Texas; Pueblo and Denver, Colorado; Springfield and Kansas City, Missouri; Chicago, Illinois; and many smaller communities in between. Within a year of his death, the line encompassed routes to Phoenix and the Grand Canyon as well. By the early twentieth century, the Santa Fe achieved an unsurpassed reputation for luxury and southwestern romance, as travelers rode on the streamlined *El Capitan* and *Super Chief,* and enjoyed speedy food service at Fred Harvey's sparkling restaurant chain as they cruised through the Land of Enchantment. Railways such as the Santa Fe domesticated the American West, making remote reaches of the nation accessible to the masses. Usually, but not always, railroads spurred economic development, lowered transportation costs, and diminished travel time, increasing the region's, and the nation's, prosperity. Declining passenger traffic caused the line to discontinue its passenger service in 1971, and a 1995 merger with Burlington Northern Company created the Burlington Northern Santa Fe Railway. Yet Colonel Cyrus K. Holliday's contributions to western railroading are still commemorated fondly. In honor of the railroad pioneer, Disneyland's Locomotive #1 has been known as the *C.K. Holliday* since the park's opening in 1955.

Bryant, Jr., Keith L. History of the Atchison, Topeka, and Santa Fe Railway. New York: Macmillan Publishing Company, Inc., 1974.

Marshall, James. Santa Fe: The Railroad that Built an Empire. New York: Random House, 1945.

White, Richard. "Transcontinental Railroads: Compressing Time and Space." HistoryNow: American History Online. Electronic resource. The Gilder Lehrman Institute of American History. www.gilderlehrman.org. Accessed August 23, 2014.

Wyman, Walker. "Freighting: A Big Business on the Santa Fe Trail." Kansas Historical Quarterly 1:1 (November 1931), 17-27.

THEODORE D. JUDAH

ENGINEERING THE FUTURE OF TRAVEL

{1826–1863}

"I have always had to pit my brains against other men's money." T. D. Judah

If the building of the first transcontinental railroad was truly America's great nineteenth-century epic, then Theodore Judah was its first great protagonist. He was so certain, insistent really, that engineers could run a rail line across the 2,000 miles of mountains and wasteland between the Missouri River and the Pacific Coast that many acquaintances questioned his sanity. Judah struck people as ambitious, humorless, and far too honest for his own good. He was highly opinionated and so single-minded about the prospects of a Pacific railroad that critics dismissed him as "Crazy Judah." Yet the practical engineer cut to the heart of the challenges blocking the construction of a transcontinental railroad. Whether in the muddy streets of Sacramento, the smoke-clouded halls of Washington, D.C., or the high, clear Sierra passes, he walked, talked, ate, slept, dreamed, breathed railroads. He personally charted the hidden route through the formidable Sierra Nevada range, and he persistently promoted the coast-to-coast line until neither Congress nor America's capitalists could afford to ignore him. He wrote the bulk of the 1862 Railroad Act, which authorized the Central Pacific and Union Pacific railway companies and provided for generous government subsidies to help get them going. He brought together many of the line's key financiers and political leaders, and he watched his beloved coast-to-coast railroad take its first baby steps across the continent. Long before he ever reached California, he repeatedly predicted "[the transcontinental railroad] will be built, and I am going to have something to do with it." Yet he never lived to see the completion of his beloved project, and for years his many contributions were largely forgotten.

Other visionaries came before, of course. Early locomotives had a way of driving people slightly insane about the future. After zipping along at a breathtaking forty-eight miles an hour on the celebrated British steam engine *Rocket* in 1830, New York shipping magnate Asa Whitney never saw life, or commerce, in the same light again. Here was a technology that "annihilated" time and distance. "We pass through a City a town, yea a country, like an arrow from Jupiter's Bow," Whitney wrote. "Steam Boats, Cars, & hotels all cramed [sic] & crowded full the whole population seems in motion. . . . Even the trees are waltzing." Visionaries such as Whitney realized how railroads offered direct passage to Asia, neutralizing Britain's commercial advantages in the Far Eastern trade. The New York capitalist became America's first missionary of steam, preaching the dream of a transcontinental railroad with almost religious fervor. Judah was his apostle.

The economic, political, and technological challenges of the 1830s and '40s proved more than a match for Whitney's considerable persuasive skills. But during the same time, the eastern states laid out an impressive railroad network. More than 200 rail companies crisscrossed the States with 31,286 miles of track before the Civil War. And Theodore Judah took the lead from nearly the beginning. The son of an Episcopal minister, born in Bridgeport, Connecticut, on March 4, 1826, Judah grew up Troy, New York, not far from the homes of his future California railroad partners. After a brief flirtation with a naval career, Judah entered engineering school, where he quickly revealed hidden talents. He worked in New York and New England, building railroad bridges, conducting grade surveys, and supervising construction of an Erie Canal section in the 1840s and early '50s. By his mid-twenties, experts hailed his design of a railroad line into the Niagara Gorge as one of the engineering marvels of the age.

Ted Judah married a gifted young New England artist named Anna Pierce. Over a period of six years the Judahs moved more than a dozen times. In 1854 the couple was on the move again. Theodore had accepted the job of chief engineer on the Sacramento Valley Railroad, California's first, and he was charged with building a line from the northern California city to the booming mining camps of the Sierra foothills.

Railroads were a completely unknown quantity in California in the 1850s, and building the state's first line was a daring assignment. As railroad historian Oscar Lewis put it, "the screech of a locomotive was yet to be heard west of the Rockies." California had no heavy manufacturing, and it was 17,000 sea miles from the nearest manufacturer of rails, locomotives, or cars. But the brash young engineer never lacked self-confidence. His motto became: "Gentlemen, raise the money and I will build your road." Judah got right to work, sighting the line, welcoming the state's first locomotive into the Golden Gate, and, with great ceremony, operating California's first handcar. After laying only seventeen miles, the railroad company became insolvent, but that suited Judah just fine. Gazing through his transit, he was already looking beyond the Sacramento foothills to the distant ramparts of the Sierra Nevada. He took a job surveying a wagon road through the mountains to the Nevada mines, assessing all the while the possibilities for locomotives. In 1856 the Judahs returned to the East Coast, where Theodore hoped to learn enough about the power structure of Washington, D.C., to convince Congress of the need for a Pacific railroad.

The year 1856 was not the most auspicious for dreamers of western railroads. Judah found easterners transfixed by a national political crisis borne out of Illinois senator Stephen Douglas's western railroad ambitions. Douglas's plan to organize Kansas and Nebraska for settlement and railroad development reignited the dormant slavery issue. Pro- and antislavery settlers flooded into Kansas Territory, elected rival legislatures, and turned Kansas into a battleground. Violence spread into the halls of Congress. Judah's arrival coincided with South Carolina representative Preston Brooks's brutal assault on Massachusetts senator Charles Sumner on the Senate floor over the slavery debate. Tempers were running high over the West, slavery, and railroads.

Judah approached his political education with the same attention to detail that he used to survey the Sierras. Armed with maps and charts, facts and figures, the well-informed engineer became a familiar and welcome face in the halls of Congress. He got to know important leaders in the railroad debate, and he impressed politicians with his powers of persuasion, his grasp of facts and figures. In time, his mastery earned him a private office in the Capitol and a seat in the councils deliberating the Pacific Railroad Act. (He would substantially write the Act that passed in 1862.) For now, he prodded debate along with a self-published booklet, "A Practical Plan for Building the Pacific Railroad," mailing a copy to each congressman as well as key federal department heads. The "Practical Plan" mixed pragmatism with zealous idealism. The two biggest impediments to a transcontinental road, Judah argued, were the perpetual impasse over slavery and the lack of a scientific survey upon which investors could form a sound business plan. Sectional rivalries would never allow the federal government to build a road through bonds or taxation. Nor should the railroad become "a stepping stone to power" for a given political party. It should be a truly national project, from which all sections could benefit. Revealing his technocratic proclivities, Theodore proposed that a council of engineers identify the most practical route for the good of all.

In dismissing the government's role in building the line, Judah swiped at the official surveys conducted in the early 1850s. Full of picturesque descriptions of flora, fauna, and landscape, the survey reports contained little practical data to attract investors. "When a Boston capitalist is invited to invest in a Railroad project," the engineer wrote, "it is not considered sufficient to tell him that somebody has rode over the ground on horseback and pronounced it practicable. He does not care to be informed that there are 999 different variety and species of plants and herbs, or that grass is abundant at this point, or Buffalo scarce at that." Practical investors wanted to know the road's length and elevation; the number of bridges and tunnels; the amounts of available stone and timber; costs and potential for revenue. As Judah argued against public funding for the roads, he also lobbied to keep the line independent of "moonshine speculators." He had learned enough about Washington to realize how little venal government officials could, or would, do "to protect themselves and the treasury from the rapacious clutches of the hungry speculators who would swarm round them like vultures round a dead carcass." Let the road be financed by public subscription and supervised by delegates from each state, selected for their reliability, honesty, and merit.

After printing his booklet, Judah returned west to continue his reconnaissance of the Sierras and drum up private support for his scheme. The first project struck pay dirt when he discovered a feasible route over Donner Pass in late 1860. The second bore fruit more slowly. San Francisco financiers kept their wallets firmly shut. But when Judah pitched his ideas in Sacramento, he found four businessmen, Stanford, Hopkins, Huntington, and Crocker, daring enough to recognize his plan's potential.

Judah liked to say, "I have always had to pit my brains against other men's money." In the Big Four, he found backers with brains and money—and something else. Thoroughly honest, Judah wanted to preserve the public trust. The transcontinental railroad was a national project, and the construction process, he argued, should be efficient, fair, and transparent. The Associates, on the other hand, never quite shared his perspective on this subject. To be fair, their concern for the bottom line was a necessary factor in justifying their risk. Building through the Sierra Nevadas would be expensive. Rival railway start-ups, telegraph companies, freighters, stage lines, and Pacific shippers opposed their efforts. The Central Pacific had to build forty miles of roadway before they could even collect the first federal dollar. Still, Judah bridled at the Big Four's efforts to wring every ounce of profit from the public treasury. When the partners awarded generous contracts to their own construction company, he objected. When Leland Stanford convinced President Lincoln that the Sierras really began on the flat plains twenty miles west of the first foothills—a necessary concession if the Central Pacific were to receive maximum federal subsidies—he fumed. Judah plotted an efficient route through Sacramento. Huntington rerouted it to increase the value of his city lots. Judah returned to Washington with Central Pacific shares in hand in order to grease the skids of the Railroad Act in 1862.

The railroad bill that President Lincoln signed on July 1, 1862, was largely Judah's brainchild. Penned mostly by the engineer, the act incorporated the Union Pacific Railroad and the Central Pacific Railroad and authorized Congress to issue generous land grants to help finance the transcontinental rail and telegraph line. It provided construction funding for private contractors at a rate of $16,000 to $48,000 per mile (between $361,000 and $1 million in 2014 dollars), depending on terrain. It granted the railroad companies land and mineral rights in alternating sections twenty miles deep on either side of the right-of-way for each mile constructed. As a vehicle of finance, the Railroad Act was a brilliant stroke. It turned an essentially worthless commodity—the unsettled land of the American interior—into expendable capital and used it to entice railroads to develop the land and its resources at their own expense. In total, the railroad companies received an immense western domain, and their stewards today are still developing the coal, oil, and gas reserves on these properties. Along with the Homestead Act, providing public land to individual settlers for a modest fee, and the Morrill Act, which funded state agricultural colleges through public land grants, the Pacific Railroad Act accelerated the settlement and economic consolidation of the West.

Despite this brilliant stroke, Judah would learn that even Washington, D.C., was not far enough away to evade the manipulations of the California-based Associates. Henry Huntington soon arrived, appropriating Judah's congressional contacts and disparaging the engineer's "cheap dignity." Soon enough, it became clear that the Big Four were making major decisions without him. Curiously, no one even mentioned Judah's name at the groundbreaking ceremony on January 8, 1863.

Judah raged, but the Big Four had decided they no longer needed their idealist. Huntington gave Judah a choice—buy the Associates out for $100,000 (about $1.8 million 2014 dollars) or get out of the way. On October 3, 1863, Judah and his wife Anna set out once again for the East, this time to secure funding to keep his railroad dream in his own hands. Crossing Panama, Theodore came down with a severe headache and a high fever. By the time he reached New York, he could barely stand. Doctors told him he had yellow fever. He died in a New York hotel room in November 1863.

During the grand galas celebrating the completion of the transcontinental railroad in 1869, few people took time to remember Theodore Judah's contribution. It was a shame. No one did more to promote the grand dream of coast-to-coast rail traffic. Judah demonstrated it was possible and wrote the legislation to make it happen. Theodolite in hand, he crossed and re-crossed the Sierras, twenty-three times by one count, looking for a feasible passage. And he garnered private and federal support for his ideas by painting a practical picture in the public's minds of how it could be done. His trust that all financiers would be fair was naïve, but admirable. As he endorsed Leland Stanford's scheme to call flatlands "mountains," Abraham Lincoln, the master of realpolitik, concluded that waste and corruption were unavoidable and necessary motivators for such a vital national project. Build the railroad, he counseled, then sort things out afterwards.

Bain, David Haward. *Empire Express: Building the First Transcontinental Railroad.* New York: VikingPenguin, 1999.

Jones, Helen Hinckley. *Rails from the West: A Biography of Theodore P. Judah.* San Marino: Golden West Books, 1969.

Judah, Theodore D. "A Practical Plan for Building the Pacific Railroad." Washington, D.C.: Henry Polkinhorn, Printer, 1857.

Rayer, Richard. *The Associates: Four Capitalists who Created California.* New York: W.W. Norton, 2008.

GEORGE MORTIMER PULLMAN

BUILDING PALACES ON WHEELS {1831–1897}

From the end of the Civil War until the early 1980s, to "Go Pullman" meant seeing America in style. Sleeping-car impresario George Pullman bet that Americans would pay a little extra to traverse the nation in safety and comfort—and he was right. His sleeping cars, dining cars, and hotel cars were really miniature palaces on wheels. Pullman reinvented long-distance travel for people all over the West, and all around the globe.

The man himself was dizzyingly complex. An engineering and social innovator, a promotional genius with an unerring memory and a gift for detail, Pullman designed, built, and marketed rail cars that redefined travel standards. He was an incurable overachiever, and a hard-nosed corporate competitor, subscribing to the philosophical consensus of his class that monopolies provided the antidote to wasteful and costly competition. He enjoyed good food, good theater, and good clothing, but avoided alcoholic excess. He worked his way up from modest beginnings, but lost his common touch. He was the nation's largest employer of African Americans. Reformers initially applauded his model company town of Pullman, Illinois. Yet his workers rebelled against his company's relentless control over their daily lives. He was described as stubborn, inflexible, "domineering," "irascible," and prone to fits of rage when he did not get his way. Although bitterly anti-union, he gave generously to educate his employees' children. He created one of the nation's first successful corporations, but was forever associated with one of America's most violent strikes.

George Mortimer Pullman was born near Buffalo, New York, in 1831. His later claims of humble beginnings were not entirely authentic. His father was a successful carpenter, building homes in the manufacturing and wheat-growing boomtowns along the western end of the Erie Canal. One of nine children, George achieved a fourth-grade education before starting work to help support his large family. An apprenticeship in his brother's cabinetmaking workshop served him well. When the builders of the Erie Canal proposed to widen the waterway, George secured a contract to move waterside buildings to make way for the canal's new banks.

Expanding railroads opened a new wheat belt in the Midwest by the 1850s, eclipsing New York's earlier wheat-growing bonanza. Pullman consequently moved to Chicago to seek new opportunities. Arriving there in 1859, the twenty-eight-year-old entrepreneur quickly made a name for himself by raising the city's skyline. The fast-growing city had outpaced its own infrastructure. City planners proposed raising every building up by an average of six feet in order to install gas, water, and sewer lines. Pullman acquired a high-profile contract to raise Chicago's Matteson House, one of the city's biggest and most expensive hotels. He hired a small army of workers to install 800 screw jacks under the hotel's foundations. Working to the coordinated rhythm of George's police whistle, the workers carefully raised the jacks a quarter turn at a time. Bit by bit, the Matteson House ascended to the level of Chicago's newly installed mud streets. Chicagoans hailed the successful project as a modern technological wonder, and the city hired Pullman to lift entire blocks of downtown Chicago out of the Lake Michigan ooze.

Even as Pullman coordinated the great Chicago uplift, he began tinkering with sleeping-car designs. The entrepreneur didn't invent sleeping cars, but he certainly improved them. Prior to the Civil War, long-distance travel was an ordeal of endurance. Railway companies jammed as many as sixty people into narrow, forward-facing wooden benches—only first-class riders enjoyed upholstered seats. Candles cast dim illumination and coal stoves alternately cooked or froze passengers, depending on their distance from the unit. Early sleeping cars had three tiers of berths. Wooden planks overlaid with filthy tick mattresses provided little comfort. Converting the crowded cars from day to night use proved challenging. Smoky wood stoves at either end of the unventilated sleeping cars emitted a suffocating funk, offering travelers the choice of smothering in their enclosed cabins or opening their windows and breathing the locomotive's smoke and cinders.

Almost from the moment he arrived in Chicago, Pullman worked to produce a better sleeping car. He hired a mechanic, Leonard Seibert, and purchased a couple of rail cars to experiment on. Working without blueprints, the pair redesigned the carriages, testing out ways to convert them from day to night use without inconveniencing passengers. Pullman demanded a high standard of luxury from the outset. His forty-four-foot-long coaches boasted cherrywood trim, ten sleeping sections, the finest fixtures, a linen closet, and two restrooms. Yet they were so elegantly engineered that they felt as roomy as regular first-class passenger coaches. Rows of seats converted into the lower sleeping tier. On the old sleepers, passengers paid the most for lower bunks, while economy-minded travelers scrambled over them to reach the upper tiers. Pullman reversed the order, making the highest berths the roomiest and most comfortable.

In 1860, Pullman contracted a severe case of gold fever. Reading about the steady returns from the Pikes Peak gold mines, he shuttered his promising Chicago enterprises and headed west. Pullman and his partners purchased a stamp mill from Chicago's Eagle Iron Works, and Pullman installed it in Russell Gulch, a bustling gold camp near Central City, Colorado. Business was so good that George spent most of the next three years engaged in various Colorado enterprises. Unlike the vast majority of ore crushers, his gold mill actually turned a profit. In time, he oversaw the mill, a log boardinghouse for his employees, a well-stocked Central City store, and the usual mix of real estate, mining, freighting, ranching, sawmills, and banking investments that attracted boomtown capitalists. He returned occasionally to Chicago to tend to family and business affairs.

In Colorado, as in Chicago, Pullman demonstrated an uncanny ability to sniff out rising business trends and to abandon enterprises just before they collapsed. By 1864, the territory's early prosperity was nearing its end. Colorado miners had extracted most of the easily refined surface gold. Chicago, by contrast, was undergoing an unprecedented boom. Sensing an end of a good run in Colorado, Pullman wrapped up his affairs, collected his profits, and returned east. The Colorado interlude educated Pullman about the economic relationship between the resource-rich West and the manufacturing-rich and capital-saturated East. Railroads, he realized, would bridge the two. And businessmen shuttling back and forth between the two regions would want to travel in style. He consequently reinvested his Colorado riches in a new generation of sleeping cars.

Legend has it that Pullman took inspiration for his sleeping car design from close-packed miners' bunkhouses. If so, then Colorado miners lived in unparalleled luxury. His next model, the custom-built *Pioneer*, boasted fold-out sleeping berths, sound-deadening doors and windows, walnut paneling, patent ventilators, and, as Pullman biographer Liston Leyendecker put it, "all the conveniences of a first-class hotel room." The entire carriage floated on a bed of steel springs, cushioning passengers from the bumpy line. Unhappy with quality problems and construction delays from his contractor, Pullman spent $20,000 (about $281,000 in 2014 dollars) to build and equip his own factory in Chicago.

Pullman's *Pioneer*, the last word in luxury travel, was a behemoth, measuring fifty-four feet long, ten feet wide, and ten feet high. Its sticker price of $18,000 ($252,000 in 2014), far more than similar sleepers, caused some critics to call it a white elephant. The railway companies concluded that no one would pay extra to ride in such splendor. Railways needed to modify their platforms, widen bridges, and raise viaducts before the new car could even travel their rails. Disappointed by their lack of interest, Pullman nearly mothballed the innovative new car before realizing that he didn't have to sell his cars at all. He offered to lease them, retaining ownership but providing hospitality staff, linen, and laundry for sleepers, along with meals made to order. Passengers would pay a little more for a ticketing surcharge based on the number of miles they traveled. The new arrangement shielded railroad companies from a losing investment, while Pullman maintained control of his company's assets. Rail carriers still balked at the necessary infrastructure modifications, and they doubted that passengers would pay more for his plush service. So Pullman offered a demonstration. Why not let the railways run mixed trains pulling both standard passenger cars and Pullmans, and let passengers decide whether or not they were willing to pay extra? Once travelers had enjoyed his cars' affordable first-class accommodations, they preferred Pullmans.

The *Pioneer* received a major promotional boost when funeral organizers tapped it to carry President Abraham Lincoln's body from Chicago to Springfield. Fortified by favorable reviews in the national press, Pullman persuaded several midwestern railways to try his plush coaches and fancy service. He organized an impressive publicity machine, hosting huge catered picnics and offering free travel to railway officials and VIPs. Like the era's steamboats and steamship liners, his cars acquired names, such as the Chicago and North Western's *Omaha,* or the Chicago, Burlington, and Quincy's *City of New York.* Soon, Pullman's sleepers and dining cars cruised throughout the South and West and began making inroads into the eastern market.

By 1867, the need for additional investment capital required reorganization. Pullman adopted the emerging practice, pioneered by the railway companies, of incorporating his company. The Pullman's Palace Car Company incorporated with $100,000 ($1.5 million in 2014 dollars) in capital stock. It quickly increased to $1 million, and then far beyond. Unlike many speculative ventures of the time, the Pullman Company never watered its stock. Pullman also developed a stable and judicious board of directors who were usually more interested in building the long-term value of the company than in lining their own pockets with short-term loot. The price of the Pullman Company's corporate stock consistently rose through good times, panics, and labor trouble.

At the time of incorporation, thirty-seven Pullman cars operated on half a dozen midwestern and Canadian lines. The corporation quickly expanded, taking orders for more than two dozen additional cars. Seeking to consolidate his construction and repair branches, Pullman moved his dispersed operations to a single Detroit plant by 1870. He continued to oversee design, commissioning a plush "drawing room" car (really a rolling hotel room) and the nation's first dining cars. He approved new comforts, such as steam heat and warming tables for prepared food. Stewards, porters, and European chefs saw to every convenience; each dining car carried enough food, staff, and equipment to serve 250 daily meals.

For hospitality staff, Pullman recruited recently freed slaves from the American South. He shrewdly guessed that middle-class white Americans would appreciate service by uniformed attendants, and he understood that liberated blacks hungered for respectable work. Pullman porters were poorly paid compared to white domestics of the time, and they endured countless indignities. Passengers addressed all porters by the generic moniker "George," to name one example. But theirs was the highest-paying job available to African Americans at the time, and their employment incubated an emerging black middle class. Historians credit their union, the Brotherhood of Sleeping Car Porters, for insisting on decent treatment and pay, laying the groundwork for the mid-twentieth-century Civil Rights Movement.

Smiling porters and gourmet chefs, clean linen, soft beds, hot meals, and extravagant private parlor cars—it was the beginning of the golden age of train travel. The only thing lacking, wags noted, were nursery cars for bawling babies, bath cars for close-packed summer travelers, and a saloon car for commuting tipplers. (Pullman took note of the last request and invented lounge cars.) Having suffered through the dirty, bumpy, suffocating experience of early train travel, passengers clearly appreciated being coddled.

Armed with capital, corporate organization, and an enviable line of high-end passenger cars, Pullman set out to dominate the market. It wasn't easy. Several firms manufactured more affordable cars nearly as nice. His largest competitor, Central Transportation Company of Pennsylvania, held senior patents and received backing from the railroad and future steel tycoon Andrew Carnegie. The competition came to a head over the Union Pacific concession in 1867. Despite Central Transportation Company's clout, Pullman seemed to have an inside track. Union Pacific patrons got a preview of his cars during Thomas Durant's lavish celebration to commemorate the crossing of the 100th meridian in 1866, and they liked what they saw. Seeking to impress Durant, Pullman introduced the *Western World*, a hotel car that lived up to the Union Pacific general manager's princely standards of luxury. The coach contained four furnished drawing rooms, a kitchen, a furnace, and yards of purple plush, gilt paintwork, clean linen, and fine china. Durant was so taken with the Pullman coach that he evicted the government commissioners assigned to it and appropriated it as his own.

Before long, Carnegie realized a merger was preferable to a costly and time-consuming war. The consolidated Pullman Pacific Palace Car Company secured the Union Pacific contract, and Carnegie saw to it that the acquisitive Durant failed to grab a controlling share. The Pullman Company next signed an exclusive contract with Carnegie's powerful Pennsylvania Railroad. Armed with senior Central Transportation Company patents and backed by the national stature of the Union Pacific and Pennsylvania Railroads, Pullman bought out his rivals' equipment, contracts, and patents. Only California's Big Four stood their ground. Hoping to cash in on their own sleeping car franchise, they banned Pullman cars on their lines. Their decision turned into a public relations nightmare when customers loudly demanded Pullmans. They relented, signing a contract with George in 1883. Pullman also entered the European market. He introduced the first English sleepers in 1873 and signed several Italian contracts the following year. By 1875, Pullmans operated on British railways from Brighton to the Scottish highlands, and a plant in Turin assembled American-made cars.

By 1885, it seemed as if Pullman could do no wrong. His corporation possessed more than $28 million in assets (almost $683 million in 2014 dollars); its capital stock was valued at $15.9 million ($387 million in 2014 dollars). It enjoyed deep cash reserves and a reputation as a net creditor, an almost unheard-of circumstance for the debt-ridden railways of the time. One condition that concerned George Pullman was the standard of living of his employees. Many of the thousands living in the Chicago area occupied filthy slums, which compromised their health, undermined their efficiency, and, in Pullman's mind, increased their discontent. Pullman responded by building an immense new factory complex south of Chicago, constructing alongside it a model company town, Pullman, Illinois.

To Pullman, the ambitious social experiment seemed like an all-around winner. The town's wide, tree-lined streets, snug brick houses and tenements, parks, and athletic and social activities contrasted sharply with the neighboring slums of Chicago. Pullman's architecture emphasized cleanliness and harmony. Town services (water treatment, sewage disposal, electrical and gas generation, firefighting) were among the best in the nation. Alcohol and prostitution were strictly prohibited. Pullman made his namesake town into a watchword for efficiency. He even installed the colossal Corliss engine used to power the 1876 Philadelphia Centennial Exhibition—the symbol of steam-powered modernism—in his new factory. To pay for it all, he charged his employees rent, demanding a steady 6 percent return in good times or bad.

The town of Pullman's population mushroomed with the growth of the Palace Car Company, from 8,500 (including 2,700 employees) in 1885 to 12,600 (including 5,500 employees) in 1893. Reformers arrived by the hundreds to inspect and praise Pullman's progressive accomplishments. An 1896 international hygienic commission, meeting in Prague, Bohemia, declared it the world's "most perfect" community. Almost all of the reviewers overlooked the town's secret decay. Pullman's climb up the economic ladder had come at a price, argues his biographer Liston Leyendecker. According to Leyendecker, a dense layer of middle managers insulated the entrepreneur from his workforce, shielding him from sympathetic insight into their true conditions. The sleeping car baron entirely missed the resentment his social experiment generated.

Intent on alleviating their squalor, Pullman gave employees no voice in their community. The company ran everything. Pullman strictly regulated his workers' social behavior, dictated which flowers they planted in front of their houses, and restricted their reading material. The company prohibited pro-union speech and meetings. Company spies kept tabs on recalcitrants; failure to toe the line meant dismissal, eviction, or blacklisting. According to historians at the Pullman State Historic Site, workers reportedly complained: "We are born in a Pullman house, fed from the Pullman shops, taught in the Pullman school, catechized in the Pullman Church, and when we die we shall go to the Pullman Hell."

The company town struck Pullman as an inevitable outgrowth of efficiency and benevolent corporate philanthropy. His employees, on the other hand, grumbled at the high rents and alarming absence of democracy. They seethed at the company's control over their lives and politics and compared themselves to the peons of a feudal prince. Resentment came to a head following the financial panic of 1893. Responding to depressed economic conditions, the Pullman Palace Car Company laid off thousands of workers and cut the wages of those who remained. Pullman stubbornly refused to reduce rents, however, even when workers' net income fell to starvation levels. Faced with the choice of food or shelter, workers walked off the job. Labor organizer Eugene V. Debs saw an opportunity and moved in with the American Railway Union, which called a national strike. More than 250,000 workers responded. Courts filed injunctions against the labor organizers. Federal marshals and troops intervened. Riots, sabotage, mass shootings, and property destruction exceeding $80 million (more than $2 billion in 2014 dollars) followed.

Pullman's business standing remained firm throughout the strike. Many Americans, and even some skilled craft unions, criticized the walkout for paralyzing a vital industry. The company's stock value never dropped below $150 per share ($4,054 in 2014 dollars). But Pullman's carefully-cultivated reputation as a reformer suffered a devastating blow. The strike spurred official investigations into the labor policies and anti-union activities of large companies, inaugurating new government reforms and further labeling capitalists such as Pullman "Robber Barons." A national investigating commission blamed Pullman's paternalistic policies for the strike and labeled his brand of civic control "un-American." In 1897, the Illinois Supreme Court ruled that operating the company town violated the corporation's charter. So, George Pullman's social experiment came to an end.

Despite this immense public relations setback, Pullman steered his corporation until his death in 1897. In his will, he left $1.2 million

($33.33 million in 2014 dollars), or more than one sixth of his personal fortune, to educate the children of company employees. Chicago's George M. Pullman Foundation has given more than $30 million to 11,000 scholars since its founding. Pullman is still admired for his innovative rail services, which allowed Americans to move freely about their country in comfort and style. His sleeping, dining, and hotel cars made travel to the American West less forbidding, connecting westerners to cities and markets around the nation. His creative corporate organization set as much of a positive example for the twentieth century as his disastrous labor relations did a negative one. All told, George Pullman epitomized the best, and some of the worst, of Gilded Age capitalism.

Gordon, Sarah H. *Passage to Union: How the Railroads Transformed American Life, 1829–1929.* Chicago: Ivan R. Dee, 1996.

Husband, Joseph. *The Story of the Pullman Car.* Chicago: A.C. McClurg & Co., 1917.

Leyendecker, Liston. *Palace Car Prince: A Biography of George Mortimer Pullman.* Niwot: University Press of Colorado, 1992.

Lindsey, Almont. *The Pullman Strike.* Chicago: The University of Chicago Press, 1942.

White, Jr., John H. *The American Railroad Passenger Car.* Baltimore: The Johns Hopkins University Press, 1978.

WILLIAM JACKSON PALMER

VISIONARY RAILROADER & TOWN FOUNDER

{1836–1909}

Mark Twain called the late 1800s the Gilded Age for its shiny, prosperous façade that often hid other problems created by politicians and businessmen alike. In his 1873 novel *The Gilded Age: A Tale of Today,* Twain satirized the period between 1865 and 1900 as a materialistic time when great business leaders emerged as national idols.

Twain apparently never met William Jackson Palmer. Palmer rose high above some of his fellow successful capitalists in demonstrating concern for his workers, his community, and his stockholders. Palmer, founding father of Colorado Springs and many other Colorado railroad towns, is best known for creating and guiding the Denver & Rio Grande Railroad (now part of Union Pacific). As he wrote in 1879 to his new bride, Palmer dreamed Utopian dreams: "I had a dream last night, while sitting in the railway car window . . . a wide-awake dream [about] an ideal railroad where every employee, no matter how low his rank, invested in the stock and profit of the line, should feel as if it were their own and not some strange soul-less corporation."

Palmer's idealism began with his upbringing. William was born into a devout Quaker family on September 17, 1836, on a farm in Kinsale, Kent County, Delaware. When the boy was five, the Palmers moved back to their former home in Philadelphia. There William attended the Friends school. His many Quaker relatives and friends became abolitionists crusading against slavery, the burning issue of those days. A surviving story of Palmer's childhood has him leaving a candy shop with a sack full of sweets. Then he noticed a poor wistful Negro boy peering in the window. Outside Palmer emptied half his bag into the waif's hat.

At age seventeen, Palmer went to work on the Hempfield Railroad, then locating its line through the Allegheny Mountains of Pennsylvania. Palmer's fascination with railroading inspired him to head for England, where railroading had begun in 1815. He inspected British railways in the nation that led the world in that new science. He noted that British rail, unlike American wood burners, ran mostly on coal. Palmer also ventured across the channel to study French railroads. Returning to the United States in 1856, he decided to study coal further and joined the Westmoreland Coal Company. Within five months he was secretary of that company.

Palmer sent his reports on coal and locomotion to the nation's number one railroader, J. Edgar Thompson, president of the Pennsylvania Railroad. Impressed, Thompson hired Palmer as his private secretary and assigned him to study switching the Pennsylvania, the country's largest and most advanced railroad, from wood to coal. Palmer experimented with coal, which he found twice as efficient as wood for powering steam locomotives. He also suggested that companies motivate workers by sharing profits—a radical idea back in the 1850s.

When he was not working on technical or employee improvements, Palmer lectured on humanitarian causes such as abolishing slavery and providing greater opportunities for Negroes. When the Civil War broke out Palmer struggled with the clash between his Quaker pacifism and his hope that the war would end slavery. Finally he decided to join the Union cause, but on his own terms. He raised four hundred men for his Fifteenth Pennsylvania Volunteer Cavalry Regiment, an elite troop of friends and handpicked soldiers.

He led troops behind the enemy lines in 1862 on a spying mission. There he was captured and spent several months in a Confederate prison in Richmond, Virginia. Released in a prisoner swap, Palmer led his regiment through fierce fighting in Tennessee, Alabama, and Georgia, earning the Congressional Medal of Honor. In his tailor-made uniform, the wiry, five-foot-ten Palmer, with his wavy reddish-brown hair, neatly trimmed moustache, and aristocratic bearing, looked every inch an officer. In 1864 the army commissioned him a brevet brigadier general of cavalry.

Palmer's war-learned ability to command large groups of men came in handy when he was asked in 1868 to help lead the survey and construction of the Kansas Pacific Railroad. Palmer relished this assignment, in which he would be, as he put it, "instrumental in carrying the star of empire westward across this Great Continent." He hired many veterans from his Pennsylvania Volunteers, some of whom would remain with him as railroad employees for decades to come. Although Palmer surveyed a route all the way to the Pacific, the Kansas Pacific never got anywhere near its nominal goal. Like so many other "Pacific" railroads, the Kansas Pacific never even made it across the Rocky Mountain barrier, terminating the line in Denver in 1870.

Meanwhile Palmer grew much more excited about discovering that Colorado was rich in coal—his black gold. The richest fields lay in southern Colorado around Trinidad. This led Palmer to another new vision. Instead of aiming for the Pacific, how about southern Colorado, New Mexico, and even Mexico? While other railroads were building east to west, Palmer reckoned it would be most profitable and helpful to build north to south along the front range of the Rockies. Feeder lines could run west to the mining camps and east to the new agricultural communities on the Great Plains. To pare down construction costs in difficult terrain, Palmer decided to use something he had investigated in Festiniog, Wales: a narrow-gauge line instead of the standard four-foot, eight-and-a-half-inch gauge that originated with George Stephenson's pioneer 1829 steam locomotive, *The Rocket*. The slim gauge had advantages. It was cheaper to build and could negotiate tighter curves and steeper grades, enabling Palmer and his Denver & Rio Grande to win rail races to new mining boomtowns. Palmer raised money among his British and Philadelphia connections. In London, he interested a renowned society doctor, William A. Bell, Sr., who advised on financial investments as well as medicine. He, his son, Dr. William A. Bell, Jr., and their wealthy patients began bankrolling Palmer's dreams. Young Dr. Bell grew especially enthusiastic and moved to Colorado to become vice president of the Denver & Rio Grande Railroad founded by Palmer in 1870. The younger Bell also wrote a book, *New Tracks in North America* (1870), promoting American railroading.

Bell helped Palmer survey and lay tracks due south out of Denver in 1871. Unlike the Union Pacific, Kansas Pacific, and many other lines, the Denver & Rio Grande received no federal land grants. So Palmer strove to make it pay for itself by town developments. The railroad left perhaps a hundred new towns in its wake, starting with Castle Rock, Palmer Lake, and Palmer's favorite model city, Colorado Springs, spectacularly sited at the base of Pikes Peak.

R.G. Dun & Company's confidential credit reports on the Denver & Rio Grande Railroad began showing up November 14, 1871: "All of the bonds have been sold in Europe . . . one of the most prosperous roads in the west. . . . credit excellent." On May 16, 1879: "250 miles in operation . . . the Pres. [Palmer] a man of large experience good ability and honest and the enterprise is regarded as very promising."

Palmer founded Colorado Springs in 1871, platting it with broad streets, parks, land for education institutions, and other amenities. He hoped his model town would also become a tourist destination.

Disembarking passengers, however, found the town cemetery next to the railway station. To squelch any doubts about the Springs being a first class health spa, Palmer had the cemetery moved to its eastern outskirts, where Evergreen Cemetery lies to this day. A large natural boulder there serves as Palmer's unpretentious tombstone.

His newly minted city's majestic setting and crisp, sunny mountain air attracted wealthy travelers and genteel invalids, who found attractive homes, tree-lined streets, numerous parks, and a focus on churches, schools, and libraries—not Colorado's usual bars, bordellos, and gambling halls.

Palmer's Tudor-style mansion at Glen Eyrie near the Garden of the Gods became a retreat for the social and cultural elite. To help make Colorado Springs a refined city, he donated land and money to build Colorado College. In addition to Palmer Hall on the Colorado Springs campus, there is also one at Hampton Institute in Virginia, a pioneer college for African Americans. Palmer founded the Antlers Hotel in 1881 and helped to make it the finest in Colorado at that time. He also gave land and money for the original Colorado Springs Public Library.

Palmer erected a splendid Queen Anne–style depot for the Denver & Rio Grande, which built spur lines up to the resort town of Manitou Springs. There Dr. Bell built his mansion, Briarhurst Manor. Of the Colorado mountains Palmer wrote to his wife, "Could one live in constant view of the grand mountains without being elevated by them to a lofty plane of thought and purpose."

Certainly Palmer envisioned lofty things for the Pikes Peak region. Working people shared in that dream. A century before profit sharing and stock options would become available to many employees, Palmer promoted that practice so that workers might become "capitalists themselves in a small way." In another letter to his wife, Queen Mellen Palmer, he declared, "We shall have a new and better civilization in the far West . . . the inner temple of Americanism out in Colorado, where Republican institutions will be maintained in pristine purity."

This grand vision inspired Palmer to build a spider web of steel, creating many new towns or reviving old ones along its reach. From its Denver base, Palmer's Denver & Rio Grande built south to Colorado Springs, then on to Pueblo and Walsenburg. From that coal town, the railroad turned west to cross La Veta Pass and built through the San Luis Valley, where Alamosa soon became the valley hub. From Alamosa the rails ventured south to Santa Fe and then up and over the towering San Juan Mountains to Durango, founded by the railroad as its southwestern hub. From Durango, Palmer built the still operating, spectacularly scenic line to Silverton. Another branch of the Denver & Rio Grande built west from Cañon City through the Royal Gorge after the company won the "Royal Gorge War" with the Santa Fe Railroad. After squeezing through that thousand-foot-deep gorge of the Arkansas River to get to Salida, Palmer's slim gauge climbed over Marshall Pass into Gunnison County and steamed on to Montrose and Grand Junction. Another branch ran from Salida north to Leadville, then over Tennessee Pass down to Minturn and the Eagle River, to the Colorado River, Glenwood Springs, and Grand Junction. From there it proceeded into Utah in 1881 and took the new name Denver & Rio Grande Western as it reached Salt Lake City and Ogden. Not until 1934 would the D&RGW acquire the Moffat Road and all-weather Moffat Tunnel route directly due west out of Denver. Meanwhile the mainline, to Denver's dismay, ran through Pueblo and over Tennessee Pass.

In Pueblo, Palmer's vision of benign labor relations ran awry. There, in 1881, Palmer founded what became the Colorado Fuel & Iron Company. This plant transformed Pueblo into the Pittsburgh of the West, with a giant operation that became the largest employer in Colorado and the owner of more than fifty company towns. The huge Pueblo plant made much of the railroad track, spikes, nails, barb wire, and other steel products for the American West. Despite sporadic attempts to improve working conditions, living conditions, and worker pay, the company became the villain in the Great Coalfield War of 1914. Palmer, who died in 1909, did not live to see his hopes for harmonious labor-capital relations smashed in one of the deadliest conflicts in the history of American labor, culminating in the Ludlow Massacre and the deaths of some two dozen people, including women and children.

Later capitalists did not always share Palmer's idealism, which shone through even after his forced sale of the Denver & Rio Grande to George J. Jay Gould in 1901. True to his commitment to share the wealth with his workers, Palmer dispensed $1 million from the sale to all employees. Even the lowliest track layer or maintenance man received a generous check. Palmer spent much of the rest of his wealth on making more civic improvements to his beloved Colorado Springs. In 1907 he gave the city a multimillion-dollar park system totaling 1,638 acres, acquired, developed, and landscaped under his direction. This included Antlers Park, the 753-acre Palmer Park, and the two-mile-long Monument Park through the heart of the city.

At a time when many U.S. citizens were contemptuous of Spanish and Mexican peoples and cultures, Palmer used Spanish names for many Colorado Springs streets. His interest in the Rio Grande River rail route also led him to collaborate with Mexican officials on building the Mexican National Railway, which he organized and presided over from 1880 to 1887. Like African Americans, whose advancement he long championed, Palmer also respected and partnered with Mexicans.

The general's concern for underdogs led him to donate in 1903 a Colorado Springs site for the still-operating Colorado State School for the Deaf and Blind. He gave 100 acres and $50,000 in cash to establish Cragmor Sanitarium for consumptives (now part of the University of Colorado at Colorado Springs campus). He donated to other healthcare institutions that would make Colorado Springs a nationally noted health spa. Beyond cure himself, he died on March 13, 1909, at his estate of Glen Eyre, now a tourist attraction. In all, Palmer would give over $4 million toward the betterment of Colorado Springs. His equestrian statue still stops downtown traffic at the intersection of Platte and Nevada and suggests the high road for America's business leaders.

Palmer improved American railroading with his widely distributed and influential research on switching from wood to coal. He became a driving force in the development of southern and western Colorado, eastern Utah and northern New Mexico, as well as Mexico itself. Besides founding numerous towns, he conquered the Rocky Mountains with brilliant engineering achievements that remain operating railroads or automobile highways today. Furthermore, he did all this while leaving a rarely matched legacy of philanthropy and successful labor relations.

Palmer's work is commemorated by large brass plaques in the Union stations of Denver, Salt Lake City, the Colonia Railway Station in Mexico City, in Palmer Hall at Colorado College, and at the Hampton Institute for Colored Students in Virginia. Besides a *bas relief* of Palmer and one of his beloved Great Danes are the words:

William Jackson Palmer 1836–1909 Union Cavalry General, pioneer railroad builder, prophet of Colorado's greatness. He mapped the routes of three transcontinental railways,supervised the building of the first road to Denver, organized and constructed the Denver & Rio Grande Railroad, stimulated the State's industries, cherished its beauties. Founded Colorado Springs, fostered Colorado College, and served our Sister Republic of Mexico with sympathy and wisdom in developing its national railways.

Anderson, George L. *General William J. Palmer: A Decade of Colorado Railroad Building, 1870–1880*. Colorado Springs: CO: Colorado College, 1936.

Athearn, Robert G. *Rebel of the Rockies: The Denver and Rio Grande Western Railroad*. New Haven, CT: Yale University Press, 1962.

Blevins, Tim, Dennis Dailey, Chris Nicholl, Calvin P. Otto, and Katherine Scott Sturdevant, editors. *Legends, Labors & Loves of William Jackson Palmer*. Colorado Springs, CO: Pikes Peak Library District, 2009.

Fisher, John Stirling. *A Builder of the West: The Life of William Jackson Palmer*. Caldwell, ID: Caxton Printers, 1939.

McCarthy, Judge Wilson. *General Wm. Jackson Palmer (1836–1909) and the D&RGW Railroad*. N.Y.: The Newcomen Society in North America, 1954.

Palmer, William Jackson. Papers. Stephen Hart Library, History Colorado Center, Denver.

Peabody, George Foster, compiler. *William Jackson Palmer: Pathfinder and Builder: A Compilation of Addresses at Presentations of Bronze Bas Reliefs and Equestrian Statue Commemorating His Life and Work*. Boston: Thomas Todd Company, 1931.

Sprague, Marshall. *Newport in the Rockies: The Life and Good Times of Colorado Springs*. Denver: Sage Books, 1961.

Storey, Brit Allan. William Jackson Palmer: A Biography. Ph.D. History Thesis, University of Kentucky, 1968.

Thode, Jackson C. "William Jackson Palmer, September 17, 1836 – March 13, 1909." In *The Encyclopedia of American Business History and Biography*.

JAMES J. HILL

EMPIRE BUILDER OF THE NORTHWEST

{1838–1916}

James J. Hill was an empire builder. The Canadian immigrant built one, and eventually controlled two, of America's transcontinental railroad lines. His Great Northern and Northern Pacific Railroads connected the Great Lakes region with the Pacific Northwest, bringing the rich mining and farming lands of Montana, Idaho, and the Dakotas into the national economy. He was ambitious, driven, and empathetic, shifting his business to meet the changing needs of his adopted home region. He was also egotistical, pushy, and he sometimes engaged in dubious enterprises. Every northwesterner had an opinion about the shipping and railroad baron's business activities. Wheat farmers in the Pacific Northwest who resented Hill's economic dominance dubbed an invasive mustard plant that plagued their fields "Jim Hill," after the capitalist. Despite their grumbling, the farmers had to admit that Hill did more than nearly any other person to develop the economy, industry, and agriculture of the Northwest.

James Hill was born in 1838 in Wellington, Ontario. His parents, James and Ann Hill, had emigrated from Ireland to Ontario in the early nineteenth century. Prosperity eluded the elder James Hill—he first tried his hand at farming and then ran an inn in the tiny town of Rockwood when his three children were young. While the Hills could not offer James, his sister Mary, or his younger brother Alexander material comfort, they fostered the siblings' love of reading and education. Hill's early education was simple, but at age eleven, he attended a Quaker academy headed by William Weatherald, often doing chores to earn his tuition. James flourished under Weatherald's tutelage, learning English, mathematics, and science. He dreamed of becoming a doctor, but dropped out of school in 1852 after his father's sudden death. Hill appreciated his mentor's influence all his life—decades later, Hill treated Weatherald to trips and gifts, referring to him as "My Dear Old Master."

Hill's education gave him pragmatic skills, but also instilled in him a love of romance and adventure. At one time, he aspired to a trading career in China or Asia, and his fascination with Napoleon inspired him to adopt the middle name Jerome, after that of the French emperor's brother. Hill's childhood also left another, more painful legacy. At nine, Hill lost his right eye during a hunting accident in the woods. A nearby doctor partially saved the imperiled eyeball. For the rest of his life, Hill would be able to move his damaged eye, but could not see more than shadows with it. Hill's eye later disqualified him from service in the First Minnesota Volunteers during the Civil War, which possibly saved his life, as the regiment suffered heavy casualties at Gettysburg.

Hill dreamed of achieving more than rural Ontario could grant him. In 1856, he left for the United States, believing his future lay there. He traveled to New York, Philadelphia, and elsewhere in the East and the South, but he settled permanently in St. Paul, then the largest settlement in Minnesota Territory. St. Paul was a raw frontier town, full of ambitious energy. It was the largest center of river transportation on the northern Mississippi River, and, for most of the year, cargo from both north and south passed through St. Paul en route to other destinations.

Hill found employment as a clerk for a local steamboat agency, where he kept the books and helped handle freight. The energetic, gregarious Hill took to life on the river levees and began learning all aspects of the Great Lakes shipping and freighting industry. He grasped the intricacies of purchasing commodities, setting shipping rates, and determining the needs of his customers. These lessons helped Hill succeed when he entered the railroad business later in life. Unlike other railroad barons, who came from the world of finance, Hill's bottom-up rise through the shipping and freighting industry gave him insights into the world of transportation others lacked.

Hill also looked for ways to earn money on his own, especially in winter, when river trade slowed. He sold horse fodder and firewood, delivering them throughout the city and St. Paul's quickly populating hinterland. These early successes, plus his growing network of friends and potential investors, spurred him to go into business himself. He first became an independent shipping agent, arranging logistics for the Northwest Packet Company, one of the most powerful shipping agencies on the Mississippi. But river transport was waning as more goods began to be shipped by rail. Hill founded his own company in 1866 to take advantage of the new technology, securing contracts with local railroads to transfer goods from riverboats to railcars. He also began dealing in coal, purchasing large quantities of the fuel in Chicago or further east and using his railroad contacts and negotiating skills to ship it cheaply to Minnesota for sale.

In 1867 Hill married Mary Mehegan, the daughter of Irish immigrants. The couple had met in 1860 and struck up a fast friendship. Mehegan, with Hill's financial help, studied music and French, an education that made her the ideal companion for a budding industrialist. Hill and Mary's partnership was close and loving, and they had ten children, nine of whom survived to adulthood. Hill wasted little time securing a comfortable life for his growing family.

Urban St. Paul lay at the edge of one of the most fertile agricultural regions in North America—the Red River Valley, which straddled the border between the United States and Canada. It was an area changing rapidly due to increased settlement and wheat cultivation. The creation of the Dominion of Canada in 1867 had brought the confederation's western plains and mountains under federal control and these regions were turning away from the fading Hudson's Bay Company and towards Ottawa. Hill focused on the region, forming a steamship company in 1870 to service the small settlement of Winnipeg. As the region boomed in the early 1870s, Hill's steamboats carried nearly 30 percent of the cargo and people traveling along the Red River.

The Panic of 1873 threw the Great Lakes railroad industry into chaos. The Saint Paul and Pacific Railroad, Minnesota's oldest railroad, was ineptly managed and poorly planned, and the panic caused it to go bankrupt. Hill spent several years carefully researching the railroad's prospects before he and several investment partners purchased it in 1878. A year later, Hill renamed it the St. Paul, Minneapolis and Manitoba Railway—a name symbolizing the growing urban network that tied together the Red River region. Hill's family and finances were already comfortable by the time he immersed himself in the railroad business. When he married in 1867, he mused that he might retire once his fortune reached $100,000 in order to spend the rest of his days devoted to learning, perhaps finally obtaining the formal education his father's death had interrupted. But Hill was too restless to spend the rest of his life reading.

The Red River Valley became an internationally important center of wheat cultivation in the 1870s, and Hill's railroad, which connected the Twin Cities and northern Dakota Territory to Manitoba and the Canadian Pacific Railway, helped it grow. Hill encouraged European immigrants to emigrate to the region, sold wood from railroad timberlands to farmers and homesteaders, and helped set up towns and industry along his railroad's path. Hill's Canadian roots and American business ties made him the ideal man to bring the flourishing border region into a broader universe of national and global economies.

The Great Lakes region, the Dakotas, and the Pacific Northwest still lacked a transcontinental line when Hill entered the railroad business. The Northern Pacific Railway, chartered in 1864, was intended to connect these regions to the Pacific, but economic instability and poor management slowed the railroad's progress. Hill envisioned a solution: why not create a transcontinental line of his own? Initial attempts to work with the Canadian Pacific failed, so Hill began expanding his own railroad—renamed the Great Northern—westward, through Minnesota, then into Montana, and finally reaching Seattle in 1893. En route, Hill constructed branch lines to Butte and Helena to capitalize on the Montana copper boom, forging an agreement with copper king Marcus Daly to offer inexpensive shipping rates and reliable transportation.

Hill's Great Northern Railroad ran north of the Northern Pacific and south of the Canadian Pacific. He scouted out much of the route himself on horseback, supplementing the work of his engineers. Great Northern trains traveled an easier path than their Northern Pacific counterparts, thanks to Hill's insistence that his railroad cover "the shortest distance, the lowest grades, and the least curvature we can build." John Stevens, a Great Northern engineer, located a route over Marias Pass, the lowest northern passage over the Rocky Mountains, allowing the railroad to cross the mountains easily and inexpensively. Unlike other railroad magnates, Hill constructed the Great Northern —the last major transcontinental railroad line to be constructed— with little support from federal land grants.

The Great Northern came out of the economic depression of the 1890s in strong financial shape. Hill cut shipping rates and offered generous credit to farmers and businesses that relied on the railroad. He cut wages and pressured his staff to increase efficiency. Other rail lines went bankrupt, and Hill began buying up struggling railroads in the early 1900s. With the help of J. P. Morgan, Hill took control of the troubled Northern Pacific in 1900 and then bought the Chicago, Burlington and Quincy Railroad in 1901 in order to connect both the Great Northern and the Northern Pacific to Chicago and areas to the west and south. Hill now commanded a near-monopoly on rail traffic in the northern Great Plains and the Pacific Northwest, frustrating area farmers and business owners, and making other railroad operators nervous. Edward H. Harriman, then head of the Union Pacific, also wanted control of the Chicago, Burlington and Quincy. He quietly began buying shares of the Northern Pacific in order to take control of the railroad and, by extension, the Chicago, Burlington and Quincy. Harriman and his partners came close to majority control, but Hill, alerted by the quickly rising price of his company's shares, countered. He notified Morgan, who had his agents buy as many shares of Northern Pacific stock as they could. The railroad's stock reached dizzying prices—up to $1,000 per share—but the Harriman-Hill feud threatened to plummet Wall Street into a panic.

To keep the market stable, Morgan crafted a truce. Harriman, Hill, Morgan, and John D. Rockefeller formed the giant Northern Securities Company. The four men and their associates now jointly owned the Great Northern, the Northern Pacific, and the Chicago, Burlington and Quincy railroads. Northern Securities was intended to calm the market and increase efficiency, but it stirred up increasing antitrust sentiment. The specter of four of America's wealthiest men dominating an industry so many people relied on for their livelihoods did not sit well with many, including President Theodore Roosevelt. In 1902 the Department of Justice sued Northern Securities for violating the Sherman Anti-Trust Act—and won. Two years later, the United States Supreme Court broke up the conglomerate. Hill remained the owner of his railroads, but the ruling prohibited him from ever merging the three into one company again. In 1970—fifty-four years after Hill's death—the three lines finally merged, forming the Burlington Northern Railroad.

Hill's impact on the West was far greater than just laying down railroad tracks. He helped build towns, promoted industry, and encouraged settlement in the Dakotas, Montana, and the Pacific Northwest. He funded the development of new strains of wheat and other agricultural research. Hill also promoted the timber industry in Washington and Oregon, selling Great Lakes lumbermen on the promise of lush Northwestern forests—an easy job, since timber lands in Wisconsin and Minnesota were increasingly cut over. In 1900 Hill sold 900,000 acres of Washington forests to lumber baron Frederick Weyerhaeuser, the largest single land sale in American history at that time.

Hill died in St. Paul in May 1916, leaving behind an immense legacy in his adopted city. Although he remained a Protestant throughout his life, his wife's devout Catholicism spurred Hill to donate generously to the local Catholic church and seminary. He was also a major benefactor of local colleges and universities. But his greatest gift to St. Paul, and much of the northern West, was connectivity. Hill's railroads linked farmers, business owners, and others in some of the United States' most remote areas to regional, national, and global markets. He developed the region from the Great Lakes to the Pacific Northwest like no other industrialist could.

Harvey, Mark. "James J. Hill, Jeanette Rankin and John Muir: The American West in the Progressive Era, 1890 to 1920," in *Western Lives: A Biographical History of the American West,* ed. Richard Etulain. Albuquerque: University of New Mexico Press, 2004.

Johnston, Louis. "James J. Hill," in *The Oxford Encyclopedia of Economic History,* ed. Joel Mokyr. New York: Oxford University Press, 2003, 529-30.

Malone, Michael P. *James J. Hill: Empire Builder of the Northwest.* Norman: University of Oklahoma Press, 1996).

Martin, Albro, James J. Hill and the Opening of the Northwest (St. Paul: Minnesota Historical Society Press, 1976).

FRED HARVEY

Fred Harvey—the company and the man were one and the same. For three generations, Harvey's name meant good food, friendly service, a superb cup of coffee, and a quality cigar, in the most unlikely places. The dapper, no-nonsense Englishman was responsible for creating America's first national brand and building an empire of restaurants, hotels, and dining cars that set high standards for quality and consistency from Chicago, to the edge of the Grand Canyon, to the Mexico border—anywhere, really, where the Santa Fe Railway connected.

Fred Harvey was the nation's first chain restaurant, serving post–Civil War travelers in rough-and-tumble western locales such as Raton, New Mexico; Winslow, Arizona; Needles, California; and Dodge City, Kansas. Under Fred's son Ford, the company exported western images and icons to the rest of the nation.

In the early twentieth century, Fred Harvey opened fancy hotels and restaurants in America's national parks, creating (and satisfying) a nearly unquenchable public thirst for Navajo rugs and jewelry, Pueblo and Mission Revival architecture, and magnificent sunsets over scenic western vistas. It's been often said—overstated really—that the fastidious Harvey and his friendly, immaculate waitresses, known as Harvey

Girls, brought civilization to the Wild West. In fact, Harvey's dining and tourism dynasty introduced the West to new forms of civilization, powerfully influencing our popular imagination to this very day.

Harvey was born on June 27, 1835 in London. His early years read like a lesser Dickens novel. Fred's tailor father struggled with failure and bankruptcy. His mother ran off with another man, and the young boy moved in with an aunt. At seventeen, Harvey left England for America. He learned the restaurant trade at New York's Smith & McNeil's dining establishment, located in the shadow of America's premiere restaurant, Delmonico's. Harvey advanced through the restaurant's ranks, from pot cleaner, to busboy, to waiter, to cook. At twenty-three, he became a naturalized American citizen, marking the occasion by opening his first restaurant in St. Louis. Harvey took care of the diners while an Irish partner handled the barroom.

The Civil War proved bad for business—Harvey's partner joined the Confederate army, taking with him the business's savings. But it was good for railroading. So Fred took a job handling mail for the Hannibal and St. Joseph Railroad, delivering mail pouches to westbound Pony Express riders at the end of the track. When the war ended, he became a traveling mail clerk and general agent for the Chicago, Burlington and Quincy. He became a perpetual commuter, traveling the lines to sort mail, collect debts, arrange for freight, and sell tickets. Long, jouncing journeys along primitive tracks, punctuated by hurried, glutinous meals, inflamed Harvey's debilitating nerve pain, migraines, and gastrointestinal problems. The spare, nervous clerk battled to keep both his health and his appointments. In time, he embraced a diagnosis invented by Victorian-era doctors to classify stressed-out traveling businessmen. They called his ailment "American Nervousness."

Harvey's illness and stress allowed him to recognize an opportunity. Intent on the task of getting passengers and freight from place to place, America's major carriers had ignored the value of decent, comforting meals. In his western memoir *Roughing It,* the American writer Mark Twain described the primitive dining conditions he encountered in a frontier stage station:

> The table was a greasy board on stilts, and the table-cloth and napkins had not come—and they were not looking for them, either. A battered tin platter, a knife and fork, and a tin pint cup, were at each man's place. . . . The station-keeper upended a disk of last week's bread, of the shape and size of an old-time cheese, and carved some slabs from it which were as good as Nicholson pavement, and tenderer. He sliced off a piece of bacon for each man, but only experienced old hands made out to eat it, for it was condemned army bacon. . . . Then he poured for us a beverage which he called "Slumgullion," and it is hard to think he was not inspired when he named it. It really pretended to be tea, but there was too much dish-rag, and sand, and old bacon-rind in it to deceive the intelligent traveler.

Railway fare proved little better. If a train happened to reach a station at mealtime, the passengers crowded into long, unadorned dining halls, where they gobbled down gray, unappetizing fare. The entire process was dismal, stomach-flipping, and rushed. Small wonder, Harvey biographer Stephen Fried observed, that railway food became known as "grub." George Pullman had made some progress, introducing plush sleeping and dining cars. But as a general rule, the farther one traveled west, the more unpalatable railroad meals became. If someone could provide decent, reliable food service to travelers at local railway depots, they might just make a killing.

Harvey hoped to be the first. In the mid-1870s, he opened three depot restaurants on the Kansas Pacific line. Still working full-time for the Chicago, Burlington and Quincy, he tried to convince their management to open commercial houses at their depots. When that failed, he approached the Atchison, Topeka and Santa Fe (AT&SF). That upstart line had little to lose. It operated stations in only two of its three namesake towns, and its railhead was still distant from Santa Fe. Harvey negotiated an enviable deal. The AT&SF provided him rent-free space, covered all utilities costs, paid for cooking and storage equipment, and transported his employees free of charge. In exchange, Harvey covered soft costs such as food, linen, labor, and "front of house" furnishings. Rather than take a cut from Harvey's profits, the AT&SF expected their customers' appreciation of Harvey's services to increase their traffic.

Quality and consistency were at the core of Harvey's strategy. He opened his first Atchison, Topeka and Santa Fe lunchroom in Topeka in 1876, and he expanded his enterprises as the railroads advanced. In time, his insistence on the best of everything, punctuated by frequent surprise inspections of his far-flung operations, became legendary. No matter how far away they traveled from home, travelers on the Santa Fe line could expect the best chefs, the freshest food, the finest cigars, and certainly the richest Chase & Sanborn coffee. Harvey required every restaurant to brew fresh coffee every two hours. He insisted they use the purest water. If none was available he shipped it in. Employees polished and repolished their signature silver coffee urns until they sparkled.

Harvey introduced standardization to the hospitality industry. Recipes never varied from station to station (although Harvey encouraged each manager to use local suppliers). Company rules dictated bread-slice thickness. The fastidious Englishmen expected dusty cowpokes, fresh off the New Mexico range, to wear dinner jackets in the main dining room. Those who had left their jacket at home were either provided one, or invited to leave.

The entrepreneur regulated everything. He penned long memoranda on company standards, which his officers translated into manuals. He expected uniform cleanliness and friendliness from his staff.

Strive to please the cranks, he counseled. Pleasing them would set standards guaranteed to please everyone. Hot, custom-made food had to arrive quickly at customers' tables—there was only a layover of twenty minutes before their trains departed. Headquarters staff designated four days' worth of menus at a time, telegraphing them out to the distant Harvey Houses. For custom orders, Harvey stewards telegraphed instructions straight from the train to the next depot so that passengers would find their meals waiting for them at table. Waitresses developed an elegant coding system for drink orders. If the waitress placed a patron's cup right side up in the saucer, the server delivered coffee; face down meant tea; tilted downwards against the saucer, iced tea, and so on. Harvey didn't abide mistakes. If he noticed a misplaced fork or smudged glass, he was known to yank tablecloths off tables, sending place settings shattering to the floor moments before customers arrived. (He of course expected everything to be restored before patrons were seated.) He constantly strove for what historian Donald Duke has called "systematized perfection," and he demanded the same of his employees. He posted encouraging customer service maxims such as "Real Service is Without Discrimination," "Radiate Cheer and Make a Guest feel at Ease and at Home," and "Preserve and Create— Never Destroy." Dedication to one's job and commitment to service constituted the "Fred Harvey Way." Those employees who embraced Fred Harvey's way could count on rapid promotion to better pay and bigger responsibilities.

His decision to exclusively staff his hotels and restaurants with single white female waitresses and maids might seem controversial today. Like George Pullman, Harvey initially relied on African American waiters and stewards. Racial tensions in New Mexico and Texas made him reconsider his strategy, especially after a waiter in Las Vegas, New Mexico, caused a ruckus when he accidentally dropped a large pistol, intended for self-defense, on the dining room floor. Harvey's motivations were not entirely enlightened. He intuited that close contact with black waiters made some of his white customers uncomfortable. Rather than confront racial anxieties, he alleviated them by recruiting young Caucasian women from midwestern farms and small towns. In exchange for a promise to remain on the job and remain single for six months, Harvey offered good pay and a chance for young women to broaden their horizons. Historians have noted how Harvey's hiring practices represented an important opportunity for single young women. Not since the beginning of the Massachusetts textile industry in the 1820s had American girls seen such a chance to break away from their parents' control and make a living on their own. And like the New England mill girls, the celebrated "Harvey Girls" were well supervised. They lived in carefully-monitored dormitories and attended chaperoned dances and social gatherings. Curfew began at eleven o'clock at night.

And yet, the most tantalizing aspect of the Harvey Girls was their potential as wives. Harvey sent thousands of marriageable young women into areas populated almost entirely by eligible young cowboys, railroaders, and miners. They had rarely seen anything like these respectable, charming young ladies. It was inevitable that unions formed. Stephen Fried has estimated that 100,000 Harvey Girls married western men, sticking around to build western communities and raise western families.

Equally important to his charming waitstaff was Harvey's deployment of technology. Harvey insisted on knowing the details of each of his hotels and eating houses. How many cups of coffee were served, how many pounds of flour consumed? Which employees were causing trouble or merited promotion? Which entrées did customers order, ignore, or send back? Maintaining consistency in such far-flung stations as Mojave, California; Deming, New Mexico; Lakin, Kansas; and Vining, Oklahoma, required strict attention. Harvey and his executives made the telegraph wires hum with inquiries; local managers filed daily telegraphic reports. And Fred and his top lieutenants never ceased to ride the rails, checking out local conditions in person and making adjustments where necessary.

Other innovations also helped. Fresh food arrived at Harvey kitchens in refrigerated railroad cars—a novelty. Harvey hotels were often the first buildings in their communities to feature electric lights and indoor plumbing. Pullman cars provided another opportunity for expansion, and it wasn't long before Harvey porters and waiters supplemented George Pullman's hospitality workforce in the nation's dining and sleeping cars, most notably in the storied *Santa Fe Super Chief*.

By the mid-1880s, Harvey's chronic illnesses kept the entrepreneur frequently abroad. Day-to-day responsibility fell to his capable lieutenant, Dave Benjamin, and to his son, Ford Harvey. In time, Ford stepped in to make larger strategic decisions. He renegotiated the agreement with the Santa Fe, expanded the company's hotels, and worked out a concession contract for America's national parks. When Fred Harvey died in 1901, Americans acknowledged the passing of a business legend. Pulitzer Prize–winning editor William Allen White observed that America had flourished on Harvey's diet: "Men who have eaten at Fred Harvey's eating houses have come home and insisted on having their meats broiled, not fried; their roasts roasted, not boiled; their potatoes decently cooked and their biscuits light."

Yet Fred Harvey's death marked the beginning of a new chapter. Under Harvey's son, Ford, and grandson, Fred, the hospitality company continued to expand and prosper. Working with the Santa Fe Railway, Ford Harvey built or operated a chain of premier southwestern hotels, including Albuquerque's Alvarado, Santa Fe's La Fonda, Winslow's La Posada, and the Grand Canyon's El Tovar. "Fred Harvey"—Ford preserved the illusion that his late father still ran things—and the Santa Fe Railway transformed Americans' perception of the Southwest from a desert wasteland to a must-see tourist destination.

While the railroad hired artists and lithographers to create and distribute romantic southwestern images, the hospitality company promoted the manufacture and sale of Indian art and handicrafts (some of it specifically designed for tourists' tastes by Harvey employees) and the consumption of "authentic" western experiences. Cowboy-clad Harvey Girls guided Indian Detours to picturesque Pueblo villages in New Mexico and Arizona. Fred Harvey dominated tourism at the Grand Canyon's South Rim, providing lush accommodations and conducting saddle-gripping burro rides down the canyon's steep trails. Harvey architect Mary Colter designed indelible southwestern and Pueblo Revival hotels and curio shops, including the 1905 Hopi House and the fantastic 1914 Hermit's Rest. Colter's work inspired a modern southwestern aesthetic known today as the "Santa Fe style," and helped fix the Harvey brand on nearly every traveler's southwestern vacation.

The fortunes of Fred Harvey rose and fell with the railroads. By the late 1940s, as rail service gave way to automobiles and air travel, Fred Harvey's empire dwindled. Harvey's heirs were unable to make the leap to airports and highway pull-offs in the 1950s and '60s. Only the Grand Canyon operation and a handful of other establishments remained by 1966. The family sold the Harvey chain to a large hospitality firm in 1968. Many of Fred Harvey's strategies, as well as his signature logo, still mark the products and operations of its parent company, Xanterra.

It's a testament to Fred Harvey's branding genius that his company is still cited as a model for brand creation in business textbooks. In time, his iconic signature (reportedly designed by Mary Colter) became known across the globe. In associating a person with a quality experience, he was the precursor (and often an inspiration) to Walt Disney, Howard Johnson, Conrad Hilton, Steve Jobs, Donald Trump, Colonel Harlan Sanders, and many others. Stephen Fried has pointed out that, because of Harvey's insistence on quality and consistency, earlier generations of Americans once wished America would become "fast food nation." Fred Harvey branded the American West and

Southwest with equal facility, fixing the region in the world's minds as an exotic, yet tame, recreation destination. Through iconic paintings, Indian crafts, buildings, and signature experiences, the Southwest that we imagine was, and is, Fred Harvey's West.

Duke, Donald. *Fred Harvey: Civilizer of the American Southwest.* Arcadia: Pregel, 1995.

Fried, Stephen. *Appetite for America: How Visionary Businessman Fred Harvey Built a Railroad Hospitality Empire that Civilized the Wild West.* New York: Bantam Books, 2010.

Poling-Kemps, Lesley. *Harvey Girls: Women Who Opened the West.* Cambridge: De Capo Press, 1994.

Twain, Mark. *Roughing It.* Hartford: American Publishing Company 1886.

HENRY E. HUNTINGTON

SHAPING THE CITY OF ANGELS {1850–1927}

"Tilt the world on its side and everything loose will land in Los Angeles." Attributed to Frank Lloyd Wright

The history of the American West is a history of cities. St. Louis, Omaha, Kansas City, Denver, Sacramento, San Francisco, Albuquerque, San Antonio, Fort Worth, Houston, Portland, Seattle, Phoenix, Salt Lake City . . . western cities, historian Carl Abbott writes, were essential political and economic hubs for the West's fast-growing regional economies. Western cities supplied capital, transformed raw materials into finished goods, operated regional ports of entry, and welcomed (and sometimes protested) millions of emigrants from around the world. In 2010 the U.S. Census Bureau announced that seven of the ten largest American cities were located west of the Mississippi River. We usually think of the Atlantic seaboard as America's most urbanized region, yet almost 30 percent of Americans live in western cities. Contrary to stereotypes, the West has long been the most urbanized part of the United States.

Transportation developer Henry E. Huntington did as much as anyone to shape the West's largest city, Los Angeles. If twentieth-century Los Angeles became America's "autopia," then Huntington's public transportation lines pointed the direction. His railway lines, electrical system, and real estate projects defined the growth and character of the biggest western metropolis. The nephew of Southern Pacific president Collis P. Huntington, Henry used his uncle's railroad fortune to build the world's largest integrated urban infrastructure of its time. Huntington tied L.A.'s unique urban lifestyle to horizontal mobility, building far-flung residential and commercial centers and tying them back together again with commuter rails. In his focus on interurban railroad development, he was a man of the nineteenth century. But through his relentless creation of a sprawling metropolis, bound together by modes of mechanical transportation, Huntington ushered in the future.

Los Angeles had already come a long way when the forty-eight-year-old businessman first arrived in 1898. In 1850, the year that saw both California statehood and Henry's birth, the former Spanish colonial village boasted a population of 1,600. After local boosters paid the Big Four a $600,000 subsidy to bend the Southern Pacific line to the City of Angels, Los Angeles County's population doubled in the 1870s, from 6,058 to 12,393. Although it lacked water and a decent harbor, Los Angeles's climate, scenery, fertile soil, and two major railroads—the Southern Pacific and the Santa Fe—attracted growth. The county's population increased tenfold between 1880 and 1900, to 127,945. The future offered even greater promise when demographers predicted that greater Los Angeles could hold 1 million residents if someone supplied the means.

Henry Huntington certainly had the credentials. Henry's store-keeping father, Solon Huntington, staked Collis Huntington, Solon's brother, to open a Sacramento dry goods store in the 1850s. Collis went on to lead California's Big Four. Henry grew up tending his father's New York shop and selling peanuts and cider at local circuses. Bored with academics and far more interested in pursuing a business career, Henry dropped out of college to work for his Uncle Collis by

1871. Strong, hardworking, and affable, Henry climbed the ladder through his uncle's businesses. His charming personality, passion for detail, and nearly photographic memory made him a financial success back east, where he operated a family-owned sawmill and supervised the construction of the Chesapeake, Ohio and Southwestern Railway. His success helped forge a strong, mutually admiring relationship with his uncle. The tactful Henry often smoothed over Collis's brusque encounters with business associates, making the famously curmudgeonly capitalist gush, "No better boy than [Henry] ever lived."

After he replaced Leland Stanford as president of the Southern Pacific in 1890, Collis Huntington promoted Henry to first vice president, placing him in charge of the company's San Francisco headquarters. Skilled at cost cutting and efficiency, Henry brought discipline and order to the ungainly Southern Pacific. He instituted fiscal reforms, trimmed the massive number of free passes officials awarded to cronies, and invested profits previously reserved for stockholder dividends back in the company. His efficiencies offended some of the company's investors, but he earned additional praise and respect from Collis by strengthening the line's financial base.

Huntington rarely took vacations. But after 1892, he increasingly traveled to southern California to seek respite from stress and fatigue. The Los Angeles region impressed Henry as an untapped southern wonderland, waiting for a visionary to tie the dispersed strings of its heartland together. Henry and Collis had already developed a successful business model for streetcar companies. Starting with San Francisco's Market Street cable railway, the Huntingtons merged several major streetcar lines and expanded them into San Francisco's shopping districts and suburban neighborhoods. Henry and Collis acquired the bankrupt Los Angeles and Pasadena interurban railway in 1898 with an eye toward using it to build new lines, commercial centers, and neighborhoods from scratch. In 1901 Henry reorganized his consolidated lines into the Pacific Electric Railway. In order to power the new system, and to provide electricity to the residents of the new real estate developments he envisioned, Henry organized the Pacific Light and Power Company the following year.

Collis's unexpected death in 1900 devastated Henry. His uncle's passing left him in sole charge of the family businesses. Until now, the middle-aged businessman's career had stalled in the shadow of his domineering, loving uncle. Collis bequeathed Henry one third of his Southern Pacific stock, along with stock in his shipbuilding concerns, almost $4 million in cash, and additional properties. The remaining two thirds of Collis's Southern Pacific stock went to his widow, Arabella, whom Henry would marry, after a divorce and long courtship, in 1913. Henry's hopes to succeed his uncle as president of the Southern Pacific met resistance from Wall Street and Union Pacific financier Edward H. Harriman. Harriman successfully blocked Huntington's election and, in January 1901, bought out Henry and Arabella's Southern Pacific shares. Huntington remained vice president and director, although his influence flagged in the face of Harriman's strong leadership.

As Los Angeles's population continued to grow in the early 1900s, Huntington realized that a third leg of development was necessary to complete his integrated strategy of rails and electricity. In 1902 he founded the Huntington Land and Improvement Company and set out on an ambitious venture to sculpt Los Angeles's future. Armed with his uncle's deep fiscal reserves, Henry departed from the standard strategy of building commuter lines to pre-existing towns. Instead, he invested in surrounding scrub and farmlands, building his lines wherever they could support profitable commercial and residential developments. Huntington recognized that the value of urban railways lay not in the lines themselves, which rarely turned a profit, but in the enhanced value of the real estate they made accessible.

Within two decades, his lines crisscrossed southern California, combining dispersed local communities into "one big family," as

Huntington wrote. One by one, Huntington connected and developed Long Beach, Huntington Beach, Pasadena, Pomona, Balboa, Santa Monica, and Beverly Hills. Centralized city planning hardly existed in the early 1900s, so in the absence of an effective city planning department, Huntington became greater Los Angeles's de facto urban planner. Los Angeles County's population boomed between 1900 and 1920, increasing from 170,298 to 936,455. Its manufacturing products jumped from $15 million to $790 million; its bank transactions from $123 million to $4 billion. Like the railroad-starved frontier towns of Henry's Uncle Collis's day, pre-existing communities were only too happy to provide cash and donate rights-of-way in exchange for Pacific Electric prosperity. Huntington's iconic Red Cars stitched together metro L.A.'s mountains, valleys, seashores, shopping centers, and neighborhoods, while his real estate ventures transformed miles of citrus orchards into new communities. Huntington built homes and provided easy access to the southern California lifestyle. Land prices skyrocketed, and southern Californians prospered.

By 1905, Huntington, now the "Old Man" of the family business, had become California's largest landowner and largest taxpayer. Success came with a price—his rail expansion brought him into direct competition with Harriman, his Southern Pacific boss. Despite serving jointly on the Southern Pacific board, the rival rail kingpins pursued conflicting objectives, and Harriman often blocked Huntington's routes when they countered his goals. The rivals signed an uneasy truce in 1903 when Huntington traded half his Pacific Electric shares to Harriman for essential Southern Pacific rights-of-way. The trade signified a surrender of some control over Pacific Electric's future extension.

Huntington retired in 1908, dedicating his substantial energy to a cherished personal hobby. Always an avid bibliophile, he focused on building his impressive book collection into one of the world's finest. He educated himself on rare books and antiquities, sought out advice from experts, and set about purchasing significant books, even entire libraries, on a massive scale. Under his careful stewardship, the Huntington collection grew to tens of thousands of rare books and manuscripts worth more than $20 million ($282 million in 2014). Covering English, American, and Western American history, Huntington's library includes first-edition Shakespeare folios, an illuminated Gutenberg Bible, and an early manuscript of the *Canterbury Tales,* as well as masterpieces of English, American, and modern Spanish art. Henry and Arabella relocated their collection from their New York home to California in 1919, opening their San Marino estate to researchers and art and nature lovers as the Huntington Library, Art Gallery, and Botanical Gardens. This internationally important collection continues to attract scholars and art patrons.

The famously media-shy businessman turned away biographers during his lifetime, demurring, "The Library will tell the story." Biographer William B. Friedricks nevertheless credited Henry Huntington with inventing southern California. Certainly others, including water czar William Mulholland, publisher William Harrison Otis, and a galaxy of Hollywood entrepreneurs, contributed. Yet Huntington's transportation "triad" (also Friedricks's term) of streetcars, electricity, and real estate created the framework for modern Los Angeles. His urban and interurban lines determined the city's geographic arrangement. Huntington laid out the grid and invited people to live in his far-flung developments, providing a ready-made infrastructure for forward-looking Californians. One of the great ironies of his achievement is that when Californians tore out his streetcar system to make way for more automobiles, they built their new superhighways along his original routes. Los Angelenos have struggled to rebuild the public transportation lines that once served them so well.

Abbott, Carl. *How Cities Won the West: Four Centuries of Urban Change in Western North America.* Albuquerque: University of New Mexico Press, 2008.

Friedricks, William B. *Henry E. Huntington and the Creation of Southern California.* Columbus: Ohio State University Press, 1992

Larson, Lawrence H. *The Urban West at the End of the Frontier.* Lawrence: The Regents Press of Kansas, 1978.

Spurgeon, Selena A. *Henry Edwards Huntington: His Life and Collections.* San Marino: Huntington Library, 1992.

Quiett, Glenn Chesney. *They Built the West: An Epic of Rails and Cities.* New York: Cooper Square Publishers, Inc., 1965; D. Appleton-Century Co., 1964.

MEYER GUGGENHEIM

A MINING AND SMELTING DYNASTY {1828–1905}

One day, an often-repeated story goes, the elderly businessman Meyer Guggenheim summoned his seven sons to talk about family unity. The sons were bickering about the fairness of Meyer's plan to divide family profits equally among the older, more experienced, brothers and their school-aged siblings. Emulating Aesop's fable of the dying father and his sons, Guggenheim handed each one a stick and asked them to break it. They did so with ease. Then, the family patriarch handed each son seven sticks tied together in a bundle. None of the brothers could snap the bound fasces. That is our secret, counseled Meyer. Many are better than one, and no one can break you when you stand together.

The Guggenheim story is the story of a humble American family rising together to power and affluence. Judeo-Swiss immigrant Meyer Guggenheim was a skilled entrepreneur who linked together a chain of production in manufacturing, mining, and smelting, until he controlled the point where the greatest profits accrued. Starting as a simple peddler, he devised new and better ways to manufacture his most popular wares. Sensing a desire among American women for lace and lye, he moved from sales to industrial production of these domestic goods. And in his autumn years he gambled everything in mining and smelting, forging the American West's greatest mineral empire, which his sons, working together, transformed into a global juggernaut.

Meyer Guggenheim learned the importance of togetherness growing up in the village of Lengnau, in the Swiss canton of Aargau. Lengnau was only one of two Swiss communities that allowed Jewish residents. Meyer was born in 1828, into a world that treated European Jews harshly. Christian Europe had blamed Jews for disasters, plagues, and troubled times since the Middle Ages. Swiss Jews endured severe restrictions on citizenship, marriage, movement, property owner- ship, and career options. The Swiss government categorized Jews not as citizens, but as "Alien Protection Fellows" or "Tolerated Homeless Persons Not To Be Expelled." Any Jew who failed to pay the state's special taxes, or came up short on hefty "protection and safe conduct" fees, faced expulsion. A Guggenheim ancestor in Legnau once pro- tested the enforced conversion of his son to Christianity; authorities slapped him with a large fine for his impertinence. In response, Jewish ghetto-dwellers fashioned a closed, insular community to take care of one another's needs.

The Guggenheims had always been leaders in the Lengnau ghetto, where generations of oppression pushed them from relative affluence to poverty. Simon Guggenheim, Meyer's father, stretched his meager tailor's salary to support his wife, Schäfeli, his son, and four daughters. When Schäfeli died in 1836, additional responsibility fell on Meyer. The boy took up his father's trade and supplemented the family's income as a traveling peddler. In 1847 Simon applied for permission to remarry a widow named Rachel Weil Meyer. Authorities denied the request on the grounds that the middle-aged couple was too poor, a qualification that only applied to Jews. Seeking hope and dignity, Simon decided to start fresh in America, inviting his nineteen-year- old son to come along. The group of fourteen, including Simon and his five children, and Rachel and her eight children, reached Philadel- phia in 1848.

If anti-Semitic discrimination in Europe stoked Meyer Guggenheim's hunger for material success, then America provided new opportunities. America in 1848 was a nation full of restless energy. The United States and Mexico had recently signed the Treaty of Guadalupe-Hidalgo, ending a two-year war. The U.S. received about 525,000 square miles of new land, comprising parts of Colorado and Utah, as well as California, Arizona, Nevada, and New Mexico. The California gold rush of the following year sent thousands of Americans leapfrogging across the continent. Railroads, telegraphs, and steam engines all foretold a future of American industrial promise. Still largely unknown outside of California was the newly expanded nation's tremendous mineral potential.

In time, Meyer pursued this important new opportunity with intense determination. At first, however, he confined his activities to proscribed "Jewish" trades, working as a tailor and peddling pins, domestic wares, and other "notions" door to door to housewives in western Pennsylvania. Among his best selling products was an inexpensive coffee alternative known as "coffee essence." Using distilled coffee beans, chicory, and other flavorings, Meyer helped his brother-in-law devise a less expensive formula than the partners could buy commercially. Another domestic bestseller was stove polish, a tincture of soot and other chemicals used to keep cast-iron stoves spotless. Standard polishes were messy, so Meyer invented an improved version, mixing the powdered polish with soap suds and stuffing the resulting stain-free paste into sausage casings for easier application.

The Civil War brought new opportunities. Meyer opened a Philadelphia store, sold bulk sundries to the army, and opened a lye factory. He also opened a lace and embroidery factory in Switzerland, sending his sons Daniel, Murry, and Solomon back to attain culture, learn German and French, and acquire the principles of business. No longer a mere peddler, Guggenheim began to prosper as a rising entrepreneur. Prosperity afforded Meyer the chance to cultivate a large family.

He married his stepsister, Barbara Meyer, in 1852. Together, the couple produced a steady stream of talented sons and daughters, eleven in total. Small-statured, focused, soft-spoken, and hardworking, sporting generous muttonchops and a bulbous nose, Meyer sought the best for his children, and especially his seven surviving sons, Isaac, Daniel, Murry, Solomon, Benjamin, Simon, and William; Robert, Simon's twin, died in a riding accident. The Guggenheims also produced three daughters, Jeannette, Rose, and Cora. Meyer was a loving but strict father who urged his children to appreciate education, culture, and classical music. He pushed each of them to acquire a cosmopolitan polish, and he worked hard to attain enough affluence to shield his family from the sting of anti-Semitic prejudice. He never fully succeeded in this. Yet he fully expected his seven surviving sons to follow in their father's footsteps, and he worked single-mindedly to create a family dynasty until his dying day.

In 1881 Guggenheim purchased a one-third share in two Leadville, Colorado, silver mines. It was a strange move for a man with such a sure business touch. The fifty-four-year-old businessman was already successful, and his family could look forward to at least one more generation of affluence. Like his immigrant father, Simon, Meyer took an exceptional risk, speculating on an enterprise he knew next to nothing about.

Meyer's new silver mines, the Minnie and A.Y. (named after Leadville prospector A.Y. Corman and his daughter), needed considerable capital and labor. Both were flooded, and both required large cash infusions, with no guaranteed rewards. Meyer plunged ahead, purchasing a controlling share and frequently traveling to the two-mile-high boomtown to inspect progress. He was at his desk in his Philadelphia dry goods store when a telegram arrived from his superintendent reporting the discovery of a rich and seemingly limitless vein of silver. Suddenly, Meyer's gamble paid off at a steady rate of $1,000 per day.

By the mid-1880s, the rich silver and lead ores of the A.Y. and Minnie made the Guggenheims millionaires. Meyer and his sons struggled with occasional breakdowns, labor strikes, and property disputes. Wealth still accrued quickly enough for the family to liquidate its embroidery and domestic goods interests and focus exclusively on mining development. Meyer sent his two youngest sons, Benjamin and William, to college to learn engineering, chemistry, and metallurgy, and instructed his five older ones to familiarize themselves with mining techniques. In 1881 Meyer organized M. Guggenheim's Sons, providing each boy with an equal share in the profits, regardless of experience or contribution.

The elder Guggenheim needed the strength of all his sons for his next expansion. It had not escaped his notice that the Globe Smelter, the Denver smelting firm that refined his ore, received a dollar and a half in fees for every dollar the family made. According to biographers Irwin and Debi Unger, Meyer fumed, "The smelters are getting all the profit." In order to avoid this "smelter extortion," he offered a partnership to the Globe's managing partner, Edwin R. Holden. The partners agreed to build a new smelting operation in Pueblo. Meyer became president, and appointed his son Benjamin vice president, of the Philadelphia Smelting and Refining Company in 1888. In expanding from mining to smelting, Guggenheim followed a lifelong pattern. The new startup involved risk and considerable expense. But, as always, Guggenheim succeeded by tracing a product through its production phases to its source, then acquiring control of the production, refinement, and distribution steps. Meyer hired the best managers, metallurgists, and chemists money could buy, and he drove his sons to become experts as well.

So long as silver mining boomed, the Pueblo smelter prospered. Yet Meyer and his sons found themselves increasingly entangled in international business and politics in order to keep its refineries operating. The 1890 Sherman Silver Purchase Act seemed to ensure long-term profits by requiring the U.S. Treasury to buy 4.5 million ounces of silver per year, propping up silver's going rate at $1.25 per ounce. Seeking new sources for their smelting business, the Guggenheims entered the underdeveloped Mexican market. Their success at undercutting rival American mines helped stimulate Congress to pass the 1890 McKinley Tariff, slapping a hefty import tax on Mexican ore. In response, Meyer sent his sons Daniel and Murry to negotiate with Mexican president Porfirio Díaz to build smelters directly in Mexico. Solomon took over the company's Mexican operations. Daniel and Murry remained in New York to supervise overall operations and sales. Oldest brother Isaac managed the family's financial transactions. Simon moved to Denver to handle ore purchases. Benjamin managed the Pueblo smelter. Meyer presided over all, sharing with his sons his experience and commercial savvy.

Depression, and a catastrophic drop in silver prices, spurred along by the repeal of the Sherman Silver Purchase Act, effectively crippled the silver industry in the early 1890s. Yet the efficiently operated Philadelphia Smelter and other Guggenheim interests weathered the storm. The Guggenheims expanded their smelting and mining interests into copper, lead, and other industrial metals, capitalizing on minerals essential to the nation's mushrooming telephone and electrical systems. The company opened smelters in Chihuahua, Monterrey, and San Luis Potosi in Mexico, and a new copper refinery in Perth Amboy, New Jersey. In 1889 Meyer moved his base of operations to America's financial capital, New York City, where a cosmopolitan atmosphere and large, affluent Jewish American community further buffered (if never entirely eliminated) anti-Semitic prejudices.

As the twentieth century approached, the Guggenheims operated the largest family-owned mining and smelting concern in the West. Their main rival was the powerful American Smelting and Refining Company (ASARCO), a conglomerate of mines and smelters backed by Standard Oil's John D. Rockefeller. ASARCO manager Henry H.

Rogers had repeatedly invited the Guggenheims to join the smelting trust, but the family balked at introducing "outside" influence into their enclave. In the meantime, the family extended its international reach, forming a global branch, the Guggenheim Exploration Company (Guggenex), to prospect for ores in the South American Andes and beyond. Rivalry between the Guggenheims and ASARCO heated up at the end of the century, as each firm tried to corner the metals market against the other.

Ultimately, the family's superior organization won out. ASARCO was mismanaged, weakened by a debilitating 1899 strike, and hurt by dropping silver and lead prices (created in large part when Daniel Guggenheim deliberately flooded the market with cheap Mexican metals). The company offered to merge with the Guggenheims. After two years of negotiations, the parties agreed to terms. The Guggenheim brothers put up key properties and capital in exchange for $45.2 million ($1.14 billion in 2014 dollars) in ASARCO stock, as well as seats on ASARCO's board. The family now exercised control over a trans-western corporation.

With the ASARCO merger, the Guggenheims joined the Astors, the Rockefellers, the Carnegies, and the Vanderbilts in the highest strata of America's financial elite. The merger centralized smelting in the West, combining the smelting trust's refineries in Colorado, Texas, and Montana with the Guggenheims' plants in Pueblo and Mexico, as well as a large new copper refinery in Perth Amboy, New Jersey. The merger vested the family with the power to consolidate western mining and smelting and to aggressively pursue global ventures. Within a decade, Guggenheim capital underwrote gold and silver mining from Mexico to Alaska's Kennecott River, as well as rich copper mines in Arizona, Utah's Bingham Canyon, Canada, and Chile, and rubber and diamond production in the Belgian Congo. By 1910, the company would open new refineries in El Paso and Amarillo, Texas, and Hayden, Arizona. The Guggenheims dominated western mining and smelting for several more generations, providing jobs and producing essential industrial metals for American industry.

Meyer Guggenheim passed away, at the age of seventy-seven, in 1905. He left behind a healthy dynasty for his sons, along with an obligation to give back to their community. Following the charitable lead of Barbara Guggenheim, Meyer's wife of more than fifty years, the family embraced the Jewish tradition of *tzedakah*, the duty to perform acts of philanthropy and justice. Daniel supported the pioneer aviation efforts of Charles Lindbergh and Robert Goddard. Solomon sponsored the spectacular, Frank Lloyd Wright–designed Solomon R. Guggenheim Museum of impressionist, post-impressionist, modern, and contemporary art in Manhattan, and his foundation financed the equally monumental 1997 Guggenheim Museum in Bilbao, Spain. Simon Guggenheim served as a U.S. senator for Colorado and gave $80,000 ($2 million in 2014 dollars) to build Guggenheim Hall at the Colorado School of Mines and the Guggenheim Law Building at the University of Colorado (now home to CU's Geography Department). Granddaughter Peggy Guggenheim assembled an impressive collection of twentieth-century European and American art, converting her Venice, Italy, home into a museum. Her father, Benjamin Guggenheim, displayed creditable character as a passenger on the doomed HMS *Titanic,* helping women and children find lifeboat seats and telegraphing his wife, according to biographer John H. Davis, "I played the game straight to the end and . . . no woman was left aboard this ship because Ben Guggenheim was a coward." He was last seen alive in full evening dress, sipping brandy and smoking cigars with his valet, going down, he proclaimed, "like gentlemen."

Under the Guggenheims, American smelting and mining reached its early twentieth-century peak. The decline of local ores and the drop in commodity prices, especially after the First World War, led to a long retrenchment in the West. ASARCO today operates as a wholly-owned subsidiary of the Mexican mining corporation Grupo Mexico. The company oversees three copper mines and a smelter in Arizona and a copper refinery in Texas. A shadow of its former self, ASARCO left a major footprint on the American West. As mining historian James E. Fell, Jr., has observed, mining and smelting infused large-scale corporate financing and technology into the American West, helping weld the region into a global economy. Mines and smelters employed an international workforce to extract regional mineral resources for a global marketplace. Small companies such as M. Guggenheim's Sons expanded into larger corporations, merging with competitors and extending their reach from the West into neighboring countries.

The rapid expansion of the western mining industry could be viewed a double-edged sword. On one hand, mining and smelting accelerated western economic development, creating "instant" boomtowns by providing employment, technological innovation, and infrastructure to support tens of thousands of workers. On the other, they left behind some challenging legacies of labor strife and environmental problems. Mining helped to shape the West, and the Guggenheims played an important role in creating the modern West as we know it.

Davis, John W. *The Guggenheims: An American Epic*. New York: William Morrow & Co.,1978.

Fell, Jr., James E., *Ores to Medals: The Rocky Mountain Smelting Industry*. Boulder: University Press of Colorado, 2009; Lincoln: University of Nebraska Press, 1979.

Marcosson, Isaac F. *Metal Magic: The Story of the American Smelting and Refining Company*. New York: Farrar, Straus & Co., 1949.

Unger, Irwin and Debi Unger. T*he Guggenheims: A Family History*. New York: HarperCollins Publishers Inc., 2005.

NATHANIEL P. HILL

FROM ORES TO METALS {1 8 3 2 – 1 9 0 0}

Nathaniel P. Hill

Nathaniel Peter Hill ventured onto the Rocky Mountain mining scene in 1864 when the five-year-old gold rush was sputtering. The mountain creeks that had yielded "free" gold seemed to have played out. Prospectors had turned to the hunt for lode gold, still embedded in underground ore. To extract the gold required skilled hard rock mining and major ore processing investment. The costliest steps in the process were the final ones: smelting and refining. Because fledgling Colorado Territory had no local reduction works, mining companies had to ship their ore to far-off facilities for separation of the ore from the waste rock and dirt. As a consequence, the industry was losing money and momentum.

Then entered an enterprising chemistry professor with as much business savvy as book smarts. Nathaniel Hill studied the faltering industry and identified the key to resparking it. Then he set about turning things around for Colorado mining, making it profitable for investors and enriching himself in the process. Few others made such a tremendous difference in the annals of gold mining.

Born the third of seven children in Orange County, New York, in 1832, young Nathaniel cut his business teeth helming the family farm after his father's death. Grander ambitions took him to Brown University in Providence, Rhode Island. Upon graduation from the "scientific course" in 1859, Hill transitioned seamlessly from teaching assistant to professor at Brown, teaching everything from chemistry to physiology.

He demonstrated a flair for the fundraising that is so crucial to a private university and an aptitude for consulting, applying his knowledge to various scientific challenges encountered by New England industrialists. Professor Hill earned a reputation for problem-solving, sound judgment, and integrity that distinguished him throughout his life.

Mutual acquaintances commended Hill to William Gilpin as a gifted scholar who might serve him well as consulting geologist and chemist, assessing the mineral resources of Gilpin's recently acquired property. Formerly the first governor of Colorado Territory, Gilpin had procured the old Spanish Sangre de Cristo land grant, encompassing much of the San Luis Valley in southern Colorado. Eastern capitalists who helped to finance Hill's participation in the survey had high hopes for the area's mineral production potential.

Thirty-two-year-old Hill requested a leave of absence from Brown to explore the western lands that had long beckoned him. Well paid for his expertise, he embarked upon the arduous journey that took him by train, steamboat, and stagecoach to Denver. The threat of attack by hostile Indians on the Plains was very real in 1864, but Hill assured his wife, Alice, in a letter written en route that she mustn't worry. "I prize my home, my wife and children too highly to take any chances."

On the Fourth of July in 1864, Gilpin and Hill set out for Central City in the mountain county named for the ex-governor. Professor Hill inspected the existing mines and met the other members of the party, including prospectors, surveyors, and mining engineers. He found that gold fever in the North Clear Creek district had cooled substantially due to the prohibitive costs of hard rock mining and ore processing. Believing in the region's possibilities, Hill tackled the scientific and economic feasibility of establishing a local ore processing facility. Regarding his intellectual tenacity, Wilbur Fisk wrote of the professor in his 1918 *History of Colorado:* "If he undertook a task, he would not give up until he had solved it or learned that it could not be solved."

The ores coming out of the district's lode mines were sulfurets, with chemically embedded gold impossible to separate out by simple ore crushing in even the mightiest stamp mills. The metal could only be recovered by smelting, a complex high-heat process in which base metals (such as iron or lead) collect and hold the precious metals in a "matte" which can then be refined into pure precious metal. These mattes had to be shipped at great expense to smelters and refineries in St. Louis, Omaha, the East Coast, or even Europe for extraction.

The need for local processing was obvious but the obstacles to such an undertaking were daunting. Lack of fuel was a huge problem. With the surrounding mountain sides stripped bare of timber by the mining companies, reduction works would have to import wood to fire their roasters and furnaces, and the cost of freighting anything into or out of the Central City area was formidable. Smelting was a complicated process that required scientific minds, technical experts, and experienced laborers—all scarce in 1860s Colorado.

Exacerbating the challenges facing mining companies in the region was the general lack of development in the virgin territory. Colorado lay hundreds of miles from the nearest outposts of civilization and was without rail connections. Transportation and technologies were primitive, at best.

Although a few others tried, Nathaniel Hill established the first successful smelting operation in the territory. The characteristics that had distinguished him as a scientist and educator also made him a prosperous businessman. He did his research, going to the source of the latest developments in the field and consulting with industry leaders. He planned carefully. He started small, then experimented, analyzed results, and made any necessary adjustments before moving forward.

More chemist than mining expert, Hill quickly learned that not all ores were created equal. Mineral composition varied. Smelting methods that worked well with ores from other mining regions might be ill-suited to Gregory Gulch sulfurets. He traveled to Europe twice in 1865 and again in 1866 to analyze state-of-the-art metal milling methods. As most of the Gilpin County ores were processed in Swansea, Wales, Hill was particularly keen to investigate operations there. He toured the facilities and met with experts. He returned to the U.S. with a renowned European metallurgist, Herrmann Beeger, and the mental outline for a Colorado smelter. Hill even paid passage for skilled Welsh and Cornish smelter workers to staff a Rocky Mountain plant.

In 1867 Hill moved his wife, Alice, and children, Nathaniel, Isabel, and Gertrude, to Central City and purchased a four-acre site in adjacent Black Hawk for his experimental smelter. Eastern capital from New England and New York investors financed the Boston & Colorado Smelting Company, which began operations in January 1868. The Swansea process proved successful in Gilpin County, and the smelter soon revitalized the mining industry with affordable local ore processing. Furnaces heated the rock to such high temperature that the embedded gold bonded to copper and separated from the molten "slag" as copper matte. This meant that only the reduced metallic compound had to be sent abroad for refining at a cost much lower than shipping the raw composite ore.

Investors were pleased. Gilpin County mines hummed anew. The appreciative folks of Central City elected Hill mayor in 1871. From 1872 to 1873, the professor also served on the Territorial Council, following the example of his father, who had always been active in local and state politics in New York.

Other smelters started up periodically, but the Boston & Colorado dominated processing in the region by 1871. When discoveries of silver refocused attention on the South Park mining district that year, Hill bought a group of claims and organized the Alma Pool Association. He persuaded Boston & Colorado Smelting Company stockholders to finance a new smelter in Alma and recruited Massachusetts Institute of Technology graduate Henry Wolcott to manage the production of lead-silver matte. By 1873, the Alma smelter monopolized the district, processing about 90 percent of Park County ore. But like the copper-gold matte produced by the Black Hawk works, the matte from Alma still had to be shipped to Swansea for final refining, adding substantially to the cost.

Nathaniel Hill always understood the strategic advantage of staffing his enterprises with the best and the brightest in the business. In an 1872 coup, Hill managed to lure Professor Richard Pearce away from the Swansea Smelting and Refining Company. A genius on par with Hill himself, Pearce had studied at the Royal School of Mines under the leading experts of the day. He experimented extensively with processes for refining not only gold but also silver and copper mattes. Soon after signing on with the Boston & Colorado Smelting Company, Pearce invented a cost-effective "secret process" that remained the company's mysterious intellectual property for more than three decades. In 1873 the separating works at Black Hawk turned out its first silver bullion—99 percent pure! At last the riches of Colorado mines could be transformed from ores to metals entirely locally.

As the production of Colorado mines increased, Hill's smelters expanded to keep pace, but by 1878 the Black Hawk plant was inadequate. Its capacity had grown threefold since 1871 to meet demand not only from Central City gold mining companies, but Idaho Springs, Georgetown, and Empire silver mines. As its reputation spread, the Boston & Colorado processed ores from Utah, Idaho, Montana, Nevada, Arizona, and even Mexico, at twenty-five tons per day.

Hill began to consider consolidating the Black Hawk and Alma operations into a single Front Range location. Conditions had changed since the early days of Colorado smelting. The territory was now a state, more economically and politically connected to the rest of the country. Railroads had linked the mining districts to supply centers and to the rest of the nation. A centralized location at the base of the mountains would mean more efficient, less costly transportation of ores and easy accessibility to better fuel, the rich coal deposits of the Trinidad and Cañon City fields.

Upon Hill's recommendation, the Boston and Colorado Smelting Company stockholders agreed to construct the Argo Smelter, named for the ship that in Greek mythology carried Jason on his search for gold. Hill chose a site along the railroad tracks and the South Platte River in a suburb of Denver since named Argo. To reduce the huge financial obligation of relocation, stockholders voted to double the capitalization of the Argo, creating 5,000 shares of new stock, all of which were purchased within a year. Hill used the opportunity to double his own holdings and become the firm's largest stockholder. The plant began operations on January 1, 1879, and by the 1880s and 1890s, the Argo's five 100-ton furnaces were treating gold and silver ores from Gilpin County, Aspen, Creede, and the Cripple Creek-Victor district.

Before the Seventeenth Amendment to the Constitution mandated the popular election of U.S senators, state legislatures anointed their federal representatives. Setting his sights on that coveted political plum, Hill acquired the *Denver Republican* newspaper and contributed generously to the GOP's fall election campaign in 1878. A Republican majority in the state House and Senate guaranteed the election of their nominee. N. P. Hill handily defeated his Democratic opponent, William Austin Hamilton Loveland, the following January, just days after the opening of his Argo smelter in Denver.

Senator Hill entrusted the new plant to Professor Pearce and Henry

Wolcott's capable leadership and headed for the nation's capital, where he served a full six-year term as a conservative and conscientious lawmaker, championing the interests of western business. Alice Hill shone as one of the best hostesses in Washington, and the Hills made many friends, including President and Mrs. Rutherford B. Hayes.

Defeated by Henry M. Teller in his bid for re-election, Hill returned in 1885 to his Denver mansion at 14th and Welton Streets and to the massive Argo plant. After the opening of the Argo facility, Hill converted the Black Hawk works into a sampling facility to maintain a strong presence in the Gilpin County market.

At the Argo in Denver, increased mechanization cut labor costs, and scientists and engineers continued to tweak the latest innovations from Europe to suit Rocky Mountain processing problems. The company even ran its own steam train between the Argo facility and Denver.

Hill also established purchasing agencies in the major mining camps to ensure adequate supplies of ore for processing. Hill's smelters achieved legendary technical and financial success. Production grew from $271,000 in 1868 to $2,260,000 within ten years. The Argo made $2,450,000 in its first year of operation, long before it reached full capacity.

The former professor continued to encourage innovation, upgrading and expanding his operations and his own business endeavors. Hill kept busy as president of the Colorado Smelting and Refining Company and the Durango Land Company. In 1891 Hill was appointed a U.S. delegate to the International Monetary Commission by President Benjamin Harrison.

Two developments in the last decade of the 1800s severely impacted the silver mining industry. When the British Parliament announced that it would no longer use the metal in minting Indian rupees, the value of silver plummeted to one fifth of its previous price worldwide. Adding to the crisis, the U.S. legislature repealed the Sherman Silver

Purchase Act, which had subsidized silver mining by committing to the monthly purchase of large quantities to back the federal currency along with gold. The 1893 repeal and rejection of "bi-metallism" sent the western silver mining industry into a tailspin and the Colorado economy into a severe economic depression.

By this time, few small smelting operations remained, most having been consolidated into larger integrated companies. Many mining and smelting giants laid off workers and cut wages. The Argo did not. Hill explained to the *Denver Times* that he could withstand the loss better than his workmen could.

Hill hoped to avoid the labor conflicts heating up throughout the 1890s and reaching boiling point in 1899, when most mining and smelting industrialists chose to ignore the eight-hour-day law approved by Colorado voters. But Hill and his associates negotiated a compromise acceptable to both labor and management, and Argo workers remained on the job throughout the 1899 Western Federation of Miners strike.

Nathaniel Hill's death in 1900 coincided with the end of a dynamic era in Colorado mining. The development of smelting and refining under his visionary leadership reflected the great themes of America's turn-of-the-twentieth-century Industrial Age: the calculated risk of bold financial investment, the quest for technological advancement, the drive for lowered production costs, the leverage of businessman politicians, the consolidation and integration of industry, and dealing with labor issues.

The evolution of ore refining in the Rocky Mountain Empire was shaped by the mobilization of eastern capital and the adaptation of European techniques. Hill excelled at both. His shrewd business alchemy combined money and metallurgy in just the right amounts to make metal mining profitable and to set Colorado on the road to long-term economic viability.

On the national stage, Hill showed how science and technology could be successfully brought to bear on challenges facing western entrepreneurs. Thanks to Hill and other highly trained scientist-businessmen, the American West developed technologies that set the pace globally.

Fell, James E. Jr. *Ores to Metals: The Rocky Mountain Smelting Industry.* Boulder: University Press of Colorado, 2000.

Fisk, Wilber. *History of Colorado.* Chicago: The S.J. Clark Publishing Co., 1918.

"Nathaniel P. Hill Manuscript Collection." Stephen Hart Library, *History Colorado,* Denver.

JOHN D. ROCKEFELLER, SR.

A FORTUNE BUILT ON OIL {1839-1937}

The son of a larger-than-life frontier sales-man and a strict Baptist mother, John Davidson Rockefeller embodied the spirit of nineteenth-century American enterprise. He came to prominence by reordering the chaotic Pennsylvania petroleum boom of the 1860s. By the 1880s, his Standard Oil refining company was the most successful business America had ever seen, and its founder became the world's first billionaire. By turns virtuous and calculating, Rockefeller found success through creating a bottleneck in the refining and distribution of American petroleum and relentlessly squeezing out competitors. Ever alert to opportunities to eliminate irrational and wasteful competition, he improved on time-honored business practices, and he invented revolutionary new strategies to challenge existing government regulations against monopolies. Overall, his innovations vastly improved the efficiency of oil refinement, distribution, and production, which, in turn, greatly impacted the progress of petroleum development in the American West.

Rockefeller's drive for control and his desire for secrecy cost him dearly in the public arena. "Muckraking" exposés written by reform-minded journalists such as William Demarest Lloyd and Ida Tarbell generated huge public outrage over Rockefeller's approach. Critics lashed the capitalist for creating a system that appeared to smother upward mobility. Rockefeller's monolithic enterprises generated years of lawsuits, congressional investigations, and occasional government-mandated breakups of Standard Oil's trusts and holding companies. J. D. and his son, John D. Rockefeller, Jr., helped restore the family's reputation by building on the elder Rockefeller's natural impulse to give back to his community more than he had removed.

Born in 1839, John D. Rockefeller, Sr., grew up in the heartland of big spiritual aspirations and millennial plans. The "Burned-over District" of western and central New York seethed with evangelical fervor, spawning influential religious groups such as the Shakers, the Millerites, and the Church of Jesus Christ of Latter-day Saints. J. D.'s Baptist mother provided strict discipline, a strong social consciousness, and a sense of divine destiny. John's father, William Avery Rockefeller, instilled other lessons. The elder Rockefeller often disappeared for weeks on end, selling bogus patent medicines and other dubious products. He boasted to neighbors about cheating his children in business deals to make them sharp. When John was ten, William Rockefeller abandoned his family to flee a rape accusation. News that he had committed bigamy with another woman in Ohio sparked a deep sense of shame and secrecy in his young son.

Together, Rockefeller's parents planted in their son the deep desire for stability and a profound sense of social obligation. Rockefeller reconciled by generating enough wealth to keep economic insecurity permanently at bay. Rockefeller earned his first paycheck at the age of sixteen, when he took work as an assistant bookkeeper. He demonstrated a keen eye for detail and a quick, analytical mind. By eighteen, he had gone into business for himself. Two years later, he discovered the commodity—petroleum—that would propel him to greatness.

Prospector Edwin Drake first struck oil in western Pennsylvania in 1859. Within a year, the region was immersed in the nation's first oil boom. But, where others found opportunity, J. D. saw economic anarchy. Unpredictable cycles of overproduction and shortages, cutthroat competition, and conflicts over distribution and refining all made the price of oil fluctuate wildly. In its first boom year, the price of a barrel of oil plummeted from twenty dollars to ten cents. Many Americans embraced healthy unregulated competition as the anchor of American capitalism. But Rockefeller saw waste, ill-planned competition, suicidal price wars, lax management, and bankruptcies. The young businessman resolved to save the chaotic petroleum industry from its own excesses.

Rockefeller avoided the risky practice of oil production, focusing instead on refining and distribution. He built his first kerosene refinery on an Ohio railroad line with direct access to the Pennsylvania fields. Seizing an opportunity to undercut his rivals, he solicited railroad rebates, receiving discounts on freight costs when railroads carried his oil over long distances. Rockefeller purchased large volumes of crude, using it to negotiate "drawbacks"—fines levied on rival companies' cargo—as well. He received a portion of these fines, essentially creating (and profiting from) a tax on his rivals so he could transport his own products more cheaply.

Rockefeller next turned to weeding out weaker rivals and increasing his hold on the refining industry. In 1870, he and his business partners organized five refineries into the Standard Oil Company. It controlled about 5 percent of the national refining trade, leaving plenty of room for growth. He forced most of his Cleveland rivals to sell out and, in 1871, attempted to establish his first monopoly in the Pennsylvania fields. His South Improvement Company pressured Pennsylvania railways to charge his competitors outrageous rates while secretly favoring companies that belonged to Rockefeller's cartel. The scheme sparked widespread outrage when it was uncovered. Independent oil producers banded together to embargo Standard Oil purchases, and the railroads quickly backed out of their agreement. Small producers struck back, in part, by building pipelines to avoid ruinous Standard Oil–sponsored railway fees. Rockefeller quickly flanked the independents, building his own network of pipelines. This made him less dependent on the railroads and better able to pressure small companies into using his own distribution services. Rockefeller garnered his first bad publicity as angry small businesspeople protested his attempt to monopolize oil refining and transportation.

By the 1880s, Standard Oil nevertheless controlled 90 percent of the American oil refining industry. Gross earnings in 1890, according to Gilded Age historian Sean Dennis Cashman, were $8 million (roughly $211 million in 2014 dollars); and by 1904, $57 million (about $1.5 billion today). Rockefeller's dominance increased the efficiency of oil refining and distribution. Yet his strategy also stoked a national debate about the relative merits of monopoly and free enterprise. Many Americans subscribed to the idea that open, competitive markets provided the most evenhanded chance of success for hard-working entrepreneurs. Until Standard Oil came along, government interference provided the greatest perceived challenge to the ideal of equal opportunity. Large corporations such as Standard presented a new test. As John D. Rockefeller continued to search for industrial order, developing innovative organizational structures to further consolidate and stabilize the oil industry, more people began to see his dominance as a threat to their own American Dream.

Rockefeller and his staff invented the corporate trust in 1882, in order to manage his far-flung oil concerns. His lead attorney persuaded Standard Oil and subsidiary stockholders to turn over their shares to nine trustees, who would act on their behalf for the good of the corporation. Rockefeller remained in charge, though, as the chair of the executive committee that supervised an interlocking structure of committees. The thirty-nine individual companies that composed the trust acted autonomously, except that each pledged not to compete with the others. By instilling unity and pooling profits, Rockefeller was able to stabilize petroleum prices and reduce the number of Standard Oil refineries by 60 percent. The oil trust gave Rockefeller the economic strength to expand from Ohio and Pennsylvania into western oilfields as distant as California.

The success of the Standard Oil trust attracted many imitators. Whiskey distillers, sugar and tobacco growers, meatpackers, and jute producers each followed suit. By 1886 Rockefeller praised trusts as the new brand of "modern economic administration. . . . The day of combination is here to stay. Individualism has gone never to return."

But Americans still valued individualism: such pronouncements further fueled anti-Rockefeller sentiments. Through the 1880s, states began passing new anti-trust laws. In 1892, the Ohio Supreme Court declared the Standard Oil of Ohio trust dissolved. Ever alert to organizational innovations, Rockefeller gravitated to an alternative corporate structure, the holding company. The laws of New Jersey allowed corporations headquartered there to purchase shares in any other corporation. The capitalist organized Standard Oil of New Jersey as a holding company for a galaxy of subordinate companies. Once again, Rockefeller had remained a step ahead of regulators in creating an umbrella institution that seemed to defy the rules of free markets. The age of merger took flight.

Rockefeller's success, combined with a public perception of his ruthlessness, made him a prominent scapegoat for Americans who remained uncomfortable with the vast, impersonal new corporate structure of industrial America. Ironically, as economic historian H. W. Brands has pointed out, the oil tycoon's strategy largely benefited his wage-workers, who avoided the strikes and labor strife caused by cost-cutting in more volatile competitive fields. Progressive writer Henry Demarest Lloyd nevertheless took direct aim at Standard Oil in his influential 1894 book, *Wealth Against Commonwealth,* which condemned the monopolistic drift of American industries. Between 1902 and 1904, journalist Ida Tarbell, whose wildcatting father had been a casualty of Rockefeller's South Improvement Company plan, also published a series of scathing essays criticizing Standard Oil and impugning John D. Rockefeller's character. The essays fueled public outrage that contributed to the breakup of Standard Oil of New Jersey by the United States Supreme Court in 1911.

Rockefeller family prestige received another serious blow during the Great Coalfield Strike against the family-owned Colorado Fuel & Iron Company in 1913 and 1914. Committed to breaking the United Mineworkers of America union, John D., Sr., and John D., Jr., delegated responsibility for ending the strike to subordinates, who in turn allowed events to spiral out of control. An April 1914 confrontation between striking miners, company officials, and Colorado National Guard militiamen ended in the deaths of approximately two dozen people, including women and children, and sparked a bloody ten-day labor war in southern Colorado. The negative publicity of the Ludlow Massacre further inflamed simmering public distrust of the Rockefellers and forced the family to institute moderate reforms to improve their relations with their workforce.

It would be easy to ascribe John D. Rockefeller's philanthropic activity as a mere reaction to public condemnation. Some of his later gifts, propelled by his son, John D. Rockefeller, Jr., perhaps served as a belated attempt to buff up the elder businessman's public image. But Rockefeller, Sr., had always equated charity and philanthropy with his Christian values. He often said, "God gave me money," and he intended to use his good fortune to advance God's work on earth. He supported Baptist conventions, missionaries, and relief efforts. He underwrote colleges for African Americans, including the Tuskegee Institute, Morehouse College, and the struggling Atlanta Baptist Female Seminary, which adopted the maiden name of J. D.'s wife, Laura Spelman Rockefeller, in the couple's honor. By 1890, he had characteristically organized his scattershot philanthropic projects in order to focus on the efforts that would do the most good. According to historian of philanthropy John Steele Gordon, Rockefeller declared, "the best philanthropy is constantly in search of finalities—a search for a cause, an attempt to cure evils at their source." He lived up to his own philosophy by providing more than $35 million to support the University of Chicago, founding the Rockefeller Medical Research Institution in New York City, a school of public health and hygiene at Johns Hopkins University, and the International Health Commission. He created a general education board to improve education, social conditions, and health care for rural blacks and whites. And he ensured continuity for his humanitarian work by creating the Rockefeller Foundation, soon to become the nation's largest philanthropic organization. By the time of his death in 1937, at the age of ninety-seven, he had given away roughly $540 million (almost $8.9 billion in 2014 dollars).

American business owes a lot to the genius of John D. Rockefeller. The petroleum tycoon revolutionized corporate organization and management, paving the way for modern multinational corporations. His Standard Oil companies shaped the American petroleum industry, providing the energy resources that Americans needed to advance from the age of steam to a modern, automobile-based global economy. Rockefeller underwrote major energy development projects in the American West, developing oilfields and building refineries in Texas (under the Humble Oil & Refining Company banner), California (as Standard Oil of California—today's Chevron Corporation), and elsewhere, and crossing the Pacific Ocean to provide fuel to Africa, Asia, and Oceania. Other spinoff companies, such as Standard Oil of New Jersey (today's Exxon), Standard Oil of Indiana (Amoco), and Standard Oil of New York (Mobil), also continue as well-known American brands. Americans struggled to come to terms with the scale and competitiveness of Rockefeller's economic enterprises. The business leader charted the boundaries of corporate development and provided fodder for healthy public debate over the proper relationship between private enterprise, a representative government, and the free market.

Brands, H.W. *Masters of Enterprise*. New York: The Free Press, 1999.

Cashman, Sean Dennis. *America in the Gilded Age*. 3rd edition. New York: New York University Press, 1993.

Chernow, Ron. *Titan: The Life of John D. Rockefeller, Sr.* New York: Random House, 1998.

Deane, Elizabeth and Adriana Bosche. "The Rockefellers" transcript. American Experience. WGBH Educational Foundation, 2000.

Gordon, John Steele. "John D. Rockefeller, Sr.," Philanthropy Roundtable: The Philanthropy Hall of Fame. Online resource: http://www.philanthropyroundtable.org/ almanac/hall_of_fame/ john_d._rockefeller_sr. Accessed August 17, 2014.

Rees, Jonathan H. *Representation and Rebellion: The Rockefeller Plan at the Colorado Fuel and Iron Company, 1914-1942*. Boulder: University Press of Colorado, 2010.

EDWARD L. DOHENY

PETROLEUM ENTREPRENEUR {1856–1935}

Gold and silver lured hundreds of thousands of Americans west in the late nineteenth century, but more prosaic minerals such as copper, tungsten, molybdenum, and especially petroleum, sustained western growth into the twentieth. At least, that's what former prospector Edward L. Doheny learned when he abandoned his dreams of becoming a New Mexico silver millionaire to settle down in Los Angeles in 1891.

Already thirty-five, the former prospector arrived in California with a lifetime of mining experience but with few prospects. Within two decades, he became one of the nation's wealthiest oilmen. His pioneering role in opening the oilfields in Los Angeles and California's Kern River, and on the Gulf Coast of Mexico, jump-started the western petroleum industry. In 1900 western oil production accounted for only 9 percent of American output. By 1911 it amounted to 72 percent. Doheny triggered the oil boom that, at least for a time, broke the Standard Oil Company's grip on American petroleum production and distribution. In transitioning from precious metal mining to petroleum development, Doheny essentially bridged the nineteenth century and the twentieth, ushering in the age of gasoline-powered automobility that continues to define California and the West.

Edward Laurence Doheny was born in 1856 in Fond du Lac,

Wisconsin. His father, Patrick, a former whaler and laborer, fled the Irish Potato Famine. His mother, a Canadian of Irish descent, taught school. What little evidence remains suggests that Edward endured an unhappy childhood, perhaps tainted by paternal alcoholism and abuse. Yet he showed promise, graduating as high school valedictorian at fifteen and receiving high marks in arithmetic. In 1876 the twenty-year-old Doheny took a job as a government surveyor in the West. Perhaps he traveled west to escape his unhappy home life. Certainly, he never looked back.

As a surveyor, Doheny often heard tales about rich western gold and silver mines. In 1874 he quit his government job to verify the stories for himself, prospecting in South Dakota's Black Hills and Arizona. In 1880 he settled down in a New Mexico mining camp known as Kingston. Success eluded Doheny, despite some early good fortune as a prospector and mining speculator. Strikes in 1882 and 1883 earned him a $12,000 windfall ($271,000 in 2014 dollars), which he sank into an unproductive mine. Losing real estate transactions further drained his resources, forcing the would-be entrepreneur to take jobs managing other mining claims, or even painting local buildings, to make ends meet. In truth, no amount of effort or skill could make the marginal Kingston mines pay. Doheny's prospects steadily declined until, in December 1889, he moved his family to nearby Silver City to take work as a notary public and mining claims registrar.

Mining was not a total loss for Doheny. He married the daughter of his boardinghouse keeper and began raising a family. He also forged friendships with two men, Charles Canfield and Albert B. Fall, who would play crucial roles in his later career. And, as his biographer Martin R. Ansell points out, he acquired valuable experience in mineral evaluation, stock investment, mining administration, land titles, and mining claims that would serve him well in the oil industry. He nevertheless arrived penniless in Los Angeles in 1892, desperate for a second chance.

According to legend, Doheny first learned about the oil business while he was sitting despondently on his rented Los Angeles porch, wondering what to do next. A wagonload of tar, known locally as brea, happened by, and Doheny impulsively enquired about its origin and use as fuel for the boilers of a nearby ice factory. His investigation led to nearby Westlake Park, where natural pools of petroleum oozed from the ground. Doheny later credited his natural mining instincts for divining the oil's worth, telling historian Bernie Forbes: "I had found gold and I had found silver and I had found lead, but this ugly-looking substance I felt was the key to something more valuable." But he also did his homework, avidly reading reports from the California state geologist's office and closely following the growth of the petroleum industry in mining journals.

Forging a new partnership with his old silver-mining companion Charles Canfield, Doheny scraped together $400 and leased an oil-bearing lot near downtown Los Angeles. The veteran prospectors used picks, shovels, a windlass, and time-honored mining techniques to sink a four-by-six-foot shaft into the ground. At 155 feet, they struck a gas pocket that reminded Doheny of popcorn as it crackled from the ground. Abandoning their prospect hole for fear of asphyxiation, they devised a crude drill bit and continued excavating. At about 175 feet their cable broke, sending their bit plummeting into the well and requiring a man to descend into the pit to free it up. At 200 feet, the walls of the shaft began weeping oil. The partners collected a few barrels' worth in discarded tallow buckets. They had made history, opening the first free-flowing oil well in Los Angeles.

Doheny and Canfield were not the first to strike oil in California. American Indians had long used native tar for lubricants and canoe sealant. Early attempts to commercially exploit Golden State oil dated back to the gold rush, although its viscosity made it unsuitable for kerosene, then the nation's primary petroleum product. About 100 wells operated in California by 1892. Doheny's advantage came from being, according to petroleum historian Martin Ansell, "in the right place at the right time." His real challenge was not discovering oil—thirty years of exploration had identified several large fields in California— but in creating a market. A handful of factories were burning heavy crude oil for fuel. Factories and railroad companies were beginning to recognize petroleum as an inexpensive, easily shipped, and conveniently stored alternative to coal. Doheny aggressively lobbied them to speed up conversion.

The Doheny Petroleum Company, and the California oil industry in general, advanced slowly as factories and railroad lines gradually switched from coal to oil. Doheny's strike triggered a local boom that quickly outpaced demand. Hundreds of new oil developers swarmed into central Los Angeles, injecting a peak of 3,500 barrels of oil a day into an unready market. Doheny alone drilled eighty-one wells between 1892 and 1897. His 350,000 barrels of oil represented far more than local businesses could handle. In addition to sparking bitter complaints about environmental damage, overproduction destabilized prices, pushing a barrel of oil to as little as thirty-five cents. Doheny made up the difference by selling aggressively to large corporate buyers. He approached the Atchison, Topeka & Santa Fe with a plan to convert locomotive engines from coal to oil. When the railroad expressed doubts about oil's efficiency, Doheny converted an ancient coal-burning locomotive to oil. His demonstration won over the Santa Fe. By 1899 the railway had converted completely, and Doheny contracted to supply the line with thirty thousand barrels per month at ninety-six cents per barrel.

The petroleum entrepreneur made additional attempts to stabilize his volatile new industry, promoting the advantages of plentiful oil over coal to industrial consumers, building storage tanks to hold oil off the market until demand caught up with supply, and running pipelines to reach new customers. Doheny also organized a consortium of Los Angeles oil producers to centralize production and supply, and to stabilize prices. Fortified by contracts from the powerful Santa Fe, Doheny slashed prices to attract new customers. Although rising prices sometimes caught him short on these contracts, he was able to build a large customer base as a buffer from the periodic shakeouts that struck the industry.

Increasing demand sent Doheny into new fields. In 1895 he contracted with the Santa Fe to develop wells near Fullerton, California, and in 1899 he pioneered the Kern River boom near Bakersfield. Sensing that the Los Angeles Basin booms were nearing their end, he liquidated his holdings there in order to seek out new opportunities. The biggest one appeared in Mexico. Albert A. Robinson, a former Santa Fe official serving as president of the Mexican Central Railway, invited Doheny to prospect for oil on railway land in 1900. The logistics were daunting. No one had produced oil commercially in Mexico. Potential suppliers would have to build the industry from scratch, cutting through jungles, grading and paving roads, and laying track just to reach the remote sites, then supplying pipeline, storage tanks, refineries, distribution systems, and trained workers. Aggressive British firms competed for official favor. Investment could lead to a dry well, and a gusher could go to waste for lack of a distribution network. Mexico's shifting politics also increased the risk. Doheny nevertheless forged ahead, incorporating the Mexican Petroleum Company and supplying oil for the Mexican Central Railway by the end of 1900. Despite early setbacks, Doheny's pioneering efforts slowly began to reap rewards. He threw all of his resources behind the enterprise, selling his profitable Kern County oil interests and pawning his wife's most expensive jewelry. To raise capital for new refineries, he sold raw crude for asphalt. He kept up appearances for investors by building a lavish new mansion in Los Angeles.

Doheny also negotiated Mexico's tricky political arena, forging friendships with Mexican president Porfirio Díaz and other high officials. Well aware of Mexico's potential petroleum wealth, Díaz's administration lacked the economic base and technical skill required to exploit it. Doheny cultivated their goodwill, even as frustrations over the lack of economic and political equity in Mexico grew among the lower classes. He walked a fine line, making sure that both elite and average Mexicans benefited from his developments, holding off British and American competitors, and navigating an unpredictable political landscape marked with sudden new regulations, taxes, and official stonewalling.

As with the Los Angeles field, Doheny exercised patience, investing in infrastructure and exploration for almost a decade before cashing in. He raised his game from mere producer to corporate exponent of vertical integration. Doheny financed production, transport, refinement, and marketing, successfully systematizing an industry previously dominated by small independent operators. He launched a tanker fleet to serve international markets. He paid high wages to both Mexican and international workers. Rich discoveries in Mexico's remote Cerro de la Pez (Tar Hill), in Casiano, and the promising Cerro Azul No. 4, the world's largest oil well up to that time, increased his profits exponentially. By 1911 Mexico's "Golden Lane" along the Gulf Coast was a net exporter of oil, and Doheny had become one of the world's wealthiest oilmen.

In May 1911 the Supreme Court ordered the breakup of Standard Oil trust. Doheny's companies were well positioned to take advantage of Standard Oil's misfortune. Earlier, when Doheny's Mexican wells were producing more than he could sell, he had approached Standard Oil as the only corporation with sufficient reserves to buy up his overstock. Now, Standard Oil of New Jersey, the largest of the remaining Standard companies, needed him. The conglomeration had refineries, tankers, distribution, marketing, but no production facilities. Doheny shipped oil to Standard processing and retail facilities throughout the United States. American factories, steamships, locomotives, and, increasingly, automobiles used all the petroleum he could supply.

With so much at stake, Doheny nervously watched the progress of the 1910 Mexican Revolution. Prosperity had not spread evenly across President Díaz's Mexico. The aging ruler relied increasingly on authoritarian control and the suppression of dissent. Doheny lost his most important patron when the revolutionary reformer Francisco I. Madero seized control of the Mexican government in 1911.

Over the next ten years, as Mexico saw a succession of increasingly anticorporate regimes, Doheny entered the political arena to protect his investments. He urged President Wilson to intervene to protect American interests, lending his company yacht as the American command headquarters when U.S. Marines briefly occupied Veracruz in April 1914. Doheny watched with dismay as each new revolutionary government edged closer to nationalization of Mexico's oil deposits. He recoiled when revolutionaries sacked his Huasteca Petroleum Company plant, burning more than 100,000 barrels of oil, in 1915.

Ironically, oil production remained the one bright spot in Mexico's unsettled revolutionary decade. Each successive revolutionary regime tightened oversight of American oil interests. Doheny continued to reinvest his substantial profits into infrastructure and to distribute Mexican oil to the Atlantic Seaboard, South America, and war-torn Europe. He also continued to lobby for an American invasion of Mexico to restore law and order.

At his most extreme, he commissioned a mercenary army to protect his holdings, creating a so-called "petroleum state" within Mexico's borders. In the chaos, it was sometimes hard to tell whether Doheny's private army was really defending his assets from revolutionary armies or extorting protection money from the capitalist to preserve his holdings from their own depredations.

Success in Mexico gave Doheny momentum to explore new fields in the American West, where his initiatives drew attention, both for good and for ill. Following the First World War, the United States Navy transferred control of its Wyoming and California oil reserves to the

Department of the Interior. Secretary of the Interior Albert B. Fall, an old mining associate, granted a no-bid contract to develop the Teapot Dome reserves in Wyoming to oilman Harry F. Sinclair. At the same time, the Navy selected Doheny's bid to pump reserves in California's Kern County in exchange for the construction of fuel storage tanks at the naval base at Pearl Harbor, Hawaii. It was later revealed that Doheny had delivered $100,000 to Secretary Fall at the same time the government was considering bids. Doheny insisted that the $100,000 was an innocent, if ill-considered, loan to an old friend fallen on hard times. The media sensationalized the loan as another sordid chapter in the "Teapot Dome" corruption scandal. Sinclair and Secretary Fall both received prison terms for their roles. Doheny spent the rest of the decade fending off criminal and civil suits and fighting a losing battle to repair his public reputation. Although twice acquitted of criminal wrongdoing, Doheny's loan cast him in the public eye as a rapacious plutocrat willing to sacrifice national security in the name of profits. It also resulted in personal tragedy when his beloved son, Edward, Jr., was murdered by Doheny's mentally unstable personal secretary during a fight over their pending court testimony.

Doheny's miscalculation led to a tragic and unfortunate fall. As one of the West's earliest and most successful oil producers, Doheny sparked western petroleum development that preceded Texas's sensational Spindletop discovery by almost a decade. His California wells gave the West a headstart in petroleum production. Large strikes in Mexico solidified his petroleum empire and made him one of the most powerful oilmen in America. Doheny helped build up the West's early infrastructure, transforming the region into one of the nation's premier oil-producing districts. More than a century after he first struck oil, nine out of ten of America's top oil producing states were located west of the Mississippi River. Doheny helped to lead the way.

Ansell, Martin M. *Oil Baron of the Southwest: Edward L. Doheny and the Development of the Petroleum Industry in California and Mexico.* Columbus: Ohio State University Press, 1998.

Davis, Leslie. *Dark Side of Fortune: Triumph and Scandal in the Life of Oil Tycoon Edward L. Doheny.* Berkeley: University of California Press, 1998.

Hall, Linda B. *Oil, Banks, and Politics: The United States and Postrevolutionary Mexico, 1917–1924.* Austin: University of Texas Press, 1995.

LaBotz, Dan. *Edward L. Doheny: Petroleum, Power, and Politics in the United States and Mexico.* New York: Praeger, 1991.

McCartney, Laton. *The Teapot Dome Scandal: How Big Oil Bought the Harding White House and Tried to Steal the Country.* New York: Random House, 2008.

GEORGE HEARST

FORTUNE'S FAVORITE {1820–1891}

"It takes a mine to make a mine." Attributed to George Hearst

Overshadowed by his flamboyant son, the newspaper publisher William Randolph Hearst, mining entrepreneur George Hearst has been for the most part forgotten. But once upon a time George was *the* Hearst—a celebrated western mining man, a millionaire with a Midas touch, and an influential United States senator. The self-educated Missouri farm boy became famous as one of the leading American mining experts of the late nineteenth century. Whereas most gold seekers turned away from the gold fields empty handed or ended up working for wages in a mine, fortune favored Hearst again and again, in multiple fields.

Hearst's properties included famous mines such as the Lecompton in California's gold belt, the Ophir on Nevada's Comstock Lode, Utah's Ontario Mine near Park City, Utah, the acclaimed Anaconda copper mine in Butte, Montana, and South Dakota's Homestake gold mine, the world's largest and deepest for more than 125 years. Operating on a vast industrial scale, Hearst's mines employed thousands of miners, sparked rapid settlement of remote parts of the West, and inundated the American economy with a flood of precious and industrial metals.

George Hearst was born in September 1820 in Franklin County, Missouri. He helped out on his father William Hearst's enterprises, planting and harvesting corn and wheat, tending livestock, keeping the family store, and taking other odd jobs. Formal education opportunities appeared infrequently—George later guessed he spent only two years inside a classroom. He acquired a more useful education underground, learning mining fundamentals in the nearby lead mining center of St. Clair.

Life might have gone on like that had George's father not died in 1846. Often characterized as too generous with customer credit and too lavish with his own earnings, William Hearst left debts totaling more than $10,000 (about $301,000 in 2014 dollars). He also left behind a widow, Elizabeth, a young daughter, and an invalid son to George's care. Now twenty-six, George Hearst struggled to manage his father's assets, as well as a failing general store, while slowly paying off his father's obligations. He devoured borrowed books on mineralogy and geology in his spare time. By the end of 1846, he began leasing lead mining claims, deploying his book learning, and introducing more efficient refining techniques, soon realizing greater profits than he had ever seen from farming. By 1849 George Hearst underwent a personal alchemy, transforming lead into gold and himself from a farmer into a miner.

The late 1840s were a favorable time for mining experts, self-taught or otherwise. On February 2, 1848, the United States and Mexico signed a treaty transferring Texas, New Mexico, Arizona, Nevada, California, and parts of Utah and Colorado to the United States. Unknown to the signatories, an American settler had discovered several flakes of gold in a millrace in Coloma, California, only a week earlier. Given the communications technology available at the time, word of Marshall's golden discovery circled the globe with dazzling speed. Clipper ships, fast riders, telegraphs, and early mass circulation newspapers spread the news, igniting a hunger for risk and reward unlike any other in

American history. According to mining historian Rodman Paul, some 250,000 adventurers crowded the California gold fields between 1849 and 1854, extracting an estimated $200 million in gold. In the colossal movement of people, in the investments required to meet their needs, in wealth generated, and in the incredible diversity of emigrants, the California gold rush was unprecedented in American history.

Of course, most immigrants quickly learned that, contrary to rumor, few gold nuggets actually lay on the ground waiting to be picked up. Few, indeed, were the experienced miners who understood the techniques and processes to coax gold and other precious minerals from their stony beds. Most gold seekers improvised, borrowing extraction techniques from the Spanish Californians they were displacing, and importing Welsh and German metallurgists to supply refining skills. George Hearst possessed only a few years' experience in mining, but he considered himself at least equal to any other American in the field. After spending a year sifting the wild stories coming out of the West, he gathered a party of relatives and neighbors and set off for California.

Following a difficult journey of five months, Hearst arrived in America's El Dorado in the fall of 1850. The trip had exhausted his savings, so he spent the first few months sampling streams and quartz outcroppings and learning more about the region. He claimed his first two quartz mines in early 1850. In 1857 he discovered the Lecompton Mine, earning his first sizable fortune and opening an entirely new district to prospectors.

It's difficult to capture the qualities that made George Hearst successful. Tall, thin, pale, with a slender nose and wide-set hooded eyes, he was an unlikely tycoon. He enjoyed beans, bacon, and other simple miners' fare. When he could get away with it, he tucked pants into his high boots and wore a battered slouch hat of the style favored by Nevada prospectors. Slow walking, slow speaking, and generally easygoing, he tugged absently on his wiry beard while thinking deeply.

His business ventures beyond mining invariably failed. Investments in a Nevada City theater and a Sacramento general store both failed, while a venture into publishing with his good friend Mark Twain led to bankruptcy. His attempts to breed racehorses and operate a newspaper required steady capital infusions from his mining riches. Yet he had an uncanny instinct for assessing mining properties, shrewdly guessing their hidden potential. Drawing on instinct, education, and experience, he read mining landscapes and accurately assessed their mineral value. Admirers insisted that the earth spoke to him. He also firmly believed in luck. In later years he handed gold coins freely to destitute former colleagues who approached him in the street, explaining, "I struck it rich. They didn't. They might have been lucky."

Still, successful gold camp entrepreneurs often made their own luck. George Hearst capitalized on his own good fortune with superior organization, first-rate information gathering skills, and a commitment to innovation. He did his homework, assessing sites firsthand, scrutinizing assays, and relying on an encyclopedic knowledge of applied geology. Hearst was often described as a prospector. Yet, unlike most individual gold hunters, he had the contacts and ability to raise large sums of investment capital. Individual miners usually worked surface claims with picks, shovels, and the tools necessary to build sluices and rockers. Hearst probed the deep veins where the most valuable gold and mineral deposits hid. Mining operations on this scale, however, required water rights, steam hoists, support timbers, pumping equipment, dynamite, mules, trackage, ore carts, and labor. These resources were far beyond the means of a traditional prospector. To secure capital, he formed a partnership with a San Francisco lawyer of Turkish descent, James Ben Ali Haggin, and Haggin's partner, Lloyd Tevis. The partners adhered to two rules: Never buy into a mine controlled by outsiders and never invest more in a mine than the value of visible ore. Using this simple formula, Hearst, Haggin, Tevis, & Company became the largest private mine-owning firm in the United States.

Although he had arrived late to the California rush, Hearst was one of the first to recognize the Comstock bonanza of 1859. Through an assayer friend, he acquired information about promising silver and gold deposits in the Washoe region of Nevada. Mining lore holds that the first Washoe prospectors were initially confounded, then elated, when they learned that a thick black ooze that gummed up their gold sluices was actually high-quality silver. Hearst was one of the first large operators to inspect the legendary Comstock Lode in 1859. Assaying a few samples, he quickly sold his profitable Lecompton Mine and staked everything on a new mine, the Ophir, situated on the Comstock Lode. Hearst had trouble convincing skeptical San Francisco smelter operators to refine his first ore shipment, so he contracted a German chemist to build a refinery and smelt the ore at a rate of $450 a ton. Mule teams transported forty-five tons of ore from Nevada across the Sierras to San Francisco for smelting. After deducting freight and smelting costs, the ore still netted $1,216 ($33,425 in 2014 dollars) per ton. In time, George's mine averaged $3,000 per ton in gold and silver. As word spread, miners flocked to the Washoe region. Virginia City sprouted up around the Ophir Mine, and America's first major silver boom began.

Hearst's operations were unusual in their large scale. In time, wags noted, the Comstock Lode supported two cities. On the surface lay rowdy Virginia City. Underground, a vast warren of tunnels hummed with activity twenty-four hours a day. In order to support this underground city, Hearst sponsored major technological innovations that made a lasting impact on western mining. Soft Comstock ore was easy to extract, but the deep shafts and tunnels excavated by miners were prone to collapse. Hearst's mining superintendent, Philip Deidesheimer, developed a new mining support system, known as cribbing, to hold back the mountain. Instead of traditional post and beam supports, Ophir miners used six-foot by six-foot timber cubes to fill the cavities left by extracted ore. Miners gradually built up a lattice of support beams, often filling the gaps between the wooden frames with waste rock. As miners delved deeper, they wrestled with excessive water and heat and inadequate ventilation. Ophir engineers designed more powerful ventilation systems and pumping devices to serve what became one of the world's most complex silver mines. Aboveground, Hearst pushed his German smelting experts to devise more efficient and higher yielding smelting processes.

Success in the Lecompton and Ophir mines allowed George to retire his father's debt and contemplate marriage. At the same time, his new status as a mining tycoon brought new legal troubles. The flood of claimants on the Comstock generated a wave of lawsuits, as lawyers battled to establish rival claims to the vein's dips, spurs, and angles. No one knew whether the lode consisted of one vein, or two, or ten, since only actual excavation could determine the extent and value of each claim.

As miners battled, sometimes physically, in their underground crosscuts, lawyers filed suit on the surface, and mine stockholders such as Hearst watched their fortunes swoop and slide. Litigation, a series of bad mining investments, and the exhaustion of the Ophir Mine by 1864 drained Hearst's fortune. Not for the last time his new wife, Phoebe, and young son, William Randolph, traded lavish surroundings for more modest accommodations. Each time George Hearst bounced back stronger than before.

Hearst spent some time in the California State Assembly and continued to invest in mining claims. He earned enough income as a mining consultant to purchase a large ranch on San Simeon Bay, the future location of his son's opulent mansion. In 1872 Hearst located the Ontario Mine, opening an entirely new district around Park City, Utah. The costs of developing the Ontario forced the Hearsts to temporarily economize once again; Phoebe and William Randolph moved into a boardinghouse, and William dropped his private tutors in favor of a less costly public education. Given time, the mine paid out $12,425,00 ($314,230,000 in 2014) in dividends as George Hearst's fortunes once again rebounded.

In 1876 Hearst convinced his doubting partners to invest in the remote and untamed Black Hills of South Dakota. He had learned about a promising prospect in a gulch boomtown called Lead (pronounced "Leed") and on his wife's suggestion gave it a sentimental name—the Homestake. Unable this time to attract investors, Hearst and Haggin staked $80,000 of their own money to consolidate 250 rival claims. As with the Ontario, the Homestake required heavy investments in crushers, stamps, and smelters, water rights, and water delivery systems. Hearst built a railroad, lumber mills, stores, and houses for workers, and squeezed the mountain to give up its ore on an industrial scale. The Homestake more than repaid the company's investments, becoming the world's largest, richest, and deepest mine.

Hearst's amazing streak made him one of the most respected judges of mining properties in the nation. He ploughed his fortune into profitable Mexican silver mines, plantations, and cattle companies, becoming a major Mexican landowner and a friend to Mexico's president, Porfirio Díaz. Even poor mining decisions seemed to pay off. In 1881 he broke his own rule about personally inspecting new claims and bought a quarter interest in Montana's Anaconda Mine, sight unseen. Hearst hoped the Anaconda would supply silver. For two hundred feet, it gave up nothing of value. Then, miners hit thick deposits of silver and copper, then a thirty-foot wall of solid copper. The Anaconda was a bonanza of industrial metal, easily becoming the most prolific copper mine of its time. Hearst and his partners, James Haggin and Marcus Daly, gradually acquired a controlling interest, taking personal charge of the mine by 1883. In that year, his Anaconda Company built one of the world's largest copper smelters. By 1898, the Anaconda produced one fifth of the world's copper supply.

Public acclaim for his achievements inflamed Hearst's long-cherished desire to seek public office. Political friends convinced the mining tycoon to purchase the Democratic *San Francisco Examiner* to bolster the Democrats' editorial voice during the 1880 presidential election. George Hearst was more interested in politics than newspaper publishing, and he became discouraged by the newspaper's tendency to hemorrhage money. But he also found an enthusiastic steward in his son, William Randolph, in 1887. Recently expelled from Harvard for rowdiness, the younger Hearst overcame George's reservations and took over the flagging newspaper. He quickly turned the paper around, hiring ace writers such as Jack London, Mark Twain, and Ambrose Bierce, and generating popular support as a crusading advocate for the public. With the *Examiner,* W. R. Hearst forged the first link of a large and influential media chain.

For his part, George Hearst parlayed his wealth and reputation into a seat in the U.S. Senate in 1886. He entered the Senate as one of the wealthiest of a prosperous and influential elite. He became friends with Democratic President Grover Cleveland and helped smooth over tensions between Cleveland's administration and the Mexican government. Hearst's personal vigor faded as he entered his seventies. A doctor diagnosed him with a fatal illness in December 1890. He died soon after, surrounded by loved ones, in February 1891.

Any one of his legendary discoveries might have earned George Hearst a place in a miners' hall of fame, as indeed they did when the National Mining Hall of Fame inducted George in 1988 and his wife, Phoebe Appleton Hearst, in 1989. Taken together, Hearst's California, Nevada, Utah, South Dakota, and Montana strikes transformed the American West. Prior to the California gold rush, the American West was politically unformed and economically underdeveloped. The California and Nevada strikes led to those territories' rapid settlement and immediate admission to the Union. Subsequent discoveries populated other mining regions with new businesses, capitalists, wage earners, small businessmen and businesswomen, and railroads. George Hearst was also greatly responsible for the industrialization of mining. The unprecedented scale of his operations in Virginia City and Lead pointed the way for America's mining triumvirate of capital, labor, and technology. Into Hearst's monumental mining landscape came a flood of emigrants, bringing with them new struggles over the relative value of capital and labor. Out of it poured the mineral wealth that stabilized and supercharged the post-Civil War American economy, and helped to make the United States into a global industrial power.

Bjorge, Guy N. *The Homestake Enterprise in the Black Hills of South Dakota*. New York: Newcomen Society of England, American Branch, 1947.

Fielder, Mildred. *The Treasure of Homestake Gold*. Aberdeen: North Plains Press, 1970.

Homestake: A South Dakota Enterprise. Lead: Homestake Mining Company, 1948.

Older, Cora M. and Fremont Older. *George Hearst: California Pioneer*. Los Angeles: Westernlore, 1966.

Paul, Rodman W. *Mining Frontiers of the Far West*. Albuquerque: University of New Mexico Press, 2001. C978.02 P281mi 2001. CHS 622 P282m 1963

Robinson, Judith. *The Hearsts: An American Dynasty*. San Francisco: Telegraph Hill Press, 1996.

Smith, Grant H. and Joseph V. Tingley. *The History of the Comstock Lode, 1850–1997*. Reno: Nevada Bureau of Mines and Geology, 1998.

SPENCER PENROSE

CREATING A HIGH COUNTRY PLAYGROUND

{ 1 8 6 5 – 1 9 3 9 }

On a sunny December day in 1892, a tall Philadelphian stood out in the crowd at the Colorado Springs railway station. Spencer Penrose sported a well waxed moustache, brown curly hair, a square ruddy face, and big piercing brown eyes. This fashionably dressed young adventurer admired for the first time Pikes Peak, commanding the western horizon and shimmering in all its soaring, snowy splendor. By that mountain he would spend the rest of his life, transforming the Pikes Peak Region into a high country playground.

Spencer Penrose, Colorado Springs's second great promoter and benefactor, picked up where town founder William J. Palmer left off. Palmer gave his town broad, tree-lined streets, sites for Colorado College, the Colorado School for the Deaf and Dumb, and other generous civic and public spaces as well as the splendid Antlers Hotel. Palmer brought the Denver & Rio Grande Railroad to town and first envisioned Colorado Springs as a genteel resort and tourist haven. That vision of a cleaner, greener, better place remained only partially fulfilled upon Palmer's death in 1909. The dream would be revitalized and furthered by Penrose. Like Palmer, he was a well-heeled Pennsylvanian. Born in 1865 to an aristocratic Philadelphia family, schooled by private tutors, Penrose went on to Harvard where his elder brothers had all excelled.

Boise Penrose shone in school and became a powerful U.S. senator from Pennsylvania. Charles Bingham Penrose earned a Ph.D. from Harvard and an M.D. from the University of Pennsylvania and became a prominent surgeon, then a renowned director of the Philadelphia Zoo. Richard Penrose received a Ph.D. from Harvard and became a noted geologist. One of his publications from the U.S. Geological Survey, *Geology and Mining Industries of the Cripple Creek District, Colorado* (with Whitman Cross), helped guide his brother Spencer to mineral riches.

Unlike his brothers, Penrose stumbled through college, barely squeaking through with an engineering degree. Spencer's distinction at Harvard consisted of consuming a gallon of beer in thirty-seven seconds, supposedly a new school record. The pressure of academic endeavors, Philadelphia formalities, and the high standards raised by his brothers inspired Spencer to flee the East Coast. Tired of the black sheep role, he headed west to New Mexico Territory. By 1892 Penrose had squandered his savings and what he could get from his family in a struggling fruit, produce, hay, and mercantile business in Las Cruces. After failing in New Mexico, Penrose headed for one of the brightest spots in America—the glittering gold camp of Cripple Creek and its supply center, Colorado Springs. His brother Richard, a prominent geologist and mining man, assured Spencer that Cripple Creek was no flash in the pan. A Philadelphia friend of Penrose, Charles Tutt, owned a successful real estate business in Cripple Creek and offered Penrose a partnership. The new partners headed up to Cripple Creek, where Tutt had staked out the C.O.D. Mine in 1891. It became the first major Cripple Creek gold mine to pay off after they incorporated in

1892 and capitalized it at $1 million. After getting more than their investment out of the C.O.D., Penrose and Tutt unloaded the spent mine on a French syndicate for $250,000.

Spencer quickly learned that the surest way to make money lay not in mining but in buying and selling mines and, even more so, in ore processing. The real payoff came with the final extraction of gold, silver, lead, zinc, copper, and anything else of value. Penrose knew well the tale of how the Guggenheims had built their fortune. They started out in Leadville not by mining, but by smelting the silver city's ores in what became the giant, worldwide American Smelting and Refining Company.

Penrose and partners built the huge Colorado-Philadelphia Reduction Company on a mesa overlooking Colorado City, on the west side of Colorado Springs. He persuaded Penrose family members to invest heavily in what was then one of the largest chlorination plants in the United States. Penrose opened this state-of-the-art plant in 1896 to process Cripple Creek's gold ores. Millions of dollars in gold refined there left behind a huge dump that still looms in the Colorado City landscape. Soon Penrose and his partners dominated smelting operations in the Cripple Creek-Victor-Colorado Springs area. They also built the Cripple Creek Short Line Railroad from Colorado Springs to the gold camp, hauling both ore and tourists along what is today a popular, scenic automobile road.

Penrose and his partners next formed the Utah Copper Company in 1903 and began excavating an open pit mine near Bingham, Utah. Dick Penrose convinced his brother that copper was the metal of the future for use in automobiles, telephones, heating, and appliances. Dick joined in this bold, inventive operation using new technology and massive equipment to mine low-grade copper on a gigantic scale. To help with the smelting, Penrose enlisted the Guggenheims, preferring to collaborate rather than to compete. In a short while Penrose found that his copper venture made his gold earnings look like spare change. He pocketed some $200,000 a month from his share of the Utah Copper Company, later reorganized as Kennecott Copper. While gold and silver mining fluctuated, copper production rose steadily. There seemed no end to that mineral in the immense open pit mine in Utah, which is still producing to this day. Penrose and the copper crowd expanded with mines in Ray, Arizona, the Chino Mine near Santa Rita, New Mexico, and elsewhere.

With copper capital, Penrose dreamed of building Colorado's greatest resort hotel. He shared that dream with Julie Villiers Lewis McMillan, a bright, altruistic, and wealthy woman whom he married in 1906. They had traveled the globe together, staying in the world's finest accommodations and making note of their amenities and design. As a connoisseur of the world's best hotels, Penrose wanted one of his own. Early in 1916, Penrose offered $87,500 for the Antlers, the grand old Colorado Springs hotel built by William J. Palmer. The Palmer estate wanted $200,000. Penrose declined, writing later, "I beg to say my associates and myself did everything possible to acquire the Antlers Hotel, in order that Colorado Springs might have a first-class, up-to-date hotel in the future, but, as little attention was paid to our endeavors, we have given up that entirely, and have now plans for building the best hotel in Colorado at Broadmoor."

A great building starts with great architects, and Penrose chose one of America's most respected firms. Whitney Warren and Charles Wetmore had designed New York City's Grand Central Station and designed such deluxe New York City hotels as the Ambassador, Belmont, Biltmore, Commodore, and Ritz-Carlton, as well as the Royal Hawaiian in Honolulu. Warren and Wetmore's design took advantage of the spacious site far roomier than New York City's cramped avenues. The nine-story central section was crowned by an open cupola and flanked by lower wings. The hotel's stepped mass resembled the clustered red-tile roofs of an Italian village and blended with the foothills setting, echoing layered mountains rising to the west. The lakeside site also enhanced the Mediterranean-style golden stucco walls and red tile roof, reflecting southwestern and Spanish Colonial Revival influences.

Penrose broke ground in April 1917, promising to pay the builders each $1,000 if the Broadmoor could open its doors by May 15, 1918. Otherwise they paid him. Story by story, the grand building rose, consuming concrete, steel and stone in gargantuan quantities. Much of the stone came from a quarry on Spencer's Turkey Creek Ranch. Construction costs exceeded $2 million, and furniture and interior decorating cost another $1 million. The project ran over schedule. May 15, 1918 passed, and Penrose collected from the contractors.

At the June 29, 1918 gala grand opening, the paint had barely dried when guests, neighbors, and curious local residents crowded into the hotel. Its 350 guest rooms far outnumbered those at the Antlers. Opening day gawkers found the lobby, halls, restaurants, and guest rooms exquisitely decorated and furnished, reflecting Julie's passion for Mediterranean decor and art. Penrose had hired an army of Italian artisans to paint frescoes and ceilings reminiscent of the craftsmanship of Italy. Julie's interest in performing arts inspired the small theater on the first floor. The swan, Julie's personal emblem, was painted near the elevator and above the fireplace in the center terrace. Several of the graceful white birds also reigned on Broadmoor Lake. The extensive grounds, including the lake, gardens, a golf course, and, ultimately, a ski area, polo grounds, rodeo stadium, and ice arena, were originally designed by the world's best known landscape architects, the Olmsteds out of Brookline, Massachusetts.

The Broadmoor gained widespread acclaim thanks to Penrose's marketing genius. He targeted affluent easterners with advertisements in *Vogue, Vanity Fair, Spur, Golf Illustrated, Western Architect,* and

Town & Country that compared the Broadmoor with a graceful Italian villa. A glossy *Life* magazine ad lauded the hotel as "Recreation's Shrine Amid the Rockies." Penrose left Broadmoor booklets and photographs in ocean liner salons and grand hotel lobbies as he traveled around the world.

From the start, Penrose coaxed the rich and famous to the Broadmoor. Among the first to arrive was the celebrated artist Maxfield Parrish. To paint a bewitching Broadmoor portrait, Penrose paid Parrish $2,100, but complained that he put the lake on the wrong side of the hotel. Julie reassured him that Parrish had become one of America's favorite painters by being "fanciful."

The Penroses funded an art school in their old downtown mansion provided it be renamed the Broadmoor Art Academy. Incorporated in 1919, it became Colorado's most famous art center, with teachers such as Randall Davey, a prominent Santa Fe artist. Spencer agreed to hire Davey for $800 a month at the art academy only after learning that he was also an excellent polo player who could beef up the Broadmoor team. The Broadmoor Academy attracted such nationally celebrated artists as Thomas Hart Benton, photographer Laura Gilpin, and sculptors Jo Davidson and Edgar Britton. That academy has evolved into today's Colorado Springs Fine Arts Center.

Adding to the Broadmoor's celebrity-studded register, Penrose entertained New York millionaire John D. Rockefeller, Jr., and persuaded him to pose on horseback for a Broadmoor booklet. Mrs. Rockefeller and daughter Abbey were photographed in a Broadmoor touring car. Edna Ferber, author of the best-selling novels *Showboat* (1926) and *Giant* (1952), posed in the Italian fountain. As perhaps his greatest publicity coup, Penrose enticed world heavyweight boxing champion Jack Dempsey to train at the Broadmoor for his 1926 title defense match against Gene Tunney.

Carmen Miranda, Bing Crosby, Victor Borge, Liberace, Jack Benny,

Bob Hope, Burl Ives, and Mickey Rooney all entertained at the hotel. Jimmy Stewart and Gloria Hatrick honeymooned there in 1949. Edgar Bergen and his daughter Candice visited the Broadmoor, as did Carol Channing and Marlene Dietrich. Penrose fancied greeting guests in the tavern, where his bottle collection still adorns the walls. In or out of his cups, he recited from memory Arthur Chapman's poem "Out Where the West Begins."

Penrose made many friends indeed, but labor leaders were not among them. He strove mightily to crush unions, and he succeeded. In conjunction with other mine and smelter owners, he defeated the Western Federation of Miners statewide 1903–1904 strike for union recognition, a $3-dollar-a-day minimum wage, and a maximum work day of eight hours. While fighting a 1939 effort to unionize Broadmoor employees, Penrose wrote to a close friend and fellow hotelkeeper in New York, Thomas Green: "As soon as you give in to a union you are gone. I have been fighting the unions since 1891 and at Cripple Creek we had a strike that lasted ten years simply because the mine owners kept compromising with the unions. Finally the mine owners took a stand and beat them."

Many Broadmoor guests asked what there was to do in Colorado Springs. Penrose answered that question by constructing an array of attractions, transforming the Pikes Peak region into a tourist desti-nation. He built an automobile road to the top of 14,110-foot-high Pikes Peak and, in 1915, started an annual road race to the summit. This allowed him to try out the new luxury car he bought each year. To give nonmotorists a quick and easy way to the top of Pikes Peak, Penrose bought the rundown Manitou and Pikes Peak Cog Railway for $50,000 in 1925. He invested in upgrading it, bringing in state-of-the art Swiss-made equipment and operating the train like clockwork, and so it continues to this day.

Friends and associates sent Penrose, an animal lover and collector, exotic pets from around the world. He housed all sorts of creatures at the Broadmoor until a monkey bit a hotel guest. Next, the elephant he used as a caddy trampled golf course greens. After paying off the complaining mother of the bit boy, Penrose established the Cheyenne Mountain Zoo to house his growing menagerie. He located it a mile from the hotel on the new Cheyenne Mountain Highway, yet another of his enterprises. Penrose promoted his Cheyenne Mountain animal haven as "The Highest Zoo in the World" featuring "The largest Elephant in the World," the "Empress of India, Gift of the Rajah of Nagpur to Spencer Penrose." In fact, Penrose bought the four-ton pachyderm named Tessie from a bankrupt traveling circus in Indiana.

After the humorist Will Rogers, Penrose's friend, died in a 1935 airplane crash, Penrose built a towering monument in his honor, the Will Rogers Shrine of the Sun, on a spur of Cheyenne Mountain overlooking the Broadmoor complex. Inside the tower, the history of the Pikes Peak region and the Penrose story is told in Randall Davey's life-sized murals. The tower also turned out to be Spencer's tombstone: his remains were laid into the chapel floor after his death from throat cancer in 1939.

His life had been enriched by his devoted wife Julie. She transformed a hard-drinking playboy into a faithful husband, responsible city builder, and philanthropist. She encouraged Spencer to establish the El Pomar Foundation, the richest foundation in Colorado, and its good work began in 1937. The foundation had deep pockets because Penrose, who came from a wealthy family, multiplied his wealth by investments in Cripple Creek gold, Colorado City smelting, and Utah Copper.

Penrose's contributions to Colorado continue long after his death thanks to the El Pomar Foundation's mission "to assist, encourage, and promote the general wellbeing of the inhabitants of the state of Colorado." El Pomar has given much to the Colorado Springs World

Arena, Cheyenne Mountain Zoo, the Central City Opera House Association, Fountain Valley School, Colorado College, the Colorado Springs Fine Arts Museum, Pro Rodeo Hall of Fame, the University of Colorado at Colorado Springs, the University of Denver, local hospitals, U.S. Olympic Complex, and the Historic Arkansas River Project that is rejuvenating downtown Pueblo.

Spencer Penrose, once a family black sheep, went west to start anew. He evolved into the biggest builder and promoter that the Pikes Peak Region has ever seen. Using copper mines as a steady source of capital, he made Colorado Springs and his beloved Broadmoor Hotel one of America's five-star, world-class destination resorts. He is probably most important for his fostering of tourism, now the second most important industry in Colorado and many other western states.

Unlike many builders, Penrose also had a genius for promotion. He transformed the sleepy hamlet of Colorado Springs into a major tourist center and El Paso county into what has emerged as the most populous in Colorado: its population for the first time surpassed Denver in the 2010 census. Building on the mystique of America's most famous mountain, he transformed Pikes Peak with a second, more sustained gold rush—tourism. The eastern dude who stepped off the train in 1892 and marveled at Pikes Peak made that majestic mountain the centerpiece of a western playground.

Bertozzi-Villa, Elena. *Broadmoor Memories: The History of the Broadmoor.* Colorado Springs: The Broadmoor, 1993.

Broadmoor Hotel Archives.

Colorado College. Tutt Library. Spencer Penrose and Julie Penroset clipping files.

Colorado Springs Pioneer Museum. James W. Starsmore Research Center. Spencer Penrose, Julie Penrose and Broadmoor Hotel materials.

Cuba, Stanley L. with Elizabeth Cunningham. *The Pikes Peak Vision: The Broadmoor Art Academy, 1919–1945.* Colorado Springs: Colorado Springs Fine Art Center, 1989.

Noel, Thomas J. and Cathleen M. Norman. *A Pikes Peak Partnership: The Penroses and the Tutts.* Boulder: University Press of Colorado, 2000, 2002 paperback reprint.

Penrose House Archives, Colorado Springs. Spencer and Julie Penrose materials.

Penrose Public Library, Colorado Springs. Spencer and Julie Penrose materials.

Sprague, Marshall. *Newport in the Rockies: The Life and Good Times of Colorado Springs.* Chicago: Sage/Swallow Press Books. 1961, 1980.

MANUFACTURING

SAMUEL COLT

INVENTIVE FIREARM DESIGNER {1814–1862}

God made all men, but Colonel Colt made them equal.

Colt's marketing slogan

Samuel Colt's life was the American story written in capital letters. A tinker and practical scientist, a promoter and flashy showman with a knack for salesmanship, Samuel Colt crafted both his guns and his legendary persona until the two were inseparable in the minds of the American public. The Connecticut Yankee thrived as a prolific firearms manufacturer and seller during a period of American history punctuated by often-violent western expansion and the Civil War. By adopting interchangeable parts, he was able to mass-produce his wares on some of the nation's earliest assembly lines. His repeating pistols and rifles revolutionized conflict in the West, speeding up the conquest of territory claimed by Mexico and dozens of American Indian tribes, and providing an indispensible tool for lawmen (and outlaws), cattlemen, hunters, gold seekers, and soldiers. Colt's marketers popularized the slogan: "God made all men, but Colonel Colt made them equal." His company sold his popular Army and Navy revolvers to both sides during the Civil War, and the single-action 1873 Colt "Peacemaker," manufactured after his death, became celebrated in popular culture as "the Gun that Won the West."

Samuel Colt was born the fifth of six children on July 19, 1814, in Hartford, Connecticut. His father was an ambitious but marginally successful farmer and manufacturer. His mother, the daughter of a prominent Hartford family, died when Samuel was six. Colt spent much of his childhood in foster care, working for his keep on various farms. Perhaps his rootlessness contributed to his early vagabond life. He learned something about practical chemistry and obsessed over fireworks and underwater explosives. He reportedly took early inspiration from the *Compendium of Knowledge,* a scientific encyclopedia containing biographies of famous inventors. Expelled after one of his fireworks experiments set his school ablaze, he went to sea, where legend has it the sixteen-year-old prodigy carved his first wooden revolver prototype in 1831.

Returning home to hawk his invention, the young entrepreneur developed a hustler's streak. He earned venture capital by performing theater routines that mixed chemistry and drug use. Clad in a fashionable coat and top hat and surrounded by smoking beakers, wax demons, mummies, and exploding fireworks, "the Celebrated Dr. Coult of New-York, London, and Calcutta" (as his playbills read) persuaded spectators to sniff a bag coated with nitrous oxide. Sam guaranteed his audience a good "half hour's laugh" at the resulting spectacle. Between shows, Colt refined his weapons designs. In 1836 he acquired his first patents and opened the Patent Arms Manufacturing Company in a rented Paterson, New Jersey, armory. The start of Florida's Second Seminole War in 1835 provided an early break. Seminole warriors learned to draw the fire of U.S. soldiers armed with standard single-shot weapons, then timed their counterattacks to occur before the troopers reloaded. Colt's repeating long rifles nullified the Seminoles' tactical advantage. The army ordered fifty.

Unfortunately, the inexperienced entrepreneur also demonstrated a habit for overpromising and underdelivering. Lacking mechanical and engineering experience, he drove his managers crazy by stopping production to fiddle with his designs. His first employees had no practical training as gunsmiths, and Colt struggled to design his own precision machinery. His early firearms consequently suffered from inferior designs and substandard manufacturing processes. Military inspectors rejected his samples for their severe flaws. They had too many moving parts; they were difficult to aim; and they jammed too easily. Users had to take his early pistols completely apart to reload them, hardly ideal in the heat of battle. The guns accidentally discharged if someone dropped or even bumped them. Lateral ignition sometimes set off all the loads at once. Colt's initial metal prototype exploded the first time someone fired it. Blowbacks and explosions plagued soldiers in the field as well.

Given these flaws, the entrepreneur understandably struggled to raise investment capital. He relied on heavy underwriting from family members, but even friends and family considered him abrasive, a big talker who managed to rub key investors the wrong way. He made airy promises to customers that he couldn't fulfill. His New Jersey factory never had enough employees, never enough capital. When Colt's first gunmaking venture failed in 1842, friends marveled that he had been able to keep it going as long as he had.

Colt spent the next six years in New York City studying mechanics and rehabilitating his reputation. He opened a workshop and attended scientific salons. He also hit the books, cramming on applied chemistry and mechanical engineering. Other projects competed for his attention; Samuel tinkered endlessly, developing electrical underwater mines and waterproof bullet cartridges. In 1842 he supplied Samuel F. B. Morse with a waterproof electrical wire that significantly advanced undersea telegraphy. His inventions won awards at scientific exhibitions, earning the entrepreneur more than a little side money. His public demonstrations of submarine mines, climaxing in the spectacular destruction of a derelict schooner in the Potomac River, mixed salesmanship with showmanship worthy of P. T. Barnum.

War put the gunmaker back in business. The Mexican American War of 1846–1848 brought a lucrative new government contract. European unrest, including tension between Turkey and Russia and political upheaval in British India, ensured profitable overseas sales for years to come. Colt now benefited from his past experiences by subcontracting the technical work instead of trying to finish it on his own. At about this time, the reputation of Colt firearms received a boost from an unexpected quarter. Way out west on the Pecos River, the Texas Rangers had acquired a supply of Colt's five-shooters. The repeating pistols caused a sensation when fifteen Rangers defeated a band of eighty Comanche warriors. Never in history had European Americans enjoyed tactical or technological advantages over the Comanches. Wielded by magnificent light cavalry, the Comanches' fast-firing bows and arrows more than outmatched the Americans' single-shot rifles and pistols. In 1847 legendary Texas Ranger Samuel H. Walker traveled to Colt's factory in New Haven to discuss improvements. He returned to Texas with a shipment of six-shooters.

By 1849 Colt's fortunes soared. He turned out the bestselling product of his lifetime, a .31 caliber pocket handgun, just in time for the California gold rush. Sales of his reliable military surplus .44 Dragoon pistols also spiked as gold seekers geared up for the western trek. The R. G. Dun credit rating company took notice, estimating his annual firearms output at 20,000 units in 1851.

Also in 1849, Colt hired Elisha Root to manage production. A superlative mechanic, Root rose from a blacksmith's anvil to become superintendent and president of Colt's armory. He perfected Colt's manufacturing system, introducing automation, precision milling, process integration, and mass production. Talented machinists gravitated toward the master mechanic, giving the company a competitive edge over rivals at Remington and Smith & Wesson. Root organized Colt's enthusiastic, but rather vague, production ideas into a workable system, and he improved virtually every piece of the company's machinery. Liberated from the technical details of gunmaking, Colt focused on opening new markets. So essential was Root to Colt's business that the gunmaker allowed the engineer to name his own salary. Colt paid Root the highest wages in the industry and even granted him exclusive intellectual rights to his own inventions. Root thrived, so did Colt. Whatever Colt promised, Root delivered.

In the 1850s Colt opened a factory in Great Britain, hiring men and children to turn out 18,000 British firearms for the Crimean War (and more than a few for England's Russian enemies). To facilitate foreign sales, he hired overseas agents to handle the assembly of his firearms in local factories. Closer to home, Colt built a gigantic factory complex and company town, known as Coltsville, outside the American manufacturing center of Hartford, Connecticut.

Colt's mounting success owed as much to his genius for public relations as his technological innovations. Sensitive to the American fascination with self-made men, he recast himself as a paragon of populism, as an "inventor," but never a "capitalist."

Although he never fired a weapon at another person, he padded his military credentials, soliciting a colonel's commission in the Connecticut militia. Colt and Root both embraced the efficacy of design, constantly striving for lighter, sleeker, more elegant products. Colt hired engravers to beautify his weapons. Curators and collectors still hail his 1860 army revolver, carefully "blued" by a chemical cooling process, as a deadly work of art, the "most perfect design of [Colt's] lifetime," according to Wadsworth Atheneum firearms curator William Hosley.

Colt solicited celebrity testimonials and paid the celebrated western painter George Catlin, among others, to feature Colt repeaters in his artworks. Perhaps most significantly, he tapped into America's early romance with western expansion and Manifest Destiny. His early business relationship with Samuel Walker and the Texas Rangers paid dividends when westbound pioneers demanded similar firearms. In time, the Colt revolver attained a mythic significance as the tool that tamed the American West.

Ever the pragmatic businessman, Colt sold firearms to belligerents on both sides of any conflict, even shipping guns from his New England factory to the South during the Civil War. When northern critics accused him of treason, he wrapped himself in the Union flag, offering to organize a regiment, "Colt's Revolving Rifles," and serve as its commander. He countered early criticism of America's emerging gun culture by promoting his products' peacekeeping capacities, writing with unorthodox spelling to a British associate, "The good people of this wirld are very far from being satisfide with each other & my arms are the best peesmakers."

Samuel Colt died of advanced gout in 1862, just as the American Civil War created a booming new market for his products. Yet the remarkable entrepreneur sold almost a million firearms during his lifetime. It's hard to say if his weapons sped up Western expansion—American Indians also acquired Colt firearms, and his rifles never matched the breech-loading Sharps and Winchesters that frontiersmen preferred. Yet Colt himself transcended mere success through a rare mix of inventive genius and entrepreneurial marketing skills. The inventor transformed his products into icons, and fixed Colt revolvers in the American imagination as the very symbol of western independence.

Edwards, William B. *The Story of Colt's Revolver: The Biography of Samuel Colt.* Mechanicsburg: The Stackpole Company, 1953.

Hosley, William. *Colt: The Making of an American Legend.* Amherst: The University of Massachusetts Press, 1996.

Houze, Herbert G. *Samuel Colt: Arms, Art, and Invention.* New Haven: Yale University Press, 2006.

Rywell, Martin. *Samuel Colt: A Man and an Epoch.* Harriman: Pioneer Press, 1952.

LEVI STRAUSS

CLOTHING A NATION {1829–1902}

Levi's blue jeans are an American icon born of need and ingenuity. Levi Strauss's story is also classic, an American narrative of initiative and savvy. Strauss was an immigrant who struck out for the West to find opportunity and adventure. He founded Levi Strauss and Company in San Francisco, and it became one of the city's major dry goods wholesale firms. He became famous for his fortunate capital investment in a design for work pants with riveted pockets, and he created a world-famous brand by insisting on quality, promoting his integrity, and aggressively protecting his intellectual property. Strauss did more than sell and invest. He was a sterling member of San Francisco's business community, and he directed his great fortune toward charitable causes.

Loeb Strauss, known in America as "Levi," was born in Bavaria in 1829. He joined his half brothers in their New York dry goods business in 1848. He trained with them to gain skill at understanding sales, supply, and demand. As a peddler, Strauss hauled a heavy sack around the city, selling items like needles, thread, and cloth. His next assignment was to sell goods from a family store in Louisville, Kentucky. At the age of twenty-three, Strauss sailed for San Francisco to partner with his brother-in-law in the wild entrepreneurial world of the gold rush West. Legend has it that he sold out of almost everything he had brought with him before he made landfall. His rapid success made him a millionaire by 1870.

The gold fields in northern California were a powerful magnet that attracted tens of thousands of men and women with visions of instant wealth. Strauss was one of a smaller group who planned to get rich by exploiting market forces. During the gold rush era, there were more prospectors than there were tents, shovels, pickaxes, buckets, and pans. Levi Strauss opened for business in 1853 with a plan that drew on his previous experiences and his shrewd assessment of the frontier marketplace. As a wholesaler, Strauss sold common dry goods such as clothes, boots, and large bolts of cloth to smaller retailers. His brothers in New York could not send merchandise quickly enough. Rather than let business suffer while he awaited the next shipment, Strauss bought goods auctioned from recently arrived ships anchored in the harbor. Not content merely to wait for customers to come to him, he freighted goods to merchants in the field by way of side-paddle steamer and mule train. Bolstered by a reputation for quality and fair dealing, Strauss opened successively larger and more elaborate establishments. His emporium on San Francisco's Battery Street, opened in the mid-1860s, was a commercial palace of gaslight chandeliers, elevators, and the latest modern amenities.

Although the gold rush economy had started to peter out by the 1860s, demand for goods in northern California remained strong. Mining activity continued, but agriculture, milling, logging, and manufacturing propped up the need for Strauss's goods. Each of these industries clamored for cloth, especially a heavy durable cotton canvas called duck. The material could be used to make tents, wagon covers, and work clothes. Levi also offered denim, a pliable but sturdy canvas that becomes more comfortable to wear after washing. People purchased both types of material from Levi Strauss and Company.

Strauss's business leaped from regional success story to international brand when he went into business with a clever tailor. Jacob W. Davis, a fellow Jewish immigrant, was doing a booming business making and selling sturdy work pants in Nevada. He cut his cloth from fabric purchased from Levi Strauss and Company. Davis noticed that although the pants held up well against abuse from loggers and miners, the pockets and other points of stress tended to tear out along the seam. Davis fastened the pockets with copper rivets. His innovation was a great success. What he did not have was the $68 to patent his improvement. He wrote to Strauss in 1872 and proposed a partnership. Strauss thought it looked like a promising investment and agreed to file a patent for the "Improvement in Fastening Pocket-Openings." Levi's jeans were born in 1873. Jackets, vests, blouses, and other clothing items would soon join the famous pants on racks and shelves throughout the West.

Quality control was an important aspect of the company's success. Strauss built a manufacturing plant next to his wholesale emporium. He hired skilled seamstresses and brought Davis, the man who designed the in-demand product, to San Francisco to oversee early production of the "waist overalls." The first pairs were made of brown cotton duck or blue denim. To control the quality of raw material, Strauss purchased the Mission and Pacific Woolen mills and contracted with New Hampshire manufacturer Amoskeag to supply their XX denim for Levi's jeans. He aimed to create consistency across his product line. The brand bore his name; it needed to have a reputation for quality.

Appearance was also important to Levi's brand. The patent on the rivets expired in 1890, so Strauss used other distinctive elements to maintain the Levi's identity. Back pockets have a birdwing pattern of double-stitched arc sutures. That design was trademarked in 1943. Copper rivets have "LS&CO" embossed on them. Starting in 1886, the leather patch sewn to the waist began featuring a design of two horses pulling a pair of Levi's in opposite directions to communicate the clothing's durability. Consumers did not need to be literate to understand that Levi's were tough. The two-horse label design, standard orange linen thread, and branded rivets told the buyer that they were purchasing a quality Levi's product. The famous 501 style and many other numbered versions of the pants would have the same cut and fit every time.

Strauss vigorously protected his innovations through the patent and trademark process and wasted little time pursuing legal action against imitators. And he never lost sight of his original working-class customers. Even as the gold and silver mining eras faded, people still needed rugged clothes for farming, ranching, logging, working in factories, and the like. Levi, who insisted his employees and customers call him by his first name instead of "Mr. Strauss," was there to supply them.

Success granted Strauss more leisure time to devote to charity. He had always been a generous provider when he lived in San Francisco. He took special interest in orphans, helping to establish the Pacific Hebrew Orphan Asylum and Home. Although Strauss was Jewish, he contributed to causes across religious lines, supporting Catholic and Protestant orphanages as well. Education was also an important cause. He established scholarships at the University of California and gave money to the California School for the Deaf. His company continues to participate in philanthropic endeavors.

Levi Strauss died in 1902 at the age of seventy-three. The city of San Francisco declared a business holiday in his honor on the day of his funeral. Flags in the wholesale district were lowered to half mast. He had never married and had no direct descendants. The business was left to his four nephews, who had assisted him in running it since the 1890s. They succeeded in keeping the family business alive after the devastating 1906 San Francisco earthquake. Although product lines differed over the years, Levi's remains one of the most recognizable brands in the world. The identity that Strauss crafted for his company endures. Strauss possessed great business acumen. He seized opportunity, cared about quality, nurtured his brand identity, and successfully managed multiple enterprises. He responded to his customers' tastes and cultivated their brand perception. He actively protected his intellectual property using tools provided by the government. Family members were integral to his businesses throughout his career and carried on his legacy. Today, we have a nearly 150-year-old American brand that is uniquely Levi's.

Cray, Ed. *Levi's*. Boston: Houghton Mifflin, 1978.

Downey, Lynn. *This Is a Pair of Levi's Jeans: The Official History of the Levi's Brand*. San Francisco: Levi Strauss & Co. Publishing, 1995.

Rochlin, Harriet and Fred Rochlin. *Pioneer Jews: A New Life in the Far West*. Boston: Houghton Mifflin Harcourt, 2000.

GUSTAVUS FRANKLIN SWIFT

REVOLUTIONIZED THE AMERICAN DINNER PLATE

{ 1 8 3 9 - 1 9 0 3 }

Gustavus F. Swift revolutionized the way Americans consumed meat. His stockyards and meatpacking facilities turned one of the most distinctive products of the American West—range cattle—into beef destined for eastern kitchens. Swift and Company's refrigerated rail cars sped meat safely and reliably to distant markets, where Swift-owned storehouses distributed it to retailers. By controlling the entire meat-processing and distribution process, Swift offered consumers high-quality beef at low prices, forever changing how Americans thought about and purchased food. Swift brought corporate organization and management to the meat industry, reducing waste and inefficiency. He became famous for using "everything but the squeal," seeking new uses for the leftover parts of carcasses, and revamping an industry once known for its wastefulness.

Swift grew up in Cape Cod, Massachusetts, one of twelve children born to William and Sally Swift. The Swifts were farmers, and Gustavus grew up with livestock, developing an eye for quality animals from an early age. Uninterested in school, he went to work in his older brother's butcher shop as a teen. Two years later, he founded his own business dressing cattle, sheep, and pigs. Young Swift often butchered the animals himself, selling the finished meat to local stores, or sold his livestock to other butchers. After marrying Anna Maria Higgins, he opened a shop and slaughterhouse. But Cape Cod was too small for the ambitious Swift. Local farmers rarely offered more than one or two animals for sale a year, and the tourist trade in the area was not yet large enough to provide a growing market for Swift's meat. Seeking a larger market, Gustavus and Anna moved to the Boston area.

Boston had more hungry mouths to feed than Cape Cod, but the New England cattle industry as a whole was shrinking when Swift set up shop in 1869. As the region became more industrialized, north-eastern farmland no longer supported enough cows or other animals to sate local appetites. More and more of the cattle coming to Boston were shipped by rail from regions to the west. Swift formed a partnership with James Hathaway, an established local meat dealer, in 1872. Swift purchased cattle and oversaw their transport to Boston, while Hathaway took care of their company's slaughterhouse and retail operations. At first, the cattle Swift purchased came from New York and the far eastern edges of the Midwest. But, as railroad service between the Plains and the East improved, cattle from Texas, Colorado, and nearby states began crowding Hathaway and Swift's slaughterhouses.

Swift moved west as more cows traveled eastward. In order to hold live-animal shipping costs down, he first relocated to Albany, then Buffalo. Finally, in 1875, Hathaway and Swift made an even more dramatic move, to Chicago, then the nation's capital of livestock processing. Operating from Chicago meant Hathaway and Swift had access to the widest variety of livestock at the lowest prices. However, the two men's partnership did not survive. In 1878, Swift and his younger brother, Edwin, formed their own firm. In short order, Swift, who had never operated a packinghouse before, introduced innovations that revolutionized the American meat processing industry.

It was an industry badly in need of a better economic model. Shipping cattle from west to east was expensive, inefficient, and wasteful. Livestock growers usually shipped their herds from distant ranges to the slaughterhouse alive, or "on the hoof." The stress of transport cost most cattle up to half their body weight. Many others perished during the journey, and all of the emaciated animals generated high fees in feed and shipping. Previous attempts to send "dressed" meat across the United States or the Atlantic Ocean had failed. The science of refrigeration was still in its infancy and, just as importantly, consumers questioned the safety of meat that had been slaughtered up to a week earlier and shipped long distances. Even frozen meat caused waste. Butchers never used an entire cow or pig; even the most efficient meat processor left bones, hooves, and other inedible parts behind. Often, only 40 percent of a carcass made it to the plate or pot. Swift conquered both the Chicago stockyards and American dinner plate by consolidating the entire process of slaughtering, butchering, transporting, and selling meat, and carefully controlling the natural cycle of spoilage—especially important with beef, more perishable than pork. Exposed beef discolored quickly, yet was easily damaged by freezing.

At first, Swift shipped beef east during winter using open railcars, when icy winds prevented spoilage. This technique only worked part of the year. He next hired refrigeration engineer Andrew J. Chase to design a refrigerated car suitable for transporting meat. Chase and Swift were not the first to combine refrigeration and rail transport: fruit and vegetable growers began using ice-cooled cars to transport produce in the 1860s. That same decade, J. B. Sutherland and George Hammond began experimenting with refrigerated cars on with the Michigan Central Railroad, shipping dressed beef from Detroit to Boston in 1869. Chase improved on previous designs by continuously circulating ice-cooled air throughout the car, ensuring every hanging carcass was kept as cool as its neighbor. The new design took advantage of recent advances in ice-making technology to allow operators to replenish the cars' ice reserves en route. Swift eventually established a series of icing stations between Chicago and the East Coast that kept company cars cool and provided storage for finished meat. He also constructed packinghouses in key markets and made deals with local butchers—who might otherwise protest Swift's encroachment on their business—to sell his dressed meat in their shops. Thanks to refrigeration, a steer could go from slaughter to stewpot without ever leaving a Swift-owned facility.

An improved refrigerator car could go nowhere without a railroad, though. Swift's plans to ship beef east bumped up against entrenched railroad interests. Rail lines profited handsomely from shipping live cattle, and refrigerated cars would reduce their return on freightage. Many railroads were reluctant to adopt specialized technology that seemed to undermine their bottom line. Swift made a deal with the Grand Trunk Line, a railroad that traveled from Chicago to New York and Boston, to ship dressed beef east. Grand Trunk agreed to work with Swift if he supplied the refrigerated cars and constructed his own icing stations. Within a year, Swift was shipping over 3,000 carcasses a year to Boston, and the Chicago meat industry as a whole began to follow his model. For the first time, in 1883, more live cattle were slaughtered in Chicago than shipped eastward. Swift's main rivals—Hammond, Phillip Armour, and Nelson Morris—quickly made their own railroad deals to ship dressed beef. By 1890, the four Chicago firms packed and shipped nearly 90 percent of American beef. Meat processing was becoming a cutthroat business, in more ways than one.

To keep volume high, Swift ran his slaughterhouses with extraordinary efficiency. His managers pioneered the "rationalized organization of work," breaking each meat processing step down to its component elements. Swift introduced innovative new technology, including overhead trolleys to transport carcasses and automated conveyer belts to move beef swiftly through the plant. Each Swift employee specialized in a specific task, repeating the same motions over and over during the course of a workday. Supervisors carefully monitored the flow of beef moving along Swift and Company's conveyor belts, ensuring that each step in reducing the carcass resulted in peak productivity. In his autobiography, Henry Ford claimed inspiration from a visit to one of Swift's slaughterhouses. Ford's industrial assembly line was Swift's "disassembly line," only in reverse. Author Upton Sinclair, a well-known critic of the meakpacking industry, nevertheless marveled at the variety of products, including soap, oleomargarine, combs, buttons, toothbrush handles, hairpins, gelatin, phosphorus, shoe blacking, isinglass, pepsin, albumen, violin strings, tallow, grease, and fertilizer, that Swift developed out of the inedible parts of cattle and other animals. In addition, Swift and Company created and distributed new food products, turning lower-quality meat into canned goods, sausages, and other low-cost fare.

Swift's methods, while extremely cost-effective, were not without detractors. Government regulators found Swift and his competitors, including Philip Armour, Patrick Cudahy, and Nelson Morris, guilty of forming trusts to fix beef prices, contributing to the passage of the Sherman Anti-Trust Act in 1890. Subsequent federal suits filed by the administration of President Theodore Roosevelt further cited Swift's company for price collusion. While his plants were marvels of efficiency, they were often criticized as dirty, difficult, and sometimes dangerous places to work, and the chemicals and meat byproducts from Swift's slaughterhouses polluted nearby neighborhoods and watercourses. Swift prided himself in selling quality meat, but consumer concerns over the lack of third-party inspectors in meatprocessing plants industry-wide, combined with concerns about the ingredients added to the canned meats and sausages Swift and other companies sold, led to calls for greater government oversight. Congress enacted the Meat Inspection Act in 1906, the Pure Food and Drug Act in 1909, and the Packers and Stockyards Act in 1921, to help ensure a safer food supply for all Americans.

Whatever setbacks it encountered, Swift and Company shipped beef on every railroad in the United States and sold its products in nearly every major market in the country by the time of its founder's death in 1903. The company, valued at over $25 million (almost $650 million in 2014 dollars), supplied European and Asian markets through a robust trans-oceanic refrigerated beef trade as well. Swift operated slaughterhouses and stockyards in Kansas City, St. Louis, and other midwestern cities. In the last decade of his life, he channeled his energies and fortune into philanthropic causes, serving as a trustee and benefactor of the University of Chicago and providing generous gifts to Northwestern University and Chicago's St. James Methodist Episcopal Church.

For four decades, Gustavus Swift turned western cattle into meat for the masses, feeding a growing nation quickly, reliably, and inexpensively. Swift pioneered the large-scale processing of affordable, quality meat products. He introduced rationalized efficiencies of production that greatly lowered the cost and increased the productivity of the meatpacking industry and inspired industrial manufacturers into the twentieth century and beyond. Swift's company independently survived its founder for eighty years before succumbing to buyouts by Beatrice Foods and ConAgra. Today, his brand survives as Greeley, Colorado, based Swift and Company, a subsidiary of the world's largest fresh beef and pork processor, the Brazilian corporation JBS, S.A.

Chandler, Alfred D. *The Visible Hand: The Managerial Revolution in American Business.* Cambridge: Belknap Press of Harvard University Press, 1977.

Cronon, William. *Nature's Metropolis: Chicago and the Great West.* New York: W.W. Norton, 1991.

Freidberg, Susanne. *Fresh: A Perishable History.* Cambridge: Belknap Press of Harvard University Press, 2009.

Smith, Andrew F. *Eating History: 30 Turning Points in the Making of American Cuisine.* New York: Columbia University Press, 2009.

Swift, Louis F. *The Yankee of the Yards: The Biography of Gustavus Franklin Swift.* Chicago: A.W. Shaw, 1927.

ANDREW CARNEGIE

THE AMERICAN VULCAN {1835–1919}

"Put all your eggs in one basket, and then watch that basket." A. Carnegie

Andrew Carnegie's life was full of paradoxes. Born into grinding poverty, he died the richest man in America. Son of a Scottish weaver crushed by industrialization, he raised industrial production and corporate organization to unprecedented heights. He cultivated a reputation as a friend of unions, then watched the goodwill he built crumble in the ruins of the bitter 1892 Homestead Strike. He was an imaginative and pitiless competitor, forcing his rivals into bankruptcy and accumulating wealth by any means necessary. And yet he worked tirelessly to give his fortune away to benefit the less fortunate. Climbing to the top as a bobbin boy, then a telegraph operator, then a railroad manager, and finally as the organizer of the colossal American steel industry, Carnegie became the American Vulcan. In the process he helped invent the structure of big business in America—and the pattern of corporate philanthropy as we know it.

Andrew Carnegie was born in 1835 in the medieval weaving center of Dumfermline, Scotland. His father, Will, was a master weaver who operated four looms and supervised several apprentices of his own. Andrew doted on his mother, Margaret, a strong-willed woman who held the family together. And he absorbed the politics of his craftsmen father and uncles, who mobilized, in vain, to oppose inequality and the changes wrought on their profession by industrialization. The opening of a steam-powered weaving mill in 1847 shattered the Carnegie family's stability. Unable to compete with the factory looms, Will never found regular employment again. Margaret opened a shop and took in mending, becoming increasingly embittered over her family's poverty. In 1848, at her insistence, the Carnegies left for America with thirteen-year-old Andrew and his brother, Tom, in tow.

Industrialization began in Great Britain in the 1780s, but it quickly took root in the United States. Squeezed by diminishing opportunities in Europe, more than 2.5 million emigrants flocked to American cities and factory jobs between 1840 and 1850. Will Carnegie never adapted to the changing economic order in the United States, but his son Andrew caught on quickly. He took work as a mechanic, tending to the power looms in a Pittsburgh textile mill. In the evenings, the teenaged factory worker took business courses, learning accounting and managerial skills. When the opportunity arose, he switched jobs to become a messenger for a telegraph company, initiating a pattern of embracing the next important technological innovation—from textiles to telegraphs, to railroads, to iron, to steel.

As a courier, then as a telegraph operator, Carnegie began to realize the value of information. He became a familiar face to Pittsburgh's business leaders and learned the ins and outs of the city's commercial alliances and rivalries. His job made him privy to negotiations, credit troubles, market conditions, and commodity prices. He learned to "read" telegraph signals by ear, and he enlisted his own cadre of apprentices to do odd jobs and gather information.

Carnegie's organizational and telegraphic talents attracted the attention of Thomas Scott, the general superintendent of the Pennsylvania Railroad, in 1852. Scott hired the charismatic, hard-working Carnegie as his personal assistant. The seventeen-year-old prodigy eagerly attended when Scott revealed to him the hidden world of investment. Investment was a revelation to Carnegie. Given the correct choices, an investor never risked a dime of his own capital. Acting on a tip from Scott, Carnegie borrowed $500 to invest in an express company. The first dividend check changed his life. "It gave me the first penny of revenue from capital—something I had not worked for with the sweat of my brow," he wrote in his autobiography. " 'Eureka!' I cried, 'Here's the goose that lays the golden eggs.' " He paid the debt back from dividends, and never looked back. By the 1860s Carnegie earned $49,300 in annual income on a salary of $2,400.

As Scott's assistant, Carnegie revealed a bold streak. One time when his boss was absent, the young clerk acted in Scott's name to instruct subordinates how to handle a railway accident. Another time, he ordered workers to burn wrecked cars to clear them quickly from the right-of-way. Such initiative earned Scott's praise, and his unorthodox solution to clearing the railway line became standard practice following accidents. Despite, or perhaps because of, his immigrant background, his short stature (he stood just five feet and three inches tall), and his father's failures, Andrew Carnegie's ambition knew no bounds. Above all, he embraced economic and managerial systems that allowed a man to go as far as his skills and drive allowed.

Carnegie's time with the Pennsylvania Railroad sharpened his managerial skills and deepened his understanding of economic theory. The railroad served as an effective graduate school, providing answers to many of the challenges of complexity, bureaucracy, logistics, and finance that Carnegie later faced when harnessing the steel industry. Under Scott's tutelage, Carnegie learned to lower unit costs while maximizing opportunities for revenue. Carnegie acquired larger cars and larger locomotives to carry more traffic at a lower price than his competition. He cut railway employees' wages and raised their hours, instituting round-the-clock service to maximize billable carrying time. When some workers threatened to strike, he learned the names of their ringleaders and arranged for their dismissal. Rising to the position of superintendent of the Pennsylvania Railroad Western Division, he used inside knowledge to make lucrative investments in rail and sleeping car factories. He formed a company to make iron railroad bridges, invested in an iron foundry, and expanded into telegraphy. And he continued climbing.

At the age of thirty-three, Carnegie took stock of his life thus far. He gloried in his ability to generate wealth, but also worried that moneymaking "must degrade me beyond hope of recovery." The son of an altruistic father, Carnegie was uncomfortable with the increasing economic gap between industrial captains and their workers. He found justification for his life's work in the writings of English philosopher Herbert Spencer, who articulated the concept of "social Darwinism." The economic sphere, Spencer argued, was a competitive modern jungle, where only the most talented survived. A prolific writer, Spencer condemned humanitarianism, but he also promoted a social trajectory to perfectionism through competition. Carnegie synthesized Spencer's somewhat contradictory philosophies with the motto: "All is well since all grows better," or more succinctly "Upward and Onward." Carnegie resolved to retire at the age of thirty-five in order to spend his life and wealth helping the less fortunate.

That was before Carnegie learned about steelmaking. Instead of retiring young, he spent the next thirty years transforming the American industrial economy into a global powerhouse. On a trip to Great Britain in the 1860s, Carnegie inspected that country's new Bessemer steel plants. Before Henry Bessemer patented his process in 1851, ironmakers were only able to transform iron into steel in small batches. The Bessemer process inexpensively converted large amounts of pig iron into steel. Carnegie immediately realized that the English roller mills offered a solution to a perennial American headache. American railroad operators cursed the brittle iron rails that supported their lines, but were unable to procure durable steel rails in sufficient quantities.

Carnegie returned home to convert his iron foundry to the Bessemer process. After proceeding in fits and starts, he opened a mammoth new steel plant in Braddock, Pennsylvania, in 1873, to produce rails for the Pennsylvania Railroad.

Carnegie's innovative steel production facility outshone all of its competitors in efficiency. He developed revolutionary cost-tracking systems to document every expense to the penny and used the data to beat down costs. His steel, consequently, was usually the best made and the least expensive on the market. Just to be safe, he bought stock in his competitors' firms, learning their business secrets through their annual reports, and he constructed or acquired larger mills to expand his capacity. He ran his foundries day and night to maximize an economy of scale. He invested heavily in new technological developments that would reduce costs. He developed new performance metrics to define, review, and promote the most effective executives. And he vertically integrated the steelmaking industry, bringing all of the components—mining and smelting ore, converting iron to steel, producing steel bars, sheets, plate, nails, and finished goods—into one company.

A transformed steel industry transformed American labor. Carnegie's steel mills were praised as the pinnacle of modern technology. Yet for many workers, the industrialist's furnaces and living quarters offered a glimpse of hell. Novelist Hamlin Garland compared the noise of Carnegie's Homestead works to "the roar as of a hundred lions" and the "thunder of cannons." Workers stirred deep pits of glowing metal while rains of sparks showered overhead. To keep the blast furnaces producing around the clock, steelmakers worked twelve-hour shifts, seven days a week. Some of Carnegie's factories mandated a twenty-four-hour shift on Sundays. Working-class neighborhoods surrounding the plants were pestilent and foul, poorly drained and unventilated. Garland observed that it took a special kind of laborer to endure these conditions for the sake of his wife and children. "A man works in peril for his life for 14 cents an hour," he wrote. "Upon such toil rests the splendor of American civilization."

A former immigrant laborer himself, Carnegie initially sympathized when workers gravitated toward the labor unions that led the movement for reform. He initially stood out among captains of industry for supporting labor's right to organize and collectively bargain, penning a widely-read essay opposing the importation of strikebreakers during labor unrest. In general, he kept his mills running steadily enough to provide his workers with stable employment. When labor troubles broke out at a coking facility that served Carnegie's plants, he pressured the firm's managers to accept the union's demands. He built libraries and community centers in his company towns, along with music venues and sporting facilities. He possessed a disarming common touch, inviting union leaders to his home, meeting with them personally, attending their mass meetings to address their concerns, and generally charming his workers into accepting his terms.

And yet, no amount of charisma or benevolence could fully disarm the tension that arose between workers and their employers in the new industrial order that Carnegie embraced. As industry grew, laborers saw their jobs deskilled, their control over workplace conditions eliminated, and their opportunities for advancement curtailed. They felt that their labor gave them equity in Carnegie's steelworks. As sympathetic as he was, Carnegie's drive to dominate the steel industry necessitated a different view. Ever vigilant about costs, Carnegie urged managers to cut wages. He also brought in a new chairman for Carnegie Steel, Henry Clay Frick, who was committed to breaking the workers' craft union at the flagship plant in Homestead, Pennsylvania.

The showdown came after a breakdown in contract negotiations in July 1892. Frick shut down the mill, locking out 1,100 union members. Soon another 2,400 workers joined them on strike. Frick fortified the Homestead mill and brought in replacement workers, guarded by 300 armed Pinkerton detectives. Battle ensued between strikers and detectives along the Monongahela River. The strikers won and occupied the foundry. An assassin tried to murder Frick, stabbing him three times and shooting him twice. Carnegie vanished into a remote corner of the Scottish Highlands, emerging from time to time to send Frick encouraging telegrams. He won the highly publicized strike, but his reputation as a friend of labor reform never fully recovered.

It has often been said that Carnegie became a philanthropist to still an inner torment about the predatory tactics he sometimes used to acquire his fortune. Encouraging other millionaires to give, Carnegie once wrote that benevolence "provides a refuge from self-questioning." Other equally valid reasons apply: the radical politics of his father and uncles, his own hardscrabble roots, and his innate humanitarianism among them. Regardless of his motivations, the capitalist dedicated much of his restless energy to good works. His 1889 essay "The Gospel of Wealth" charged industrial capitalists with a social responsibility to redistribute their fortunes in order to create opportunities for the worthy poor. Carnegie lived up to his own standards by building more than 2,000 public libraries. He also endowed universities, scholarships, teachers' pensions, and institutions to promote arts, literature, music, science, ethics, international studies, and world peace. He funded the lavish Peace Palace in The Hague, Netherlands, that is today home of the International Court of Justice. Realizing that he would never be able to give money away faster than he made it, he founded the Carnegie Corporation to continue his benevolence after his death. By 1911, it was estimated that Carnegie had distributed 90 percent of his fortune to worthy causes.

Carnegie Steel had become the largest steelmaking firm in the world by 1901. It also faced a serious challenge from financier J. P. Morgan. Morgan had acquired two rival firms and announced his intention to run Carnegie Steel into the ground. Carnegie was more than game for a fight—his plants were the most efficient and best managed in the nation. But he was also sixty-five years old and ready to devote his remaining years to philanthropy. When Morgan expressed an interest in buying Carnegie out, the capitalist accepted. Morgan acquired Carnegie Steel for $480 million (about $13 billion in 2014 dollars), the largest financial transaction in the nation up to that time. Morgan merged Carnegie's firm with the others to create United States Steel.

Andrew Carnegie passed away in 1919, disillusioned somewhat by the ways in which the industrial systems he had devised were used to sustain the First World War. His name had nevertheless become synonymous with the birth of large American industry. He refined it, reorganized it, consolidated it, and defined it. Carnegie steel built America up and out. Americans traveled west on his steel rails and lived and worked in skyscrapers supported by his steel beams. He pioneered new managerial systems and business practices that made efficient, large-scale production possible. If his aggregation of money and power made some Americans uncomfortable, Carnegie addressed their concerns by giving back as much as he could to improve the chances of others, and he encouraged his fellow businessmen to do the same. The son of a down-at-the-heels immigrant craftsman had lived the Horatio Alger story word for word, becoming the face of modern America and impacting both the momentum and the products to sustain the growth of American industry.

"American Experience: Andrew Carnegie." Transcript. WGBH Educational Foundation, 1997.

Carnegie, Andrew. *The Autobiography of Andrew Carnegie*. Boston: Northeastern University Press, 1986; 1948; 1920.

Hacker, Louis M. *The World of Andrew Carnegie, 1865–1901*. Philadelphia: J.B. Lippincott Company, 1968.

Krass, Peter. *Carnegie*. Hoboken: John Wiley & Sons, 2002.

Nasaw, David. *Andrew Carnegie*. New York: The Penguin Press, 2006.

Livesay, Harold C. *Andrew Carnegie and the Rise of Big Business*. Boston: Little, Brown & Co., 1975.

CHARLES A. PILLSBURY

AN ENDURING BRAND {1842–1899}

After the Civil War, Americans experienced a period of rapid technological transition unlike any that had come before. They released their pent-up energies in rapidly settling the West and developing new industrial innovations to catapult the nation economically ahead of Europe. As historian Sean Dennis Cashman has pointed out, the United States lagged behind Europe in industrial production in 1860. Just three decades later, it led the world; the value of its manufactured products equaled the combined effort of the three leading European nations, England, France, and Germany. During that period, the United States became a net exporter of wheat and flour—the breadbasket of the Northern Hemisphere. Innovations such as Cyrus McCormick's mechanical reaper helped increase agricultural production, as did the development of urban grain exchanges, while improvements in transportation and communication made it easier to plan and distribute America's bumper crops.

In Minneapolis, Charles Alfred Pillsbury and others concentrated on converting hard western grain into soft white flour, adopting new techniques to achieve a scale of production undreamed of during the Civil War. Pillsbury helped turn Minneapolis into a global milling powerhouse.

Born in New Hampshire in 1842, Charles A. Pillsbury graduated from Dartmouth College with training in languages, engineering, physics, and chemistry. His classmates considered him an unremarkable scholar, but he was an admirable conversationalist, equipped with a broad-ranging curiosity. He told anyone who would listen about his determination to succeed in business. Upon graduation, he found work in a Canadian produce commission company, avoiding the Civil War draft by hiring a substitute. Pillsbury moved to Minneapolis in 1869, joining his uncle John Pillsbury, a successful hardware merchant and future Minnesota governor. Charles and his father, George, bought a one-third interest in Minneapolis Flour Mills, on the west bank of the Mississippi River near the falls of St. Anthony.

According to company lore, Minnesota businessmen scoffed that the Pillsburys' flour milling investment was a sucker bet. Like the rest of his family, Charles Pillsbury was a flour-milling novice. But, then, so was everyone else in Minneapolis. Although the city had all the ingredients for successful milling, including substantial wheat farming, railroads, and an abundant power supply in the Falls of St. Anthony, the city's handful of flour mills were poorly regarded and barely profitable. In large part, this was because of the quality of available grain. Unlike southern granaries, which produced soft winter wheat, Minnesota and Dakota farmers grew hardier spring wheat that resisted time-honored milling techniques. The traditional way to turn wheat into flour was to remove the chaff, then grind the wheat kernels between two large rutted millstones. After grinding, millers sifted the pulverized wheat through a fine cloth to separate it from the bran. Milling historian William J. Powell described the dilemma that western millers faced in his corporate history of the Pillsbury Company:

> Because of its much harder coating, millers of spring wheat placed their stones close together and turned them at a high speed. This method of "low grinding" scorched the flour and pulverized

portions of the hard, brittle bran coat so much that they could not be separated from the flour in the sifting step. If the miller set his stones father apart to avoid scorching and pulverizing of the outer coat, incomplete separation of the glutenous mass of cells just below the bran caused much of the gluten to remain with the bran and be lost to the flour (Powell, *Pillsbury's Best,* p. 21).

Offered the choice of discolored, less nutritious, and unpalatable northern flour and the pure white winter wheat varieties available from flour mills in St. Louis and elsewhere, consumers invariably selected the latter. Fortunately for Charles and his family, millers in southern Minnesota had begun experimenting with an additional step to recover some of the lost gluten, or "middlings," that escaped the first grinding. Engineers developed a middlings purifier that ran the unground gluten and bran through a vibrating sifter that separated the bran from the remaining wheat. Millers reground the separated gluten, producing a whiter, tastier, and more nutritious flour. Charles paid careful attention to the new developments and watched closely as his primary rivals at Minneapolis's Washburn Mills installed new purifiers in 1871. The results were successful enough for Pillsbury to hire away a Washburn expert, George T. Smith, to supervise the installation of a "new process" middlings purifier at his own mill.

Equipped with middlings purifiers, Pillsbury's mills reorganized under the banner of C. A. Pillsbury & Company and expanded through the 1870s. The firm increased its capacity from a couple of hundred of barrels per day to over 3,000 by purchasing two additional mills, the Empire and the Anchor, and building a new flagship facility, the Pillsbury A Mill. Charles ensured that his new mill was state-of-the-art. It was the first to boast electric lighting and the first designed by an architect. More importantly, it embraced a revolutionary new milling process. Traveling to Europe in 1873, Pillsbury learned that Hungarian and French millers had replaced their millstones with chilled rollers made of porcelain or iron. By running wheat through an incremental series of rollers, they were able to break down kernels more efficiently and with greater grade variation than was possible with traditional grinders. The roller mills took up less space, consumed less power, and eliminated maintenance costs, while producing more flour. After a period of scrutiny—after all, retooling his mills to accommodate the new process represented a major capital investment—Pillsbury became an early adopter.

These gradual reduction mills catapulted Pillsbury, and Minneapolis, to the top spot in American flour milling. By 1877, Minnesota was a net exporter of flour, shipping the white powder to the rest of the nation and to Europe. Pillsbury continued to improve his millworks, adding steam power by 1884 and continually rebuilding burnt mills— fire was a common hazard in the flour milling industry—with greater capacity. To keep up with farmers' output, he built storage facilities and grain elevators throughout the upper Midwest and West. By 1884, the Pillsbury A was the world's largest flour mill, capable of producing more than 6,000 barrels of flour each day.

Charles Pillsbury hustled to find new markets for his record-breaking flour production. He advertised heavily, and "Pillsbury's Best XXXX" developed into a powerful brand. He pioneered new lines of bran, mixed-grain flours, pancake mixes, and cereals for the retail market, and placed the first regular advertisements in the industry's trade journal, *The Northwestern Miller,* to attract wholesalers and exporters. In 1874 he opened a baking laboratory to test the quality of the products made with his flour. He cultivated strong loyalty among his workers, paying high wages—$3.25 for skilled millers, $1.90 for unskilled workers—and compensating employees for holidays and unanticipated work stoppages. In 1883 C. A. Pillsbury & Company instituted one of the nation's first profit-sharing plans.

C. A. Pillsbury & Company weathered the economically turbulent 1870s and flourished in the 1880s. In a twenty-year span between

1869 and 1889, Minneapolis mushroomed from a backwater flour production center with a few low-capacity mills to America's flour-milling capital. Grain poured into the Mississippi River city from all over the Midwest and West and departed as flour to destinations around the world. Charles Pillsbury diversified his portfolio, investing in timber, railroads, banking, urban railway and electrical systems, and the woolen-underwear manufacturer Munsingwear. He won a seat in the Minnesota state senate. He also invested his good fortune back into his community. Charles and his wife, Mary Ann, underwrote the Plymouth Congregational Church in Minneapolis, and donated $150,000 to build the Pillsbury Science Hall at the University of Minnesota. He shipped tens of thousands of barrels of flour to Russia during an 1891–1892 famine. His family endowed the Pillsbury Settlement House and the Pillsbury United Communities organization to provide a safety net for Minnesota's down-and-out population.

Meanwhile, flour milling was undergoing another seismic change. The increased complexity of milling technology, combined with Minnesota's immense capacity, began to shake out smaller concerns, while the larger operations consolidated. An English syndicate bought out the Pillsbury family, along with their Washburn Mills rivals, in 1889. The combined Pillsbury-Washburn Flour Mills Company retained Charles Pillsbury as managing director. Pillsbury spent his final years shepherding the concern through the 1890s, a decade marked by depression, drought, charges of price fixing, and overproduction. Exhausted by thirty years of effort, he died of heart failure in 1899. Charles Pillsbury is remembered as one of the nation's most gifted milling entrepreneurs. He succeeded through an insistence on quality and adaptability to technological change. He was a first-class marketer who developed an enduring brand, and he created a market for wheat that sustained farmers throughout the American West—sending their produce in finished form to consumers around the world.

Cashman, Sean D. *America in the Gilded Age: From the Death of Lincoln to the Rise of Theodore Roosevelt.* New York: New York University Press, 1993.

Convery, William J. *Pride of the Rockies: The Life of Colorado's Premiere Irish Philanthropist John Kernan Mullen.* Boulder: University Press of Colorado, 2000.

Kuhlmann, Charles B. *The Development of the Flour-Milling Industry in the United States.* Boston: Houghton Mifflin Co., 1929.

Pillsbury, Philip J. *The Pioneering Pillsburys.* New York: The Newcomen Society in North America, 1950.

Powell, William J. *Pillsbury's Best: A Company History from 1869.* Minneapolis: The Pillsbury Company, 1985.

Sturdevant, Lori, with George S. Pillsbury. *The Pillsburys of Minnesota.* Minneapolis: Nodin Press, LLC, 2011

ADOLPH COORS

MASTER BREWER {1847–1929}

"My grandfather, Adolph Coors, never thought backward, only forward," said William Kistler Coors. "He didn't talk about the past, which had its tragedies. He focused on making the best beer in America." In his book *Citizen Coors: An American Dynasty,* Dan Blum added that Adolph Coors, Sr. was a "mule headed ass-kicker with a genius for mechanical invention and vertical integration" but "an aversion to advertising and publicity."

The best known of all western brewers frustrated contemporary biographers and did not care to reflect on his life, which began and ended with tragedy. He started out as an orphan and ended leaping from a hotel window.

His father, Johann Joseph Kohrs, was a miller like his father before him, and perhaps his grandfather and great-grandfather. Joseph became a master miller in the small town of Barmen in the west-central German province of North Rhine Westphalia There he married Helene Hein. The couple's first child, Adolph Hermann Joseph, appeared the following year.

Shortly afterwards the family moved to nearby Dortmund, where Adolph grew up across the street from the Wenkler Brewery. There the youngster went to work at age fourteen. The brewery fascinated him. He watched with particular interest as the brewers bolted down their first steam engine.

A year later Adolph's world turned upside down. Tuberculosis killed both his parents and authorities installed him and his younger brother and sister in a Catholic orphanage. At least the nuns there respected his pleas to continue working at the brewery.

At age twenty-one, Adolph faced being drafted into the Prussian Army and its endless wars. Like hundreds of thousands of other Germans, instead he fled to America. He stowed away on a ship headed for Baltimore. There he either changed Kohrs to Coors or immigration officials did it for him. Either way, Adolph gladly left his old name and old country behind to begin life anew.

The pale blue eyes of the young immigrant focused on a future away from orphanages and a lifetime at war. In the new country, he headed west. He did not stop until he reached Naperville, Illinois, twenty-five miles west of Chicago. There Coors found work in John Stegner's brewery. In Naperville, Coors heard talk of a booming new western city where Germans were the single largest foreign-born group, and he knew that where there were Germans, there would be brewing opportunities. Following his dream of running his own beer works, in 1872 Coors climbed aboard the three-year-old transcontinental railroad headed for Denver.

Coors took a shine to Colorado after stepping off the train that April. At first, he blinked in Denver's bright sunshine. He felt the dry climate and wondered at the lack of vegetation. In the brown and tree-less town, Coors, an avid horticulturalist all his life, found work as a gardener. The intense western sunshine may have left him thirsty for his old brewery job. Most Colorado breweries were small operations that relied on separate firms for bottling. On May 1, 1872 Adolph Coors and a partner, John Staderman, opened a bottling works. Their company bottled ale, porter, cider, and seltzer water. Coors bought out Staderman in November 1872, then sold the business in October

1873. He had learned and earned enough to get back to brewing. Bottles did not interest him as much as what was in them.

The Coors Brewing Company originated with Adolph's Sunday ramble up Clear Creek in 1873. He lingered beside that jubilant mountain stream, studying and then tasting its clear, cool water. Poking around the cottonwood-lined banks, he found springs. He learned that Clear Creek had been the mother lode of the Colorado gold rush, attracting some 100,000 fortune seekers in one of the greatest mass migrations in U.S. history. Coors did not seek the heavy, yellow metal in Clear Creek. He figured its water could be transformed into liquid gold.

And, indeed, the brash, booming, young Mile High City would prove a thirsty market. Beer also sold well in the mountain towns where miners poured out of hot, dusty holes in the ground and headed for the nearest saloon. Coors began looking for a partner with capital. Jacob Schueler was impressed with Coors. Presumably over a beer or two, the pair dreamed of the possibilities.

Schueler had retail experience with his Larimer Street shop where he sold candy, baked goods, ice creams, beer, wines, and soda water. He put up $18,000 and Coors $2,000 to buy a vacant tannery in Golden. Whereas Denver had seven breweries by 1873, Golden had none. Golden welcomed the new business. George West, a founder of Golden and editor of the *Colorado Transcript,* reported on November 12, 1873, that "Messrs. J[acob] Schueler and Adolph Coors of Denver have purchased the old tannery property of C. C. Welch and John Pipe and will convert it into a brewery. They propose large additions to the building, making it one of the most extensive works of its kind in the territory . . . . We welcome these energetic gentlemen among us."

"A brick brewery of the most modern plan," noted an agent of the R. G. Dun credit firm in his May 2, 1874 report. Coors, he added, "is a young man of good character & habits . . . a practical brewer [with] but little means and gets an interest in the business for his services."

While Schueler remained in Denver, Coors moved to Golden in October 1873 to oversee operations. He installed a steam engine that could pump sixty barrels an hour to the mash tub and aging vats. The July 22, 1874 *Golden Transcript* noted that "Schueler & Coors have leaped to the front rank of brewers in a remarkable short time, and their beer is now regularly sold in Denver and the mountain and valley towns."

To supply customers, Schueler and Coors expanded the boiler room, added a new steam engine, and opened a beer garden, Golden Grove, where visitors might sample their lager. Customers arrived on the Colorado Central Railroad, which built a spur line across Clear Creek to the brewery. Today the Burlington Northern Santa Fe still operates that "beer line."

In 1879 Coors produced 4,000 barrels of beer, half of which were sold in bottles. Breweries opened—and closed—every year in the Denver area. Many failed because they did not capitalize on inventions that revolutionized the beer business. Anybody could make beer. Making it well and getting it to market in fresh, tasty condition was trickier. Coors used the crown cap, which replaced corks and ceramic seals with gas-tight, cork-lined metal caps that made possible long-range shipment in bottles with minimum spoilage. The advent of the refrigerated railroad car enabled Coors to ship beyond local markets. He grew tired of haggling with various Golden, Denver, and eastern bottlers, who could not give him the quantity, quality, or price he wanted, and opened his own bottling works. In 1878 Coors also built a large, three-story malt house to manufacture his own malt from barley. And he became a major ice producer, harvesting ice from the brewery ponds in winter and storing it in large wooden icehouses for year-round use. Besides providing the brewery with ice for cooling beer, the ponds enabled Coors to sell ice to the public. Coors ice wagons delivered five pounds every morning for $2 a month, or ten pounds for $3.

Flush with success, Adolph Coors borrowed $90,000 and bought out his partner Jacob Schueler in 1878. At last, Coors owned a brewery all by himself. He renamed the Golden Brewery the Adolph Coors Golden Brewery and replaced the original "Golden Lager Beer" in 1880 with two new brands: "Coors Golden Beer" and "Coors Golden Bock."

In 1879 thirty-two-year-old Adolph Coors married sixteen-year-old Louisa Magdelena Weber, the German-born daughter of the superintendent of the Denver & Rio Grande maintenance shops. With his beery bachelor days behind him, Coors converted his beer garden's old dance pavilion into a family home. Initially, Coors kept half the house filled with his precious barley—until the wall broke one night and it flooded the house. Louisa must have been relieved to have the barley out, as eight children rapidly began appearing; six lived past infancy.

The key to his success, according to Adolph Coors' grandson, Bill Coors, was reinvesting in the family business and handling all steps in making, distributing, and selling beer. After Denver's Union Station opened in 1880, Coors built a large Coors depot next door to expedite shipping by rail. He set up other depots at Aspen, Black Hawk, Buena Vista, Como, Creede, Del Norte, Durango, Fort Collins, Gunnison, Leadville, Meeker, Pueblo, Salida, and elsewhere. To this day brewery buildings survive in many Colorado towns with large brown porcelain plaques over their entries stamped COORS. Porcelain became another Coors product when he discovered good clay for making it in the Golden area.

Adolph Coors had few close friends or hobbies. He was devoted to his work and his family. He supervised both closely, insisting that they run efficiently and on time. In his surviving ledgers, he carefully noted household expenses along with business expenditures. He paid Adolph, Jr., a $15-a-month allowance and made frequent payments to his wife Louisa for household expenses, including donations to the

Ladies Relief Society, the Artists League, and the Colorado School of Mines. Coors ran his family as well as his brewery with Teutonic firmness. Promptly at 6:25 every evening Adolph and Louisa arrived in the living room. Hands washed and hair combed, the six children marched in for inspection. "They always had to be on time," recalled longtime housekeeper Alma Brushwiller. "Mr. Coors senior was always looking at his pocket watch."

At 6:30 he took Louisa's arm and led the way to the dinner table. The six children followed in a straight line, Alma Brushwiller recalls, "just like ducklings."

After dinner the old man would go out on the porch and exercise with his pair of dumbbells. Alma Brushwiller remembers Adolph Coors, Sr., as "very German, very precise about everything. He spoke with a German accent. He was very prim, neat. Every hair in place. Even for his breakfast in the dining room nook, he would be all dressed up in coat and tie. You could set your watch by that man. His life was the brewery. Even on Sundays he would go walk through the plant, just checking on things."

Adolph became a U.S. citizen in 1889 and, a year later, a millionaire. He was the only brewer west of the Mississippi to win a medal at the Chicago's 1893 World's Fair. In an era of bitter labor wars, Coors avoided strikes by treating his workers well. He gave them frequent breaks and had "beer boys," including his own sons, serve workers buckets of beer. Coors even allowed his workers to join the United Brewery Workers and honored union requests to reduce the work day from ten to nine hours.

Coors's growing empire faced a major threat during the 1890s. Brewing, like every other industry, encountered the growing trend towards consolidation and monopolization. The first big challenge came from faraway London, where a British syndicate organized Denver United Breweries, Ltd. The syndicate bought Colorado's largest and oldest brewery, the Zang Brewing Company, in 1889 for $3.5

million. The British capitalists also acquired the Denver Brewing Company, which had been founded and built into a major beermaker by one-time Denver mayor Joseph E. Bates.

In 1890, the British approached Adolph Coors with an offer. He declined it. Denver United Breweries, Ltd. put pressure on Coors— and on saloonkeepers who sold Coors. The Golden brewer responded by opening up his own saloons around the state. He also hired agents such as former Denver mayor Wolfe Londoner to represent Coors in the escalating beer wars. Coors clashed early on with Anheuser-Busch, the St. Louis brewery that would eventually reign in the beer business. The *Golden Globe* newspaper on June 21, 1890 reported a beer battle in Wichita, Kansas, where "The saloon men kicked vigorously at the prices the Anheuser-Busch charged." To the rescue came "C. M. Webb, representing Coors Beer Co., of Golden, Colorado. The Golden beer, which is said to be superior to the Anheuser-Busch, is now being sold at 25 cents less on the keg and the saloon men have pledged them- selves to buy the Golden no matter how cheaply the other may be sold, and the war is on. The Golden men are 'hustlers' and seem determined to carry on the war."

The mule-headed Coors not only fought off hostile takeovers and competition but saw to it that his sons and grandsons would also resist being swallowed by any rival, no matter how lucrative that might be for the Coors family. Rather than pile up a fortune, Coors reinvested nearly everything he had in expanding the brewery. He did not stop until the Golden plant became the world's largest brewery under one roof.

Coors also believed in horizontal integration, in making every- thing needed, including the bottles, cans, barrels, boxes, glasses, ash- trays, placemats, and napkins needed to get his beer to a customer's lips. His favorite slogan did not exactly sing but it did ring true: "The more we do ourselves, the higher quality we have."

To scientifically safeguard the quality of his product, Coors sent his sons and grandsons to Cornell University to study chemical engineering. Their knowledge came in handy after Coloradans voted for Prohibition three years ahead of national Prohibition. As of January 1, 1916, it became illegal to sell alcohol in Colorado. Bitterly but obediently, Coors dumped the final barrels of his beer into Clear Creek—and began making near beer, malted milk, and porcelain. Those three products enabled the Coors Brewing Company to survive Prohibition, which dried up nearly every other Colorado brewery. Prohibition embittered Adolph Coors, who feared it would never end. In 1923, he turned the brewery over to his son Adolph, Jr.

In 1929, ailing with the flu, the eighty-three-year-old beer king went for a rest at the Cavalier Hotel in Virginia Beach. On June 5, looking into a future without beer and no longer needed at his brewery, Coors climbed out an open window and jumped. Prohibition was repealed in 1933.

Coors's leap concluded the tale of a poor orphan whose determination and commitment to his chosen craft made him one of a handful of brewers whose companies survive to this day. His descendants continued his work and slowly outgrew the old man's belief that a superior product and word of mouth made advertising an unnecessary frill. The third-generation Coorses came around to advertising and transformed what had been a regional beer into a national bestseller, third only to Anheuser-Busch and Miller.

Few other Americans have created a nationally known and loved brand that is still showcased in nearly every liquor store, grocery, restaurant, and tavern in America. With his dedication to quality and insistence on keeping the business in the family, Adolph Coors built a brand that has long outlived him and become uniquely identified with the Rocky Mountain West.

Adolph Coors Brewing Company Archives.

Banham, Russ. *Coors: A Rocky Mountain Legend*. Lymne, CN: Greenwich Publishing Group, Inc., 1998.

Baum, Dan. *Citizen Coors: An American Dynasty*. New York: William Morrow, 2000.

Bellant, Russ. *The Coors Connection: How Coors Family Philanthropy Undermines Democratic Pluralism*. Boston: South End Press, 1988.

Brushwiller, Alma, longtime Coors family housekeeper, interview with Tom Noel

Burgess, Robert J. *Silver Bullets: A Soldier's Story of How Coors Bombed in the Beer Wars*. New York: St. Martin's Press, 1993.

Conny, Beth Mende. *A Catalyst for Change: The Pioneering of the Aluminum Can*. Golden, CO: Adolph Coors Company, 1990.

Coors, Adolph. *Introduction to the Brewing Process: A Training Manual*. Golden, Co.: Adolph Coors Company, 1978.

Coors, Peter Hansen interviews by Tom Noel.

Coors, William Hansen interviews by Tom Noel.

Holden, Fred. *Adolph Coors Company: A Marketing Analysis: Literature Supplement*. Golden, CO: Coors Container Company, 1977.

Kostka, William. T*he Pre-Prohibition History of Adolph Coors Company, 1873–1933*. Golden, CO: Adolph Coors Company, 1973.

Krajeski, Anita, E. *A Taste of the West from Coors*. Des Moines, IA: Meredith Publishing Services, 1981, second revised edition, 1985.

Yetzbacher, Bill, ed. *Caps & Taps: Adolph Coors Company, 1873–1973*. Golden, CO: Adolph Coors Company, 1973.

HENRY FORD

PUTTING AMERICA BEHIND THE WHEEL

{1863–1947}

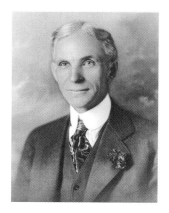

"M y ambition is to employ still more men; to spread the benefits of this industrial system to the greatest possible number, to help them build up their lives and their homes." So said Henry Ford, who did more than anyone to move the majority of Americans into the automobile-owning middle class.

Henry Ford revolutionized industry in the United States and the world by introducing techniques of mass production, standardization, and streamlined labor and management that shaped the twentieth century. Ford believed that enlightened management methods could ensure harmonious relations between workers and capitalists. He reinvested profits to expand production, raise wages, and reduce prices to the consumer. Though his opinions and business practices in the world arena proved controversial, Ford always maintained that international trade was the key to world peace. His stunning success made him a global icon of the American way of life.

Henry Ford was born July 30, 1863, on a farm in Greenfield Township, Michigan. His father, William Ford, emigrated to America from Ireland to escape the Irish Potato Famine. Henry's mother, Mary, was the youngest child of Belgian immigrants. Henry, the Fords' eldest child, had two brothers and two sisters. As a young man growing up on his father's farm in Greenfield, Ford early demonstrated his mechanical aptitude by dismantling and reassembling the timepieces of friends and neighbors. When his siblings received windup toys for Christmas, they had to hide them from Henry or he would take them apart to see their inner workings. Driving the family's horse-drawn wagon to Detroit one day, Henry saw for the first time a self-propelled machine, a portable engine and boiler mounted on wheels, operated by a single man standing on a platform behind the boiler shoveling coal, steering, and operating the throttle. The huge iron monster gave Henry the idea of a vehicle that moved under its own power. His father wanted him to take over the family farm, but Henry disliked farmwork. He left home in 1879, at sixteen, walking to Detroit. There he found work as an apprentice machinist and began studying bookkeeping.

In 1888 Ford married Clara Ala Bryant. The couple had one child, a son they named Edsel. Henry joined Thomas Edison's Edison Illuminating Company as an engineer in 1891. His promotion to chief engineer in 1893 gave him enough time and money to pursue personal experiments with gasoline engines. With encouragement from Edison, Ford designed and built a motorized vehicle in 1898. Financial backing from Detroit lumber baron William H. Murphy and others allowed Ford to leave the Edison Company and found the Detroit Automobile Company in 1899. The perfectionist Ford used the infusion of capital to further his experiments, but refused to rush a vehicle into production despite the fact that nascent competitors such as Oldsmobile were already selling hundreds of cars. Frustrated shareholders dissolved the Detroit Automobile Company in January 1901.

Ford put all his energy into building a twenty-six-horsepower race car, which won a prestigious race at Grosse Pointe, Michigan in 1901. The victory gained Ford a new group of backers. An improved version of the racer, with the engine moved from the back to the front, won again at Grosse Pointe in 1902 and broke all speed records. Ford refocused on building an affordable passenger car for sale to consumers.

Henry and his business partners incorporated as Ford Motor Company in 1903, and Ford's Model T automobile reached the market in 1908. This relatively light, sturdy, and inexpensive car emphasized simplicity and standardization over style. It was easy to drive and cheap to repair. Ford created a huge publicity machine to promote the Model T, along with a national network of independent dealers across the country to distribute it to consumers. The company put out a hundred cars a day, but Ford aspired to produce a thousand. Seeking greater efficiency and lower costs, in 1913 Ford introduced the moving assembly line to his plants, enabling an enormous increase in production.

Sales of the Model T initially doubled almost every year, passing 250,000 in 1914 and reaching 472,000 in 1916. By 1918, half of all cars on the road in the United States were Model Ts. As production increased, the price of Ford's cars shrank, from $900 in 1909 to $440 in 1914—almost $500 less than its nearest competitor.

Ford shocked the world in 1914 by offering his workers a wage of $5 per day, more than double the rate he had been paying previously. Furthermore, rather than pocket profits, he plowed them back into expanding his business operations, much to the chagrin of his early investors. Although they had enjoyed spectacular gains, investors resented that Ford did not distribute the bulk of his profits to them but instead reinvested them, both in high wages and new factories. When in 1916 shareholders sued to compel Ford to distribute three fourths of Ford Motor Company's cash surplus as dividends, Ford explained his philosophy of high wages and reinvestment in court: "My ambition is to employ still more men; to spread the benefits of this industrial system to the greatest possible number, to help them build up their lives and their homes. To do this, we are putting the greatest share of our profits back into the business."

Ford championed higher wages to improve the lives of his workers, to reduce the turnover of employees, which hindered efficiency, and to produce a class of workers who could afford to contribute to the economy by buying Fords. The $5-a-day wage attracted the best mechanics in Detroit and from around the country—and the ire of other industrialists. But Ford's high wages came with strings. His employees were subject to intrusive supervision from his "Sociological Department," made up of more than fifty agents who visited employee homes to make sure they kept up a code of conduct that frowned upon drinking, gambling, and child neglect.

Henry Ford quickly spread his distinctly American vision of industrial production across the world. Ford Motor Company set up numerous subsidiaries that manufactured and sold cars and trucks abroad. Ford assembly plants opened in Canada and Great Britain in 1911 and soon became the biggest automotive producer in those countries. A factory in Cork, Ireland, provided trucks to much of Europe by 1919. The same year saw the first Fords produced in Copenghagen, Denmark, and sold in Germany, Scandinavia, Poland, and the Ukraine. From a plant in Trieste, opened in 1922, "Fordita" sold cars in Italy, the Balkans, Turkey, Cyprus, Egypt, and other Middle Eastern locations. Even the communist government of the Soviet Union welcomed this arm of capitalism. "Throughout the nineteen twenties," according to Ford biographers Allan Nevins and Frank Earnest Hill, "it was almost impossible to overestimate the reputation which Henry Ford enjoyed among German businessmen as the apostle of mass production." Ford plants operated in Germany beginning in 1926. In 1925 a Ford assembly line outside of Paris produced 150 cars a day. By 1932 Ford was manufacturing one third of all the world's automobiles.

At home, the success of the Model T and the publicity surrounding the $5-per-day wage made Henry Ford a major national figure. He used his wealth, power, and profile to promote his views and beliefs on various subjects, which did not always prove popular. Ford viewed war as a terrible waste, concocted by unethical financiers and industrialists to fill their coffers. In 1915 he funded a Peace Ship to Europe, where the terrible bloodletting of World War I was underway. The plan was to transport a team of respected advocates to neutral cities in Norway, Sweden, and Holland to undertake "continuing mediation" with the belligerent parties until a settlement could be reached. Upon arriving in Europe, Ford became ill and hastily returned to the United States while his fellow delegates continued the goodwill mission. Despite Ford's avowed pacifism, Ford plants in the United Kingdom produced trucks and aircraft engines, as well as tractors to increase the Allied food supply. When the United States finally entered the war in 1917, Ford became a major military supplier.

Sales of the Model T began to decline in the mid-1920s. Other automakers offering more modern and varied features and styling than the simple, uniform, black Model T cut into Ford's market share. Other automakers also offered payment plans that allowed prospective drivers to buy on credit. Finance companies offended Ford's personal code of ethics, and he refused to create one to move his merchandise. But the main factor in the Model T's decline may have just been consumer fatigue; the car saw no real design changes between 1908 and 1927.

Ford and his son Edsel retreated to the drawing board. With Edsel taking the lead, Ford Motor Company completed a prototype of the Model A. Every Ford factory had to be retooled and every worker retrained. The Model A debuted in 1927. The first day it was displayed in showrooms, 100,000 people squeezed into Detroit dealerships, mounted police were called out to control crowds in Cleveland, and the New York City branch manager had to move his cars into Madison Square Garden to accommodate the crowds. For the launch of the Model A, Ford set aside his repugnance for consumer credit and created the Universal Credit Corporation, funded by Ford Motor Company. By 1929, Ford produced 1,851,092 Model A cars, 34 percent of the total sold in the United States that year. By 1931, 4 million of the new models were sold. Ford Motor Company had climbed to the top of the auto industry again.

Ford disliked government interference in business and adamantly opposed labor unions. He believed unions restricted productivity to promote employment and balked at technological gains that increased productivity but eliminated jobs. No admirer of President Franklin D. Roosevelt, Ford ignored the mandates of Roosevelt's National Recovery Act. Given Ford's reputation as the creator of the $5 daily wage, FDR's administration hesitated to take him on. Ford fought the unions, leading to ugly clashes at several plants. Edsel finally prevailed on his father to allow a vote on unionization. In 1941 more than 95 percent of 83,000 workers at three Detroit-area Ford plants voted to unionize. Henry Ford's delusion that his workers preferred his benign dictatorship to organized representation shattered. The contract he signed with the UAW contained some of the most generous provisions in the industry.

Ford's reputation will always bear the stain of his public campaign against the world's Jews. Though never accused of discrimination against black, female, or handicapped workers, Ford harbored a deep ill-will toward Jews and published screeds against them. In 1918 Ford's aide and private secretary, Ernest G. Liebold, purchased *The Dearborn Independent,* an obscure weekly Michigan newspaper that began anti-Semitic rantings. Ford franchises nationwide distributed it to their customers. Lawsuits and a boycott campaign caused Ford to shutter the *Independent* in 1927 and recant his anti-Jewish rhetoric in a public letter to the Anti-Defamation League.

As the Second World War loomed on the horizon, Ford opposed America's entry, continuing in his belief that international business could generate the prosperity that would head off wars. He reiterated his belief that "greedy financiers" pulled the strings in world conflicts. Nonetheless, he continued doing business with Nazi Germany, including the manufacture of war materiel. When the United States entered the conflict, however, Ford fell in line with the Allied war effort. Ford's German plants were seized and became property of the Third Reich.

A year before the Pearl Harbor attack, the United States Air Force asked Ford to build the B-24 bomber. Ford agreed, and by 1944 the company's Willow Run Plant was turning out 428 B-24s a month at a 3.5 million-square-foot plant that claimed to have the largest assembly line in the world.

Edsel Ford passed away in prematurely in 1943. An aging, mentally impaired Henry Ford resigned in favor of his grandson in September 1945. He died in 1947 of a cerebral hemorrhage at eighty-three in Fair Lane, his Dearborn estate. Some 5,000 people per hour filed by his casket at a public viewing held at Greenfield Village, after which Ford was laid to rest in Detroit's Ford Cemetery.

Ford's legacy is complex and still vigorously debated today. His unique combination of populism and capitalism continue to resonate powerfully in the American imagination. While his values were deeply rooted in the agrarian past, no one is more responsible for the advancement of industrialization and its attendant social changes. Though he identified with the common man, his management style was authoritarian, not democratic. His techniques of vertically integrated production reshaped world industry. Ford controlled iron-ore deposits, coal mines, timber, rubber plantations, a glass works, and ships and trains to move his products. While getting the world into Fords, Henry pursued what he called "a theory of business that looks toward making this world a better place in which to live." Ford's genius for efficient production—and vision of the positive social changes that could result—made him a lasting symbol of uniquely American industrial greatness.

Because of Ford, many middle-class folks could become motorists. Automobiles were no longer just toys of the rich. This was particularly important to the American West, a land of vast distances and rugged obstacles. Westerners bought and used cars more than easterners or southerners. Los Angeles, the prototype western city, set the pace for automobile cities. Ford, more than any other individual, also allowed millions of Americans to go west as tourists. Visitation at national parks and other western wonders soared once families could drive themselves cheaply and reliably in Model T and Model A Fords. And many who toured the West later moved there—in their Fords.

Ford, Henry and Samuel Crowther. *My Life and Work*. Garden City, New York: Doubleday, Page & Company, 1926.

Gelderman, Carol. *Henry Ford: The Wayward Capitalist*. New York: The Dial Press, 1981.

Levinson, William A. *Henry Ford's Lean Vision: Enduring Principles Form the First Ford Motor Plant*. New York: Productivity Press, 2002.

Nevins, Allan. *Ford: The Times, the Man, the Company*. New York: Scribner, 1954.

Nevins, Allan and Frank Earnest Hill. *Ford: Expansion and Challenge 1915–1933*. New York: Scribner, 1957.

Rae, John B., ed. *Great Lives Observed: Henry Ford*. Englewood Cliffs, New Jersey: Prentice-Hall, Inc., 1969.

Watts, Stephen. *The People's Tycoon: Henry Ford and the American Century*. New York: Random House, Inc., 2006.

JAY COOKE

RESILIENT FINANCIER {1821–1905}

The path of the gifted financier Jay Cooke symbolized the volatile financial climate that sometimes characterized business in the American West. The financial chaos caused by the spectacular plunge of his bank, which collapsed in 1873 under the burden of the hard-pressed Northern Pacific Railroad, illustrated how deeply western finance interlocked with the national economy. Before the fall and the consequent Panic of 1873, Jay Cooke and Company was the darling of Wall Street, and its principal investor was revered as a national hero for his contribution to the North's Civil War victory. As a private investment banker, Cooke transformed war bond sales in the 1860s and set the standard for future bond campaigns. With innovative strategies, Cooke sent agents across the nation and sold bonds at an unprecedented rate. Cooke sold $1.3 billion (more than $18 billion in 2014 dollars) worth of bonds, garnering a reputation as the "Financier of the Civil War" and earning approximately $7 million in commissions. He was an ardent proponent of the idea of Manifest Destiny and was aware of his own place in American history. Cooke took the financial reins of the Northern Pacific Railroad in 1870, but there, the fundraising tactics he had so successfully deployed during the Civil

War failed him. With unforeseen construction challenges, investment difficulties, and mismanagement, Cooke (literally) wrote checks he couldn't cover. When his liabilities surfaced, depositors rushed his New York banking house and precipitated a national depression in 1873.

Biographers agree that at times Cooke's success emerged more from his enthusiastic dedication than from a particularly astute mind, oration skills, or sound business practices. A man of average height and weight with blue eyes, neatly combed white hair, and a long beard to match in his maturity, Cooke was indistinguishable from many Americans except in the category of wealth, which he acquired far more abundantly than most. He loved to fish, but was extremely afraid of water, and he collected art not for its beauty or cultural importance, but through a sense of duty to his affluence.

Cooke was born in August 1821 in Sandusky, Ohio. His father, Eleutheros, was a prominent business lawyer who served in the House of Representatives as an Ohio Whig from 1831 to 1833. Eleutheros placed heavy emphasis on formal education for his children and, blaming a lost election on his difficult name, insisted that they have easily-pronounced names to ease their future political and business endeavors. Hence the Cooke brothers' names: Jay, Pitt, and Henry.

Jay Cooke's ambitions derived not merely from the pursuit of financial gain, but from an adamant conviction that his ventures were divinely ordained. Reflecting in his memoirs, Cooke wrote, "Like Moses and Washington and Lincoln and Grant I have been—I firmly believe—God's chosen instrument, especially in the financial work of saving the Union."

Everything Cooke did was influenced by his Christian faith. He read only religious texts, built an Episcopal church in Ohio, taught Sunday school, and entertained the idea of financing a national evangelical tour for a famous Boston minister. Cooke hosted more than 250 poor clergymen for all-expense-paid vacations at his luxurious home, with the stipulation that he participate in their prayers and theological discussions. His generous "sense of social responsibility," as biographer and economic historian Henrietta Larson characterized it, inspired the capitalist to tithe 10 percent of his profits to charities each year. An equally zealous patriotic fervor drove his Civil War bond drives and Northern Pacific ventures. He regarded the American Northwest as valueless without the railroad and sought, above all else, to settle the region with small towns, churches, schools, and Christian families.

As a businessman who wished to travel the moral high road, Cooke wrestled with several potential ethical and social dilemmas. He harshly scolded employees for any public activity on the Sabbath, but struggled to decide whether or not to run his trains on Sundays. Raised in a staunch abolitionist family, Cooke supported the northern cause wholeheartedly, yet African American soldiers were not allowed to ride his Georgetown trolley cars. He held "progressive" views towards American Indians while simultaneously encroaching on their land with the Northern Pacific. When necessary, Cooke was not above offering bribes and favors to political friends, and as biographer Henrietta Larson tartly observed, he drew a fine distinction between stealing from his neighbors and urging them to invest in a railroad with shaky prospects.

Pitt and Henry Cooke went on to college, but young Jay, at the age of fourteen, showed a propensity for business as a clerk at a local dry good and hardware store. Cooke considered himself a "full-fledged merchant" by 1836 and accepted a bookkeeping position in St. Louis for $600 a year. In 1839, at eighteen, Cooke received his first banking experience at the E.W. Clark and Company firm in Philadelphia.

Philadelphia treated young Cooke very well. At E.W. Clark and Co., Cooke kept books, handled publicity, and earned the "power of attorney" position for the company in two years. At twenty-one, he was admitted into partnership with E.W. Clark. During the 1840s, he learned about the western land business and the potential for wartime gains during the American-Mexican War in 1848. He left the firm in 1857, and, aside from a small venture securing loans and selling bonds for the Sunbury and Erie Railroad, "rested" for a few years. Cooke later wrote that the "preparation of rest and of disentanglement from all business providentially fitted me to carry cheerfully, energetically, as well as faithfully and trustingly, the most enormous financial burdens I verily believe that were ever placed on the shoulders of one man."

As the Civil War was brewing in 1861, Cooke and his brother-in-law, William E. C. Moorhead, established the Jay Cooke and Company private banking house in Philadelphia. Cooke received two thirds ownership and Moorhead one third. The firm dealt in bank notes, bills of exchange, and stock, and accepted deposits. Cooke immediately went to work trying to secure government loans and bond sales. Pennsylvania's state representatives wanted to raise $3 million (about $77.5 million in 2014 dollars) for the war effort. Their success came largely through Cooke's salesmanship, and the U.S. Treasury Department took note.

By 1862, Secretary of the Treasury Salmon P. Chase needed first-rate bond salesmen such as Cooke. The Treasury Department had budgeted for a quick resolution to the secession crisis; by the war's second year, the government was desperately short of cash. Cooke and his partners established another Jay Cooke and Company house in Washington, D.C. There, Cooke and his brother Henry cultivated a friendship with Secretary Chase, lubricating the way with investments in the U.S. Treasury as well as gifts and favors to their new friend. Chase first treated Cooke as his "unofficial advisor," then officially appointed him general agent for the disbursal of $500 million worth of "five-twenty" bonds (bonds that paid a fixed 6 percent interest, redeemable in five years, and fully matured in twenty). In October 1862 Secretary Chase wrote to the House of Representatives, noting that "many experienced and able financial men expressed their belief that it would be impossible to negotiate bonds redeemable after so short a period as five years, and bearing an interest of only six per cent., and for a time appearances were decidedly against the success of the loan." Cooke, however, proved the dissenters wrong with an innovative campaign that would transform government bond sales for decades to come.

Instead of focusing his pitch on bankers and investors (who of course gave generously as well), Cooke pushed for widespread distribution to the middle and lower classes. Cooke hired over 2,000 traveling agents, sent them all over the nation, and aggressively promoted bond sales through patriotic appeals. Agents spent a month on the road, traveling by boat, horse, or wagon to the far reaches of the Union, to docks, suburbs, and even rugged western mining camps. Agents received $10 a day for expenses and were paid $50 to $330 per month. Bond offices were open early in the morning and late in the evening to accommodate all walks of life. Cooke paid well for favorable articles in newspapers, publicly recognized bond buyers by listing their names on congratulatory posters, and actively advertised in religious and trade papers. To support the troops at the front, Cooke launched an irresistible propaganda campaign, making it feel as if everyone were buying bonds.

No town was too small, no settlement too distant, and no part of the war zone was off limits for Cooke and his agents. Agents followed the army to sell bonds to soldiers with fresh paychecks and traveled to newly-occupied towns in the South to promote bond sales. Agents sold to young and old, black and white, war hawks and pacifists. Cooke even managed to sell war bonds to Quakers by persuading them the bonds would be used for soldiers' medical care. By June 30, 1863, Cooke's inventive sales tactics met the $500 million loan with 5,000 subscribers. Cooke, paid on a commission of less than 1 percent, received $1,350,013 (almost $25 million in 2014 dollars).

Some criticized the government for paying Cooke such a large sum and scrutinized Cooke for profiting from the war. The majority of the nation, however, considered Cooke a hero for his involvement in the northern victory and keeping the Union together. Cooke became known far and wide as a trustworthy investment banker. With his wartime gains, he built an ostentatious fifty-three-room mansion on 200 acres near Philadelphia. A host with "patrician grace," Cooke greatly enjoyed entertaining at his home as well as fishing with politicians, partners, lawyers, relatives, Japanese diplomats, and members of the Upper Brule Sioux Tribe. Oil and gold speculators flooded the financier with investment offers, only to return disappointed. Cooke established a third banking house in New York and watched comfortably as his company netted $1 million annually. By 1869, Cooke was a contented family man and the owner of the most powerful banking house in the nation.

By the end of the 1860s, Cooke had every reason to settle back and watch his profits accumulate. Instead, in the wake of the national excitement following the first transcontinental railroad's completion, he sought investment opportunities in transportation. With options to invest in the Union Pacific and the Central Pacific limited, he turned to the hard-pressed Northern Pacific Railroad. Proposed as the second transcontinental railroad and chartered in 1864, the Northern Pacific promised to connect the Northwest to the East and to open that region's resource-rich lands for agriculture, mining, timbering, and settlement. Beginning in the Great Lakes region, the 2,000-mile route was planned to traverse present-day South Dakota, Montana, and Idaho, emerging on the Puget Sound in Washington. The Northern Pacific struggled to secure financing until Jay Cooke arrived on the scene.

With its strong national objectives, the Northern Pacific seemed a good match for the financier celebrated as the savior of the Union. Cooke believed the Northern Pacific's development of the Northwest, like the North's Civil War victory, could only improve the nation by opening commerce between the ports of the Pacific Northwest and the Great Lakes via Seattle, Washington, and Duluth, Minnesota. But before committing fully, the experienced risk-taker insisted that two surveying parties—one for the proposed eastern route and one for the western coastal and mountain route—inspect the feasibility and estimate construction costs. Both surveying parties reported favorably. The experienced engineer W. Milnor Roberts concluded that the land "had great intrinsic value" and if the Northern Pacific was "honestly constructed, and properly administered, [it would be] within a few years a fair dividend on its cost." With the successful surveys and an estimation of $85,277,000 for construction, Cooke was convinced of the Northern Pacific's potential.

In 1870 Cooke became the Northern Pacific's chief financier and banker, with responsibility for selling $100 million worth of bonds, payable at a 7.3 percent interest rate. Henrietta Larson, an economic historian from Harvard, concluded that the Northern Pacific would have faltered without the agency of Jay Cooke and Company. The railroad needed the nation's most accomplished capitalist to complete "the biggest single business enterprise that had up to that time been undertaken in the United States." Cooke advanced $500,000 for construction and equipment, acquired a three-fifths share in the company's stock, and earned twelve cents of every bond dollar sold. As he had during the Civil War, Cooke threw all his energy into the endeavor. He evangelized in newspaper advertisements, nicknaming the Northwest "The Fertile Belt" and the "Seat of the Empire" to entice publicity. He sent agents to various towns with patriotic brochures illustrating the Northern Pacific's value to the nation—and to investors—and displayed grains, fruits, and minerals from the Northwest in his eastern banking houses. "I am very glad," wrote Cooke cheerfully in a letter, "that my lot is cast in the glorious Northwest."

Cooke not only financially backed the Northern Pacific, but

took charge of its public relations. Always an ardent promoter, he insisted that the railroad was a public improvement and set out to secure land grants and government loans. He donated substantially to political campaigns and appealed to the federal government and its agents to assist with the endeavor. According to John M. Lubetkin, Cooke "never hesitated in distributing cash, stock, jobs, consultancies, waivers of debt and other gratuities to politicians to further the [Northern Pacific]." He contended that the railroad would increase the production of gold, silver and other minerals and opened land offices in Europe to encourage European immigration to settle the region. Grasping the tourism potential for Yellowstone country and its implications for the Northern Pacific, Cooke sponsored a speaking tour for Nathaniel P. Langford, lately of the 1870 Washburn, Langford and Doane Yellowstone Expedition, to promote the region's national wonders. He also commissioned artist Thomas Moran to join the United States Geological Survey of the Yellowstone region in 1871. Upon Moran's return, Cooke hosted an exhibit of Moran's pieces in Washington, D.C., to demonstrate the region's beauty. (Moran's paintings of the region's scenic wonders played a critical role in Congress's decision to create Yellowstone National Park in 1872.)

The years 1871 and 1872 proved fateful for Cooke and the Northern Pacific. Despite Cooke's "financial wand," the endeavor faced several obstacles. Without a known completion date, investors balked at buying bonds. Cooke's surveying teams met resistance from the Lakota and Sioux warriors as the railroad encroached on their land. Construction reached present-day North Dakota in 1871, then halted when the team encountered swamps and dense forests. To Cooke's chagrin, dishonesty plagued the project. Construction overseers lied about their accomplishments, and expenses drastically overran the budget. Cooke might have done more to shore up concerns; his name still carried credibility in the financial world. Instead, he went on extended fishing trips and refused to meet with foreign investors.

Even worse, Cooke's personal life fell into shambles when his beloved wife, Elizabeth, died unexpectedly in July 1871. Following Elizabeth's death, Cooke became, in the words of a biographer, "increasingly more reclusive—his life rigid, his dress outdated and almost bizarre."

The effects of Cooke's personal tragedy began to tell in his professional life. He overextended his banking houses to meet Northern Pacific obligations and used the bank's deposits to leverage acquisition of 75 percent of the railway. Rumors of Cooke's high liabilities surfaced and investors began to withdraw money from the banking firm. Cooke, who could not manage to sell railroad bonds based on speculative promotion any longer, froze his banking houses' assets in the enterprise and failed to meet the Northern Pacific's obligations. Depositors panicked and rushed to Jay Cooke and Company's New York offices. Despite Cooke's insistence that he could save it, the banking house closed under pressure. Equities on the New York Stock Exchange collapsed over the news, precipitating a chain of bank runs that heralded the Panic of 1873. Cooke declared bankruptcy, lost his properties, and scrambled to repay more than $11 million in liabilities (almost $211 million in 2014 dollars). A broken man, Cooke moved in with his daughter in Ohio.

When asked if he would pursue business ventures after the bankruptcy, Cooke responded, "I have gone up in the tower and looked around and it will not be necessary to do so again." Yet the veteran capitalist did not wait long to recapture some of his former wealth. Cooke repaid his liabilities within three years and, perhaps drawing on hidden reserves, invested in the Horn Silver Mine in Utah. He earned annual operating profits for two years from the mine and eventually sold his shares for $1 million. With the profits, he repurchased some of his former properties and converted his mansion into a seminary for girls. Cooke refused an invitation to attend the Northern Pacific's "final spike" ceremony in 1883, but he traveled the entire Northern Pacific line in 1891. He passed the final two decades of his life quietly focusing on fishing and small-scale farming. Jay Cooke, who had been at times the darling and at other times the pariah of Wall Street, passed away on February 16, 1905.

Cooke was an eastern banker with western ambitions. An economic frontiersman at heart, he pursued a vision for the development of the Northwest into a land of productive farms, forests, and cities. He invested emotionally and financially in the Northern Pacific. Ultimately his investments led to a setback in his career. Yet he set a new standard for war bond campaigns and is credited with establishing the organization of government security distribution. Cooke's example as an investment banker inspired J. Pierpont Morgan and Jacob H. Schiff to succeed. Cooke, the hailed financer of the Civil War, tried mightily to promote the American West, and mostly succeeded. His vision for the economic potential of the region was sound, but his failure to fully achieve it forced him to quietly abdicate his position as the nation's largest private banker.

Larson, Henrietta M. *Jay Cooke: Private Banker.* New York: Harvard University Press, 1936.

Lubetkin, M. John. *Jay Cooke's Gamble.* Norman, OK: University of Oklahoma Press, 2006.

Oberholtzer, Ellis Paxon. *Jay Cooke: Financier of the Civil War*, Volume 1 and 2. Philadelphia: George W. Jacobs Publishers, 1907.

WALTER SCOTT CHEESMAN

LAND AND WATER {1838–1907}

W.S. Cheesman [signature]

One of the West's shrewdest pioneers knew that the fur trade, mining, railroads, and agriculture were all risky ventures. He bet on commodities nearly everyone wanted or needed—land, water, power. To build a city, Walter Scott Cheesman also became a key player in making rail connections. Cheesman reckoned that real estate, despite occasional dips, would pay off in booming western cities. He spent his career collecting corner lots and building up what ultimately became one of Denver's largest and longest-lived realty firms, Walter S. Cheesman Realty Company. Among many other achievements, he put together the land parcel for Union Station.

Cheesman also plunged into the water business, where he ultimately monopolized service in the Denver area. He faced growing public criticism about high water rates and minnows popping out of open faucets. This led the water company to ultimately sell to the city of Denver—at a considerable profit. But the money Cheesman sank into a visionary water system to provide Denver with water for centuries to come is one of the greatest legacies any entrepreneur could leave behind. Even his many critics marvel at Cheesman Dam, that beautiful stone landmark that is still the proudest monument of what is now Denver Water.

Born June 27, 1838 at Hempstead Harbor, New York, Cheesman grew up in a prominent Long Island clan. Young Walt graduated from public high school and received private tutoring before entering the family mercantile and banking endeavors. In 1854 he moved to the flourishing city of Chicago to try out the pharmacy business with his older brothers, Edward Talbot and William Henry. The older siblings expanded in 1859 to open a pharmacy in the one-year-old town of Denver. After his brothers failed to thrive with the Colorado pharmacy, Walter moved to Denver in 1861 to rescue the faltering family venture. Ignoring the advice of his older brothers—"We all feel that you have made a great mistake"—Cheesman came up with a new pharmacy product. In the thirsty little town, he made bottled water a mainstay of the business, along with drugs, rye and bourbon whiskies, brandies, wines, bitters, and other libations.

During the late 1860s Cheesman joined former governor John Evans and *Rocky Mountain News* editor William N. Byers in coaxing railroads to Denver, which was stagnating because of its isolation and high transportation costs. Cheesman had far too much money tied up in Denver real estate to see the city die. He had bet nearly everything he owned on the town where his Cheesman Block reigned as one of the largest structures. Yet many businessmen moved to Cheyenne, Wyoming Territory, with its Union Pacific rail connection, figuring that city was destined to become the Rocky Mountain metropolis. Cheesman and the rest of Denver's power elite must have bristled when the *Cheyenne Daily Leader* of September 24, 1868, crowed: "Denver is too near to Cheyenne to ever amount to much."

Cheesman and other persistent, able business leaders decided that if the railroad would not build to Denver, Denver must build to the railroads. In 1867 they formed the Denver Pacific Railway to construct a 106-mile-long steel lifeline connecting Denver with the transcontinental railroad at Cheyenne. Cheesman became the major financial backer of the city's first railroad, the Denver Pacific, which named its first locomotive for him.

After the Denver Pacific reached town in June of 1870, the city blossomed. Many other railroads soon made Denver either their hub or a destination. Cheesman became involved with many of these roads, including the Denver & Boulder Valley, the Denver, South Park & Pacific, the Denver & New Orleans, the Denver & Rio Grande, and the Denver Texas and Gulf.

Initially each of the pioneer lines had its own separate passenger and freight depot. Cheesman realized that Denver needed a consolidated station and spearheaded organization of the Denver Union Depot and Railway Company. As the first president of Union Depot—a post he held for decades—Cheesman brought in one of New York City's wealthiest and flashiest capitalists, Jay Gould. Gould, who had come to control the Union Pacific and other railroads, invested heavily in the Denver Depot Company, which capitalized at $400,000. Cheesman's "personal influence with Jay Gould was the prime factor," according to Cheesman's biographer, Edgar C. McMechen, "in securing the funds used in building Denver's Union Station."

Cheesman selected a depot site and put together a vast real estate parcel—the land bounded by Wynkoop and Wewatta Streets, between 16th and 18th streets adjacent to the South Platte River. Cheesman issued $300,000 in stock to buy the land and begin construction of the largest and most impressive building that Colorado would see during the 1800s. On July 26, 1881, Coloradans thronged the grand opening of the new depot. They marveled at the gigantic structure, measuring 503 feet long and 65 feet wide, under an 180-foot-high tower that soared heavenward as Denver's first skyscraper. The Mile High City rode the rails to prosperity, mushrooming from 4,759 residents in 1870 to 106,713 by 1890. Thanks to Cheesman and a few other movers and shakers, the little city in the middle of nowhere had become second in the West only to San Francisco, larger than Los Angeles or any town in Texas.

Cashing in on the flush times after railroads revitalized Denver, Cheesman and his closest longtime business associate, David H. Moffat, joined James Archer to form the Denver City Water Company in 1870. By the end of that year, that firm celebrated delivery of the first piped water to paying customers. Thanks to the new pumps and underground water pipes, Denver boasted running water and indoor plumbing, allowing outhouses to be abandoned. The firm's fire hydrants helped Denver avoid any significant blaze after the great fire of 1863. Cheesman took a special interest in fire hydrants because the great fire that destroyed much of central Denver had consumed his drugstore. Cheesman rebuilt a handsome two-story brick building on the same corner site at 15th and Blake Streets.

To assure a steady water supply, the Denver City Water Company created Lake Archer. The site of that reservoir at West 12th Avenue and Shoshone Street is now home to Denver Water. That public utility serves a vast metropolitan area and hydraulically engineers both the Colorado and the South Platte Rivers.

Besides railroads, water, and real estate, Cheesman also became a co-founder and longtime board member of the Denver Gas & Electric Company, established in 1870. A year later, gas street lights illuminated the city and private citizens could also purchase service. In 1880 Denver became one of the first cities in the world with electric light. Cheesman took pride in helping to envision and capitalize such civic progress. That little firm of Denver Gas & Electric would evolve into Public Service Company of Colorado and then into today's Xcel Energy.

Cheesman's multifaceted business activities kept him busy and—after 1880—on the telephone. He was one of the first Denverites to buy a line on that new-fangled contraption, according to the Colorado

Telephone Company's first phone book. In the *Denver City Directory* his many railroad and real estate activities are hidden behind the only occupation he usually listed, vice president, First National Bank of Denver. He helped make First National Colorado's leading bank and a source of capital for his many entrepreneurial endeavors. He also invested in mines in Leadville, Creede, Redcliff, and Gilman.

Cheesman, as his biographer Edgar C. McMechan puts it, "had little time or inclination for recreational activities, preferring to employ his leisure hours in making plans for the future." Real estate was Cheesman's passion," as McMechen put it. "When others became disheartened during periods of depression, he bought more real estate, and bought and bought again until he made himself the largest taxpayer in Colorado." The portly, mustachioed capitalist also owned more property in Denver than anyone else. The *Denver Times* of September 29, 1901 praised Cheesman for "the most rock-ribbed faith in Denver real estate. He is acknowledged as the most clear-headed realty student Denver has ever had. And his cash has been always ready to back it up." Among the major Denver buildings Cheesman constructed were the Cheesman Block, the Burlington Block, the Empire Building, the Colonial Block, the Columbia Block.

R.G. Dun & Company, the New York City firm judging credit risks for its subscribers, also wrote highly of Cheesman after investigating his business career. In their 1867 confidential report the Dun firm characterized Cheesman as "worthy [of] all confidence." Dun's agent added in 1873 that he was "one of the staunch . . . good credit."

Cheesman seemed to have a Midas touch, but he could shift directions with changing circumstances. He bought as much land as he could on Larimer Street when it was Denver's main street. Then as prime development turned uptown toward the Brown Palace Hotel and Capitol Hill, he began buying up land along 16th and 17th Streets. After Cheesman's daughter, Marcia, married John Evans II, the grandson of Governor John Evans, the Walter S. Cheesman

Real Estate Company served Cheesman and Evans family interests. Cheesman's legendary real estate speculations included the 1500 block of Broadway. While holding out for the highest offer, he grazed cattle on the site, leading town wits and wags to joke about Cheesman's cow pasture on one of the city's most valuable chunks of real estate.

Water, as well as land, continued to fascinate Cheesman. His Denver City Water Company faced a dozen different competitors over the years. In 1888 Cheesman and his closest ally, David Moffat, left Denver City Water Company to set up a rival firm, Citizen's Water Company. By acquiring many upstream water rights and offering cheap or free water—which Citizen's did for two years—Cheesman forced other competitors out of business or into merging. The final 1894 consolidation, which Cheesman called Denver Union Water Company, established a near monopoly on water service in the Denver area.

To assure water for twentieth-century Denver, Cheesman constructed a mountain reservoir behind a state-of-the-art dam. He hired Charles L. Harrison, a noted engineer who had worked on the Panama Canal and the Pennsylvania Railroad, to design a gravity arch stone dam. Besides being one of the world's first gravity arch dams, when completed in 1905 it was also the highest. That engineering marvel measured a quarter mile long, a solid 176 feet thick at the base and eighteen feet at the crown. Each granite block had to be chiseled to fit the curve of the structure. When the water rose behind the 212-foot-high dam without a single leak, Cheesman rewarded his chief stonemason with a fancy new $50 suit of clothes.

Two years after finishing the dam named for him, Cheesman died of influenza, aggravated by asthma, on May 31, 1907. In his honor, Denver renamed the western part of Congress Park, calling it Cheesman Park. As a centerpiece for the park, his widow Alice donated $100,000 to construct the Cheesman Pavilion in 1910. Denver finally had its own Parthenon, a Colorado yule marble neoclassical Greek pavilion overlooking the park, the city, and the Front Range of the

Rockies. The Cheesman Pavilion's architects, William A. Marean and Albert Norton, also designed the Cheesman Mansion (now the governor's mansion) at the southeast corner of E. 8th Avenue and Logan Street. Completed in 1907, the Cheesman Mansion is a Colonial Revival–style showplace. Like Cheesman himself, it is very large, formal—some might say pompous. Stately fluted Ionic columns guard the porte cochere, entry portico, and west side portico overlooking the mountains where Cheesman had built his dam and acquired so many water rights. Cheesman died before completion of his mansion but his widow Alice and daughter Gladys moved in upon completion in 1908. Mrs. Walter S. Cheesman continued to live there at 400 E. 8th Avenue until her death in 1923.

Judge Benjamin Barr Lindsey, a leading Colorado reformer and founder of the nationally celebrated Juvenile Court and juvenile justice reforms, publicized a more critical view of Cheesman and his park. Lindsey called it "Corporation Park" and a monument to controlling corporate interests, such as Cheesman's water company. In his classic exposé of Colorado corruption, *The Beast,* Lindsey criticized Cheesman as a mainstay of the Mayor Robert W. Speer's political machine. Lindsey attacked Cheesman for political maneuvering to have the Denver Union Water Company's taxes rebated and its assessment reduced. According to Lindsey, the company overcharged for water and high-handedly decided "to force the people of Denver either to pay $14,400,000 for the waterworks or to grant the company a new franchise."

Lindsey argued that Cheesman and his water company had manipulated elections, giving them an exclusive franchise to provide water to Denverites. Lindsey in *The Beast* portrays Cheesman as grumbling about how much he had to spend to elect Mayor Speer.

Others grumbled about Cheesman's water company. Despite rates higher than in other cities, Denverites complained of low pressure during dry summers and of dirty tapwater according to the April 15,

1907 *Denver Express.* Stung by such criticism, Cheesman offered to sell the company to the city in 1899. In 1906 Cheesman again offered to sell it, complete with the new Cheesman Dam, for $14.4 million. Critics, however, claimed the company was only worth $7 to $8 million. Judge Lindsey and other reformers argued for municipal ownership, which finally happened in 1918 after prolonged haggling over the price.

Even Lindsey, however, acknowledged that Cheesman had at least one virtue. The man loved animals. Back in the days when the two men worked together on children's aid and the Juvenile Court, Lindsey says he motored with Cheesman on his jaunts around Denver. On their way to inspect Cheesman Dam, Lindsey recalled in *The Beast*, "I saw him stop his car, pick up a stray cat mewing by the roadside, and take it to the dam were he caught fish to feed it."

Cheesman helped found and presided for fifteen years over the Bureau of Child and Animal Protection (later the Colorado Humane Society). He led its fight against animal abuse, pushing through Colorado legislation that forbade docking (cutting off) horses' tails. He led the fight to ban rodeos after the first major Denver event was staged in 1887 at Riverfront Park. Rodeos did not return to Denver until 1931, long after Cheesman's death. The September 29, 1901, *Denver Times* praised Cheesman as "foremost in charitable and humane work," but "modest in these regards and no one knows how many tens of thousands he has given away." Cheesman supporters pointed out that, among many charitable gifts, he gave financial support and donated 600 volumes to the Denver Public Library. Using his real estate experience, he also helped the library find a home after its 1889 creation.

Cheesman was a prototypical, highly efficient robber baron, but also a brilliant capitalist and city builder and a major philanthropist. Perhaps he should be summed up in his own boast, as reported in the *Denver Times,* September 29, 1901, that his many efforts always were "a Denver enterprise, with Denver capital used in its construction and enlargement, and Denver men ever in control." In more recent times, of course, most major Denver utilities, banks, railroads and other enterprises have succumbed to out-of-state ownership and control.

Thanks in part to this controversial tycoon, Denver still has one of America's strongest water departments. The city is well watered with cool, clear, mountain water. So are Cheesman Park and Fairmount Cemetery, where lies Walter Scott Cheesman's impressive tombstone. Besides the water system, Cheesman built Union Station, a major landmark, revived in 2014 as a hotel and a multi-modal transit hub. As a founder and heavy investor in Denver Gas & Electric Company, Cheesman also figured heavily in bringing electric power and gas heating to Denver ahead of many communities. Few have done so much to build up and to green a city in the Great American Desert. Albeit enriching himself, Cheesman was Denver's greatest city builder.

Arps, Louisa Ward. *Denver in Slices*. Denver: Alan Swallow, 1959.

Forrest, Kenton H. and Charles Albi. *Denver's Railroads*. Golden: Colorado Railroad Museum, 1981.

King, Clyde Lyndon. *The History of the Government of Denver with Special Reference to Its Relations with Public Service Corporations*. Denver: Fisher Book Company, 1911.

Lindsey, Benjamin Barr, 1869-1943, and Harvey J. O'Higgins. *The Beast*. NY: Doubleday, Page & Co., 1910. 2009.

Limerick, Patricia Nelson with Jason L. Hanson. *A Ditch in Time: The City, the West, and Water*. Denver: Fulcrum Publishing Company, 2012.

MacMechan, Edgar Carlisle. *Walter Scott Cheesman: A Pioneer Builder of Colorado*.

Mosley, Earl L. *History of the Denver Water System, 1858–1919*. Denver: Board of Water Commissioners, 1962.

Noel, Thomas J. "All Hail the Denver Pacific: Denver's First Railroad," in *Colorado Magazine*, Spring, 1973. pp. 92-116.

A.P. GIANNINI

THE PEOPLE'S BANKER {1870–1949}

Giannini was a modest man. He and his wife, Clorinda, lived in the same humble home in San Mateo, California, for years. He dressed simply, owning only a few suits and pairs of shoes. When he died in 1949, he left behind only $489,278—a small sum, considering that Giannini founded and owned what was then the world's largest bank. Giannini's Bank of America defied all traditional rules of banking. It was headquartered in San Francisco, a continent away from East Coast financial capitals. It had the son of Italian immigrants at its helm, an oddity in an industry stocked with elite white Protestants. And, most importantly, Bank of America provided banking services to the many, not just the few. Giannini's innovation was simple: he created a bank that catered to the needs of ordinary people. Many banks ignored working- and middle-class customers in favor of wealthier clients. Bank of America was built on customer service. Giannini's banks were open late to let customers make deposits after they finished work. Bank of America targeted immigrants, publishing ads and bank documents in Italian, Spanish, Chinese, and other languages.

Generous to his customers, Giannini competed ruthlessly with his banking peers. Bank of America grew because Giannini took over small community banks across California, sometimes skirting the edges of banking regulations and drawing his business into skirmishes with state legislators and federal regulators. Yet Bank of America grew as California grew, and Giannini's innovative strategy became one of the dominant business strategies of the industry.

By the late 1940s, Giannini's bank served nearly 4 million customers at over 500 branches across California. Bank of America dominated the financial landscape of the Far West, holding the bank deposits of over one in three Californians. But it wasn't just the checking and savings accounts of millions that made the bank prominent: Bank of America also financed infrastructure projects and the state's entertainment and construction industries.

Amadeo Peter Giannini was born May 6, 1870 in San Jose, the first child of Luigi and Virginia Giannini. His father emigrated to California from Italy in 1863, attracted by gold mining's promise. Luigi was a farmer rather than a miner at heart, and the fertile landscape and favorable climate of the Santa Clara Valley reminded him of his Italian home. After returning to Italy to marry Virginia DiMartini, Luigi tried his hand at running a boardinghouse for Italian immigrants, then moved his family to a nearby farm, where the Gianninis grew produce for the San Francisco markets. Tragedy struck in 1876, when Luigi was killed by one of his employees in a quarrel over wages. Virginia, just twenty-two, and her two children found themselves without an economic anchor.

In 1880 Virginia married Lorenzo Scatena and persuaded him to move the family to San Francisco, where he found work as a commission clerk for a produce-wholesaling firm. Wholesalers were the brokers that made California's agricultural economy flow—they bought produce from rural farmers and sold it to urban grocers and restaurants. It was a tough business. Bidding on produce, transporting crates of fruits and vegetables around the city, and negotiating with customers meant long days on one's feet and lots of mental and physical labor. Scatena excelled at it, eventually opening his own firm. His success meant the family could afford to move from San Francisco's waterfront to the bustling Italian neighborhood of North Beach.

Scatena was an excellent businessman, but his firm's greatest asset was his ambitious stepson Amadeo. Although he was a bright student, school never interested the boy as much as wholesaling. When he was twelve, he secretly spent his after-school time writing sales pitches, promising growers fair prices and good service if they did business with L.S. Scatena and Company. He sent them off without informing his stepfather, who was surprised when these growers began inquiring about doing business with his firm. Giannini began spending more time at the waterfront than in the classroom and dropped out of school at fifteen.

Tall, imposing, and confident, Giannini was a wholesaling natural. His instincts about when to buy and at what price, and when to sell, served him well in a competitive market that historian Felice Bonadio calls "entrepreneurial warfare." In 1887, Giannini earned $50,000 for Scatena by cornering the northern California pear market on a hunch that the year's harvest would fall short of expectations. He restlessly sought out new information that could give the family firm an edge, traveling from farm to farm across northern California inquiring into local growing conditions and talking to growers about their needs and concerns. He promised fair prices and reliable service, always paying farmers in cash and on time. His reputation for fair dealing set him apart from most wholesalers, who often put farmers off with their sharp practices. Giannini's groundwork helped Scatena and Company expand into new produce markets no other San Francisco wholesaler had tapped. While most jobbers confined their efforts to nearby farms, Scatena's firm reached as far as the Sacramento, Santa Clara, Salinas, and San Joaquin Valleys.

Seeking new challenges, Giannini retired from wholesaling in 1900. He searched around for a replacement profession, dabbling in politics and real estate. Then, an unexpected opportunity fell into his lap. When his wealthy father-in-law, a major stockholder and director of the Columbus Savings and Loan, passed away in 1903, the bank's owners selected Giannini to replace him. Columbus S&L was a rigid institution that poorly served the North Beach Italian community where it was located. Originally founded to provide financial services to new immigrants, its directors preferred to do business with wealthier and more established, and perhaps more reliable, customers. Giannini was distressed by the conservatism of his fellow directors and shocked by the number of spurned customers who took their banking elsewhere. He pressed for change and was rewarded by being removed from the board.

Giannini recovered by starting his own bank. San Francisco had plenty of banks to serve the wealthy—what it needed was a financial institution that served the city's large immigrant population, small business owners, and other people of modest means. The city's large banks, such as Crocker-Woolworth, disdained small loans and looked down on immigrants. From his work as a wholesaler, Giannini knew that immigrant growers and other small business owners needed reliable access to credit. His ties in the Italian community showed him that immigrants needed an institution that welcomed them, spoke their language, and would loan them small amounts of money. And everyone, he knew, wanted better financial services.

Giannini's Bank of Italy opened its first location in October 1904, and the newly-minted banker hustled to drum up business. He eagerly advertised his new bank, touting the services it could provide. To the city's conservative financial elite, soliciting business this way was unseemly and unethical to the point of madness. But Giannini delighted in shaking up an industry that he believed actively sought to keep people like him out.

His bank cultivated Italian immigrants, helping them overcome their deep suspicions about savings accounts. Giannini's staff helped former Italian peasants fill out paperwork and showed them how to use their new accounts. Despite its name, Bank of Italy didn't stop with Italians. The bank catered to immigrants from all countries—its numerous "foreign divisions" developed advertising, solicited customers, and provided services in Spanish, Portuguese, Greek, Russian, Chinese, and other languages. Bank of Italy focused on mortgage and small-business loans, and lent out thousands in unsecured "character loans" to people who Giannini believed needed the help. His bank also remained open after regular business hours to accommodate factory workers, merchants, and others whose days did not follow standard bankers' hours. Bank of Italy's customer service reflected Giannini's belief that if you treated people well and responded to their needs, they would be loyal to you in return.

Bank of Italy flourished due to its innovative marketing and service, but it took a natural disaster to make it a financial powerhouse. When a massive earthquake destroyed San Francisco in April 1906, Giannini and his employees managed to safely transport all the bank's gold, currency, and records to his home across the bay in San Mateo. Three days after the quake, Giannini announced that Bank of Italy was open for normal business, even though its building and its safe were destroyed. Bank of Italy addressed customer needs months before any other bank in the city reopened. He announced he would lend money to any San Franciscans ready to rebuild their damaged city, accepting their enthusiasm as collateral. Offering stability and security during a difficult time proved to be good business. Giannini dodged another disaster the following year, cutting back on Bank of Italy's generous lending policies temporarily to moderate the effects of a nationwide financial panic that brought down many well-established San Francisco banks.

Bank of Italy was wildly successful, but the restless Giannini craved expansion. His experiences in rural California persuaded him that smaller towns also needed high-quality financial services. In 1909, he opened a bank in his hometown of San Jose. Bank of Italy expanded by buying up small-town banks and providing financial services of local farmers and merchants. Economy of scale allowed Giannini to focus on better customer service, lower interest rates, and looser credit than most small rural banks. Each branch drew on the capital reserves of Bank of Italy as a whole, so they could absorb losses more readily than smaller local banks. He expanded Bank of Italy much the same way he expanded his stepfather's wholesaling business. Giannini built personal relationships with his customers, catered to local needs, offered reliable terms, and ruthlessly squeezed local competitors.

Giannini began eyeing fast-growing southern California, buying his first Los Angeles bank in 1913. Despite southern California's promise, establishing a successful bank there brought new challenges. Anglo migrants from the American Midwest, rather than immigrants, made up most of the city's population, and Giannini had to learn new techniques to attract their business. Efforts by the city's established bankers to keep Giannini out failed, but Bank of Italy never achieved success in the southland equal to its northern California triumphs.

California banking laws and growing opposition to Bank of Italy's size and power created other problems. Branch banking had a bad reputation in much of the West. Many states either banned or seriously restricted banks from opening branches, a legacy of Populist-era fears of monopolies and distrust of financiers and outside capital. California's laws were relatively lenient regarding bank expansion, and Giannini stretched them as far as they could go, actively cultivating allies in state government along the way. But public regulators and other bankers in the 1920s feared Giannini was creating a monopoly in the guise of serving the common man. Charles Stern, the state banking commissioner, began rejecting his plans to expand.

Giannini responded by expanding anyway, using any technique he could. Bank of Italy was part of the Federal Reserve system, so it could absorb California banks that were nationally chartered, and thus not under state control. He created separate holding companies to expand under state regulations, and created or purchased subsidiary banks that were only technically separate from Bank of Italy. Giannini also specialized in hiring former public officials to help him negotiate with state and federal agencies. By 1925, he was the head of several branch-bank systems and owned banks in New York and Italy. In 1930 his banks were consolidated into one entity: Bank of America, a name that signified Giannini's ambitions.

Giannini helped millions of ordinary customers, but he also invested heavily in public infrastructure and California's growing industries. Bank of Italy created special loan policies for the motion-picture industry at a time when other bankers were suspicious of the industry's future. The Great Depression and Second World War profoundly shaped Giannini's policies. A supporter of Franklin Roosevelt, Giannini helped influence new federal banking and mortgage-lending laws during the New Deal. During the Great Depression and the war, Bank of America became the largest private lender in the West for government-subsidized projects. Giannini's support of Henry Kaiser, for example, meant that Bank of America underwrote the construction of Hoover, Grand Coulee, and Bonneville Dams, and the construction and operation of Kaiser's vast California shipyards. Giannini also lent money to the aerospace and defense industries and provided mortgages and other loans to thousands of Americans flocking to California to work in wartime jobs that Giannini himself helped finance.

For all the money that passed through his bank, Giannini seemed uninterested in wealth. He and his family owned few shares of Bank of Italy or Bank of America. He promoted employee ownership. By the 1940s, more than 40 percent of his company was owned by his employees. Small shareholders—most holding five to ten shares—controlled much of the rest. Giannini ran his company through loyalty and his strong personality, but the fact almost no one else owned enough of the company to challenge him certainly didn't hurt.

Bank of America's effect on California and the larger western expansion was profound. Giannini created the world's largest bank in the early twentieth century out of the modest deposits of millions. He recognized that the West was a land of promise for ordinary Americans, and he created a bank that helped fund that promise.

Felice A. Bonadio. *A.P. Giannini: Banker of America.* (Berkeley: University of California Press.)

Lynne Pierson Doti and Larry Schweikart. *Banking in the American West: From the Gold Rush to Deregulation.* (Norman: University of Oklahoma Press, 1991).

Gerald Nash, A.P. *Giannini and the Bank of America.* (Norman: University of Oklahoma Press, 1992).

J. P. MORGAN

A NEW AGE OF FINANCE {1837-1913}

John P. Morgan was a lightning rod of a man: Americans either loved him or hated him. Historian Frederick Lewis Allen, writing in the 1940s, noted, "What evidence had accumulated about Pierpont Morgan was strikingly divided between the one-sidedly laudatory and the one-sidedly derogatory." Arguments over the pros and cons of America's capitalist economy, and the men who drove it, weren't new, of course. But what Morgan accomplished was new. He ushered in a new age of finance, recognizing the importance of a stable, robust economy to both private industry and the public sector. Morgan was a consolidator, rather than a creator, but he recognized the interdependence of America's growing railroad, steel, and other industries, as well as the mutually supporting connection between the public and private sector. By making peace between rivals and turning around struggling companies, he brought order to economic chaos.

Unlike Andrew Carnegie or John D. Rockefeller, J. P. Morgan was born into relative affluence. His father, Junius Morgan, was a prosperous New England importer/exporter. In 1837, the year of J. P.'s birth, Junius weathered the worst financial crisis in American history up to that time by forging close ties with the London banking house operated by George Peabody. Together, the transatlantic partners shipped southern cotton to British textile mills. Pierpont, as he was known, was a relatively solitary child who preferred reviewing his father's account books to outdoor sports. He was an avid, hard-working, intelligent student, but physically frail. Long illnesses interrupted his years in private and public schools in the United States and Europe. He became a devout Episcopalian and diligently studied French, German, art history, and mathematics at the University of Göttingen, in Germany. Upon graduation, Pierpont went to work for a Wall Street subsidiary of his father's London firm, George Peabody & Co., in 1857. He quickly demonstrated the ability, sound judgment, and nerve that would serve him well through the rest of his career. Sent to New Orleans to learn the cotton business, J. P. came across an unconsigned shipment of coffee at the city's wharves. He secured individual orders for the coffee throughout New Orleans, then used a company draft to purchase the entire lot, without consulting his superiors. Their reprimand crossed paths with a report on the deal's profits that significantly lessened his bosses' alarm. In New Orleans and elsewhere, Morgan learned the value of information. He scrutinized later business deals until he understood the workings of a given company or industry more thoroughly than the people working in it.

The Civil War provided new opportunities for enterprising businessmen. Morgan started his own firm, J. Pierpont Morgan & Company, in 1862, speculating in gold and providing military supplies to the Union Army. His incidental involvement in a plan to sell defective rifles to the army at a large profit earned a public rebuke. Pierpont nevertheless prospered during the period of national unrest, emerging from the war as one of America's most influential financiers by dealing in goods and commodities—and securities—necessary to win the war. His sound reputation was underscored by his imposing physical appearance. Allen described the once-frail youth as "a hulking, solid-shouldered young man with strong, large-featured face and an emphatic moustache and striking hazel eyes." Gazing into his penetrating eyes, photographer Edward Steichen observed, felt like looking into the headlights of an oncoming train. Morgan's features added to his not-entirely-warranted reputation as an ogre, especially when the disfiguring hereditary disease rhinophyma swelled his nose into a bulbous, pitted, purple mass.

At war's end, Morgan turned his considerable resources and attention to the development of national railway lines. The enterprise suited Morgan's nationalistic ambitions. Railroads expanded local markets regionally, regional markets nationally, and national ones globally. Morgan contributed by linking investors in the East and overseas with American railway companies. He studied the business of rail transport intensely, developing nationwide intelligence networks, until, by the 1880s, he became America's most respected expert on the railway industry. His mastery of railroad finance made Morgan's approval of a stock or bond offering worth its weight in dollars or pounds sterling for many investors. The capitalist used his clout to reorganize faltering railroads, including the Albany & Susquehanna, the Philadelphia & Reading, and the Chesapeake & Ohio.

In 1879 Morgan organized an initial stock offering for Cornelius Vanderbilt's New York Central Railway, taking a seat on that corporation's board of directors. From that perch, he witnessed a destructive war between the Central and the neighboring Pennsylvania Railroad. The Central started to build a rival line between Pittsburgh and Philadelphia. The Penn retaliated by building a new road from New York City to Buffalo. To Morgan, the whole business appeared senseless and wasteful. Why should two rival companies squander resources to reduce one another's trade when both could benefit from cooperation? Morgan forged a deal among the railways' principals that reaffirmed their original territories and restored peace and prosperity to both. The agreement cemented Morgan's reputation as an industrial peacemaker, even as farmers and certain government officials voiced alarms about the combination's threat to competitive free markets.

In 1887 the federal government responded by passing the Interstate Commerce Act, banning corporate collusion on prices and other activities. But Morgan had barely started his quest for corporate order. In 1889 he organized a summit of major railway officials to divide up the companies' national territories and to further discuss means of cooperation. When word of the meeting leaked out, progressive reformers and farmers fearing the negative impact of railway monopolies on their own livelihoods responded with outrage. Political leaders from rural Democratic strongholds in the South and Midwest angrily denounced Morgan, and politicians of all stripes distanced themselves from the financier.

When the Panic of 1893 struck, consequently, it was doubly difficult for the Democratic administration of Grover Cleveland to reach out to Morgan for financial aid. The Panic, America's largest depression up to that time, stalled business activity nationwide and led to an exodus of foreign and domestic investors from the stock market. As capital investment dried up, investors increasingly converted their savings into gold specie. By January 1895, the United States Treasury's gold supply, the foundation for America's system of currency, began to evaporate, falling below the benchmark of $100 million deemed essential to the government's fiscal solvency. As the national economy continued to plunge, the reserve dropped to $60 million, then $50 million. It looked as if federal bankruptcy were imminent.

With nowhere else to turn, President Cleveland appealed for J. P. Morgan's help. Fortunately, Morgan considered the United States too big to fail. No friend of government interference, he nevertheless understood, more than anyone, that if the dollar collapsed, his investments would go with it.

Morgan offered to secretly arrange the sale of $50 million in government bonds to a syndicate of investors, with an option to sell $50 million more. He was, in short, offering his reputation to help shore up the faltering government. When Cleveland balked, Morgan took the next train to Washington. At a meeting with the chief executive, he calmly demonstrated his mastery of the situation. The run on gold would continue, his sources agreed, until either the Treasury collapsed or the government made a creditable defense of the dollar. Mere rumors that Morgan was involved in negotiations with the feds had temporarily rallied the stock market. His actual commitment, he asserted, would serve as a further tonic. Morgan assuaged Cleveland's fears that such an initiative was unconstitutional by reciting from memory an all-but-forgotten Civil War–era law that authorized the president to buy gold coin in exchange for bonds. Cleveland could restore the public confidence in the dollar without even involving Congress. Even the politically-sensitive Cleveland could not refuse such terms. Despite loud protests from many of his fellow Democrats, Cleveland embraced Morgan as, he later wrote, a paragon of "clear-sighted, far-seeing patriotism."

Morgan next turned his considerable skills to the consolidation of the American steel industry. He helped several competitors of Carnegie Steel form a new corporation called Federal Steel, then took on Carnegie himself. Carnegie was more than ready for a fight; his steel foundries were, after all, the best in the business. Ever adverse to a wasteful industrial war, Morgan chose instead to buy Carnegie out. With the help of Carnegie's wife and his primary advisor, Charles Schwab, Morgan found a price point with enough leverage to move the nation's steelmaking colossus. Federal Steel and Carnegie Steel merged into the $1.4 billion-dollar United States Steel, the world's largest steel corporation.

Morgan's urge to eliminate waste through consolidation made him Wall Street's darling, but the sheer scale of his activities continued to hurt his reputation among America's farmers, wage laborers, and their advocates. When the capitalist intoned, "America is good enough for me," William Jennings Bryan's Populist newspaper, the *Commoner*, retorted, "Whenever he doesn't like it, he can give it back to us."

Negative public opinion regarding monopolies and trusts made Morgan an irresistible target for President Theodore Roosevelt. When Morgan, E.H. Harriman, James J. Hill, and John D. Rockefeller organized the Northern Securities Company in 1901 to consolidate railroad operations in the Pacific Northwest, Roosevelt pounced. He ordered the Department of Justice to file suit against the trust; in 1904, the Supreme Court ordered its breakup. (Roosevelt later had to eat some of his own crow when, like Cleveland, he appealed to Morgan to sponsor a bond drive to shore up the federal government during the Panic of 1907.)

John Pierpont Morgan died during a trip to Italy in 1913. No nineteenth-century financier left a larger mark on American industry. As biographer H.W. Brands has concluded, "he knew railroads as well as William Vanderbilt, steel as well as Andrew Carnegie, and government finance better than Grover Cleveland." He consolidated the American railroad and steel industry and arranged the merger of Edison General Electric and Thomson-Houston Electric into General Electric. Uncertain they would ever see his like again, government officials created the Federal Reserve System after Morgan's death to replicate his ability to bail out the U.S. Treasury during times of economic turbulence. His reorganization skills shored up shaky companies, eliminated wasteful competitive practices, and forged a new era of American industrial might. But his success challenged many Americans' ideas about democracy and opportunity. They, in turn, classed him among the despised "Robber Barons" who dominated industry during the late nineteenth century.

Yet Morgan loved his nation, saving it from economic collapse on more than one occasion, and lavishing his fellow Americans with art and culture, museums, and educational institutions such as the modern world has rarely seen. Among many other humanistic activities, he served on the board of New York's St. Luke's Hospital and volunteered his time and skills to the Y.M.C.A. He helped found the

Metropolitan Museum of Art and the Museum of Natural History, serving in various official capacities and supporting each with generous gifts of money, research grants, and objects. He underwrote three new buildings for Harvard Medical School and served as a vestryman at his local Episcopal church. A patriot in his own gruff way, Morgan made enormous economic and philanthropic investments in his nation. As he optimistically remarked: "The man who is a bear on the future of the United States will always go broke."

Allen, Frederick Lewis. *The Great Pierpont Morgan.* New York: Harper & Brothers Publishers, 1949.

Brands, H.W. *Masters of Enterprise: Giants of American Business.* New York: The Free Press, 1999.

Chernow, Ron. *The House of Morgan: An American Banking Dynasty and the Rise of Modern Finance.* New York: Grove Press, 2010.

Strouse, Jean. *Morgan.* New York: Random House, 1999.

HARRISON GRAY OTIS

PUBLICIZING THE WEST {1837–1917}

"What Southern California has done for the LOS ANGELES TIMES, *and what the* TIMES *has done for Southern California, it would take a book to relate."* Charles Lummis

Los Angeles, more than any other American city, is an idea as much as it is an actual community, a place that attracts dreamers and strivers. If anyone can be credited with creating this idea, it is Harrison Gray Otis, a printer and Civil War veteran who became publisher of the *Los Angeles Times* in 1882. With the help of his financially savvy son-in-law, Harry Chandler, Otis constructed the popular image of Los Angeles as a city of dreams, a place with unlimited promise. Anglo-Americans flooded into the fledgling city by the thousands in the late nineteenth and early twentieth centuries, lured by visions of orange groves, sparkling beaches, and limitless opportunity that the *Times* helped disseminate nationwide. Otis's unabashed promotion of his adopted home helped the *Times* grow from an undistinguished four-page broadside to the city's most influential publication, while his boundless booster optimism ensured that Los Angeles expanded with it.

Like many California dreamers, Otis was born elsewhere. A native of Marietta, Ohio, he was the youngest of sixteen children born to Stephen and Sara Otis. His parents were stern Methodist farmers who migrated to Ohio from Vermont and Nova Scotia. The Otises made up for a lack of money with distinguished family roots. They named their youngest son for his cousin Harrison, a former Boston mayor and Massachusetts senator. Stephen Otis was a staunch abolitionist descended from Revolutionary War hero James Otis, Jr. Stories of ancestral political and military achievements inspired Harrison Gray Otis to pursue an active public life.

Otis apprenticed to a local printer at age fourteen, training briefly at Granger's Commercial College in Columbus, Ohio. There, he fell in love with Eliza Wetherby, the well-educated daughter of a local manufacturer. The two married in 1859, against her father's wishes, and moved to Kentucky, where Otis worked on the *Louisville Journal.* The paper was deeply pro-Republican, and young Otis began to take a stronger interest in politics, becoming a delegate to the Republican National Convention in 1860. For the rest of his life, Otis was an impassioned supporter of the Grand Old Party. His writings in the *Times* and other papers would parallel the party's pro-business platform nearly to the letter.

Otis quickly enlisted in the Ohio Volunteers after the outbreak of the Civil War. He was a natural soldier and leader, comfortable with giving orders. He advanced quickly through the ranks of the military, and was discharged after four years with the rank of lieutenant colonel. He fought alongside two future presidents—Rutherford B. Hayes and William McKinley—in the Ohio Infantry. Otis eagerly exploited his Washington, D.C., connections in his civilian life, and he never quite gave up the trappings of the military. For the rest of his life, he insisted on being called Colonel Otis (later, General Otis after he fought in the Spanish-American War). He often wore full army dress uniform into the *Times* office, and he often ran his business as if he were fighting a war. He called his staff his "phalanx." At the height of the *Times*'s strife with the city's organized labor movement, Otis stockpiled arms in the newspaper's castle-like building in downtown Los Angeles and ran his employees through military-style drills in case of attack.

After the Civil War, Otis and Eliza returned to Ohio, trying their hand at publishing their own newspaper. Otis was bored after the excitement and challenges of war. He used his military and political connections to gain posts first at the Government Printing Office and then the U.S. Patent Office. Bureaucracy was a stable job, but the Colonel remained restless. Attracted by an advertisement touting the potential profits to be had raising Angora goats on the West Coast, he and Eliza made their first trip to California in 1874.

Goats didn't relieve what ailed Otis, but southern California did. "It is the fattest land I was ever in," he wrote home to Ohio. Two years later, the Otises left the East for good, settling in Santa Barbara, where Harrison became editor and publisher of the local newspaper. In his short time at the *Santa Barbara Press,* he cultivated the bellicose writing style he would later perfect at the *Los Angeles Times.* Santa Barbara was pleasant, but too sleepy for an empire builder. After a brief sojourn in Alaska, where he worked to curb seal poaching as an agent of the Treasury Department, Otis moved his family to Los Angeles.

Los Angeles was on the verge of an economic transformation when the Otises arrived in 1882. Long home to native California peoples and a center of Spanish and Mexican settlement, it nevertheless claimed only 5,000 residents in 1870. (San Francisco, then the state's economic and cultural center, had a population of 149,473 the same year.) But times were changing. Large-scale ranches were turning into smaller, more profitable farms. The Southern Pacific Railroad connected Los Angeles to the rest of the state in 1876. Banks and other businesses began popping up, and brick buildings replaced the adobe structures downtown. A new, Anglicized, Los Angeles was a city on the make.

The *Times* was barely a year old and on the verge of bankruptcy when Otis took over as editor in 1882. He and a partner (whom Otis later bought out) purchased the paper and its sister publication, the *Mirror,* and founded the Times-Mirror Company. Los Angeles was full of partisan papers; Otis aimed to attract Republican readers. He vociferously supported favored candidates, while denouncing Democrats, union supporters, and anyone else who didn't seem to believe in his vision of southern California's "progressive" destiny.

His promotion of Los Angeles took its purest form in the *Times's* "Midwinter Edition," which he began publishing in 1885. Each January, the Midwinter Edition was sent to Americans shivering through a frigid midwestern or East Coast winter. The Midwinter Edition featured rapturous booster tributes to southern California through the nearly seven decades it was published. It portrayed the city as an everyman's and everywoman's paradise, boasting, in the words of historians Louis and Richard Perry, that "a person could live with more grace in Los Angeles than in most other cities; a minimum of winter clothing was needed, a hat was a nuisance, clothes were easy to wash, house rents were cheap, fuel bills and utilities were low, and the simple pleasures of a streetcar ride to the beach were within everyone's reach."

Otis's vision of Los Angeles included many things, but it had no room for unions. He saw L.A. was a city for strivers, self-made men and women who didn't need a union to advocate for their needs. Otis's politics influenced his views on unions, but they also reflected his perception of the city's needs. Lacking major manufacturing and shipping facilities, Los Angeles needed to attract investors. San Francisco was a union town; Los Angeles would distinguish itself from its northern rival by offering manufacturers and employers pools of cheap, plentiful labor.

Otis once supported unions as a young newspaperman, and inherited a union printing shop when he acquired the *Times*. He initially tolerated the International Typographic Union local that drove the *Times* shop, but when southern California's boom busted in the late 1880s, Otis saw an opportunity to rid his newspaper of organized labor. He declared war on his own printers, importing "scab" laborers whom he paid twice what he had paid his previous workers. Otis's anti-union tactics didn't stop at his own paper. In the decades that followed, his paper, which carried the words "Industrial Freedom" on its masthead, was the leading voice for the open shop, organizing local businessmen and industrialists against the city's unions. Otis's war on unions reached a fiery climax on October 1, 1910, when the *Los Angeles Times* building exploded, killing nearly twenty employees and injuring 100 more. Brothers and union members John and James McNamara were convicted of the bombings, which they planned to occur when no one was in the *Times* building.

Otis hated the Southern Pacific Railroad almost as much as he disliked unions. Los Angeles boasted many things, but it lacked a natural deep-water harbor. In 1890, Congress agreed to help fund a harbor project. The question was, where? Otis and his supporters favored the coastal town of San Pedro, which had served as a port for decades and was already connected to downtown via rail. But Southern Pacific magnate Collis P. Huntington had other ideas. He began constructing a pier at Santa Monica, to the north, believing that deep connections in the national capitol would ensure a Southern Pacific franchise. Otis and other city leaders found this intolerable. How could a San Franciscan tell Los Angeles what to do, Otis rhetorically asked? And if Huntington succeeded in creating his harbor, land sale profits would drain into outside hands. Otis formed the Free Harbor League to fight Huntington. After three years of deliberation, Congress favored Otis's plan, appropriating $2.9 million to build a harbor at San Pedro.

Growing Los Angeles also needed a more secure water supply, and Otis played a crucial—and profitable—role in that battle. Booster literature rarely mentioned the desert city's lack of precipitation, but by the late nineteenth century the growing municipality was quickly using up its aquifer. Mayor Fred Eaton and his chief water engineer, William Mulholland, found an answer to the city's water problems in the Owens Valley, 250 miles north of the city. Watered by Sierra Nevada snowpack, the valley was perfect for farming and ranching—and for a gravity-fed water system that would pipe water to the distant city. Through land speculation and other means, Eaton and Mulholland began sending Owens Valley water to Los Angeles via the San

Fernando Valley. Otis, who had once downplayed the city's lack of water, now threw his support publicly behind the project. The *Times* began issuing reports on the dire state of Los Angeles's water supply, while Otis, along with other investors, began buying up land in the San Fernando Valley. Otis's newspaper drummed up support for the Los Angeles Aqueduct, which eventually ran through the publisher's 44,000 acres of prime land.

Behind his bluster, Otis had an eye for talent. One of his early editors was Charles Fletcher Lummis, who offered to walk the more than 3,000 miles from Ohio to southern California, filing travel reports for the *Times* along the way, if Otis gave him a job at the end. Lummis arrived in California in 143 days and settled straight into the city editor's chair. Lummis left the *Times* after suffering a stroke, but became famous as a chronicler of the western past and advocate for preserving California's Spanish missions.

Otis's most important recruit was Harry Chandler, an East Coast "lunger" who sought to recover from tuberculosis in California's climate. The Colonel was a shrewd businessman, but Chandler was even better. Even before he began working at the *Times,* he quietly bought up the newspaper's key distribution routes, along with others, giving him a near-monopoly on newspaper delivery in the city. If a rival paper was threatening the *Times,* Chandler simply told his newsboys to stop delivering it, while he promoted his paper as a more reliable morning read. Chandler also recognized the value of Los Angeles real estate. He accepted seemingly worthless land deeds as payment for ads and other money owed to the *Times,* building a property portfolio that helped make him and Otis rich. Chandler rose up through the ranks of the newspaper, eventually promoted to the coveted position of son-in-law, after he married one of Otis's three daughters, Marian, in 1894. Chandler strengthened Otis's relationships with the city's power brokers and helped channel family money into numerous profitable real-estate ventures.

Harrison Gray Otis died in July 1917, collapsing at breakfast after a massive heart attack. But the *Times* did not die with him. Harry Chandler took over his father-in-law's paper and, until 2000, the Chandler family continued to publish the *Los Angeles Times,* turning it into one of the most influential newspapers in the United States. Under the family's leadership, Times-Mirror became one of the largest media companies in the world, publishing not only the *Times,* but other major American newspapers, books, and magazines, and operating television stations, until it was sold to the Tribune Company in 2000.

For decades, Harrison Gray Otis envisioned a bigger, better Los Angeles as the anchor city of California and the American West. His newspaper shaped public opinion and marketed the city as a place where anyone could succeed. For Otis, boosterism was good business: for the *Times,* for himself, for his industrial allies, and for the millions of Angelenos who benefitted from the water and infrastructure projects that his newspaper promoted. Otis unflaggingly promoted his city's and state's virtues, even if he sometimes had to make them up along the way. As the *Times* grew and prospered, so did Los Angeles. And so did California, and the American West.

Boyarsky, Bill. *Inventing L.A.: The Chandlers and their Times.* Santa Monica, Calif.: Angel City Press, 2009.

Deverell, William. *Railroad Crossing: Californians and the Railroad, 1850–1910.* Berkeley: University of California Press, 1994.

Gottlieb, Robert and Irene Wolf. *Thinking Big: The Story of the Los Angeles Times, Its Publishers, and Their Influence on Southern California.* New York: Putnam, 1977.

Kahrl, William L. *Water and Power: The Conflict Over Los Angeles' Water Supply in the Owens Valley.* Berkeley: University of California Press, 1983.

McDougal, Dennis. *Privileged Son: Otis Chandler and the Rise and Fall of the L.A. Times Dynasty.* New York: Da Capo Press, 2002.

Perry, Louis B. and Richard S. Perry. *A History of the Los Angeles Labor Movement, 1911–1914.* Berkeley: University of California Press, 1963.

CARL LAEMMLE

CREATING THE WESTERN IMAGE {1867–1939}

The 1890 closure of the American frontier, at least in United States census reports, neatly dovetailed with the rise of the motion picture industry. French cinematographers began experimenting with moving pictures by 1892. Two years later, the American inventor Thomas Edison began screening his patented Kinetoscope films in New York City. Motion picture prototypes flickered in the West even earlier. To settle an 1878 bet over whether a galloping horse's feet entirely left the ground, California businessman Leland Stanford underwrote the pathbreaking cinematic experiments of Eadweard Muybridge in Palo Alto. (Muybridge's remarkable sequence of stop-motion photographs demonstrated that horses indeed flew for brief periods.)

In 1903 filmmakers began their love affair with the western genre. Although filmed in New Jersey, that year's western-themed silent film, *The Great Train Robbery,* electrified audiences. Film historians still consider the ten-minute "oater" the world's first cinematic blockbuster. By 1910, filmmakers had discovered the West's congenial year-round climate, abundant sunshine, breathtaking scenery, and relaxed intellectual property laws. Like any western emigrant, the business of filmmaking arrived in Hollywood with high hopes for the future.

Organized while the Old West was still a living, breathing reality in some parts of the nation, the Hollywood motion picture industry arguably did more to cement popular perceptions about the American West than any other medium. And Jewish immigrants such as Samuel Goldwyn, William Fox, Adolph Zukor, and Louis B. Mayer, marked the earliest paths. Carl Laemmle, the father of Universal Studios, represents the best of the immigrant contributors. He was an unlikely character in Hollywood's formative years. Rising from humble beginnings, Laemmle pioneered the nascent film industry and fought a definitive battle against Thomas Edison's attempt to monopolize film production and distribution. Laemmle led the charge for independent film producers and secured a free market for the film industry. He was one of the first to envision southern California's potential as the industry center, and he transformed hundreds of acres into a groundbreaking studio-city. Laemmle's insistence on making inexpensive films available to modest movie theater owners and their customers was a true underdog story. With westerns, horrors, classics, and wartime propaganda films, Laemmle produced a variety of genres for mass consumption, implemented innovative strategies, and effectively shaped the future of Hollywood and the imagined West.

Carl Laemmle was born January 17, 1867 in Laupheim, Wurttemberg, in southwest Germany, the son of a poor Jewish land speculator. Laemmle's mother apprenticed him at thirteen to a wealthy family in a nearby village. Initially distraught with the situation, Laemmle gradually became a successful clerk at the family's stationery store. He learned English and, intrigued with American dime novels, set his sights on the United States. In 1883 Carl's mother died unexpectedly. His father, understanding his son's American dream, purchased Carl a steamship ticket to New York.

Laemmle arrived on the New York docks armed with $50 and plenty of ambition, but opportunity did not come fast or easy. Laemmle flitted from job to job for the next eleven years. He was employed as an errand boy in New York and Chicago and then a farmhand in South Dakota. Farm wages were good, but Laemmle was not cut out for manual labor. He returned to Chicago, where he clerked at wholesalers' businesses and department stores and kept books for a jeweler and a livestock company. All the while, Laemmle delivered newspapers on Sundays to supplement his $18 weekly income.

Laemmle moved to Wisconsin in 1895 to serve as the bookkeeper for the Continental Clothing Company's Oshkosh branch. Promoted to salesman, he began to experience career success for the first time. He created clever seasonal window displays, published large promotions in the local papers, distributed the company's catalogue, and established an impressive mail-order operation. His innovative advertising techniques led him to a manager's position and a $40 weekly income. After twelve years of employment, Laemmle traveled to the company's Chicago headquarters to negotiate a raise. In a quick turn of events, Laemmle walked into his boss's office (his boss was also his wife's uncle), engaged in a heated argument, and walked away without a job. Suddenly unemployed and nearing his fortieth birthday, Laemmle stumbled to find new job prospects. When a friend advised, "Don't be a salary slave!" Laemmle took the advice literally. With eager urgency, he moved his family to Chicago in 1906, bent on purchasing a five-and-dime or small clothing shop with his $2,500 savings.

With cash in his pocket, Laemmle recognized an alternative opportunity. By 1906, nickelodeons, the first indoor motion picture houses, were flourishing nationwide. Nickelodeons appealed to the masses for their affordability. Before closing on a five-and-dime shop, Laemmle attended a short silent comedy at a Chicago nickelodeon. During the show, he realized that he too could "charge people and make them laugh," according to biographer Neal Gabler. Laemmle calculated potential profits by counting the audience and set out with a determination to learn the business. He abandoned the idea of owning a shop and, in January 1906, converted a vacant storefront on Milwaukee

Avenue into a picture house for $900. Budgeting for a $200 weekly expense, Laemmle spent $50 on the building rental, $27.50 for film rentals, $24 for a manager (himself), $20 for projectionist, $15 for a doorman, $15 for a pianist, $15 for a porter, and $12 for a cashier. Laemmle installed 190 seats, named his operation "The White Front," and insisted on courtesy, cleanliness, and comfort for his patrons. For a nickel, patrons watched a six- to seven-minute film and two illustrated songs (still images accompanied by a recorded musical number). Within two months, Laemmle averaged a daily profit of $180. He opened a second theater, The Family Theatre, on Halsted Street and doubled his price to ten cents per showing. Laemmle joined the nickelodeon industry at the height of its nationwide craze. It took very little to convince the entrepreneur that motion pictures represented the future of leisure activity.

Entering a burgeoning and unregulated industry, Laemmle encountered unethical business practices. He bristled when his film distributors charged premium rental prices for films they had reproduced without authorization. Instead of resigning himself to low-quality knockoffs, he purchased the rights to a motion picture, *The Pearl Fisher's Dream,* and showed it in his houses before renting to neighboring movie houses. Discovering the profit potential of distribution, the businessman established Laemmle Film Service in October 1906. Buying from production agents and renting to exhibition houses, Laemmle reaped success as a film broker. He enlisted an old advertising friend, Robert Cochrane, to help on a promotional campaign and an impressed Cochrane invested $2,500 in the company. The popularity of his services allowed Laemmle to establish branch offices in Des Moines, Omaha, Memphis, Salt Lake City, Portland, Winnipeg, and Montreal. By 1909, Laemmle's film exchange was the largest distributor in the world.

Laemmle enjoyed rapid success and sizeable profits, but ominous clouds were on the horizon. In 1908, Thomas Edison owned patents for the most efficient cameras and projectors, along with the largest camera manufacturing company. Edison invited eight of the top motion picture producers to join his Motion Picture Patents Company, known as the "Edison Trust." The Trust signed an exclusive contract with Eastman Kodak, the largest manufacturer of raw film stock. By early 1909, Edison's alliance owned virtually every aspect of film supply and production. In some respects, the trust improved the motion picture industry by standardizing production and achieving economies of scale. At the same time, it threatened the independence of smaller companies by stipulating that any producer, distributer, or exhibitor using the Motion Picture Patents Company's pool of patents (which was virtually everyone in the business) was subject to membership, license, and royalty fees.

Laemmle paid his dues for three months before resolving to oppose the film cartel. At five feet, two inches tall, with a receding hairline, the pudgy, gap-toothed Jewish immigrant did not seem to pose much of a threat to Edison's corporate allies. But in the fall of 1909, Laemmle and thirteen other producers founded the rival Independent Motion Picture Company. Since early filmmaking required little technical skill, Laemmle decided it was time to start producing films on his own. He avoided patent infringement suits by using cameras not covered by Edison's patents, or by hiding his Edison devices in iceboxes, wagons, and studio cellars whenever Trust inspectors arrived on the set. Laemmle bought raw film stock from Europe to circumvent restrictions on Kodak film and sent his production team to film in Cuba to avoid further scrutiny. In October 1909, Laemmle released his first motion picture film, an adaptation of Longfellow's poem "Hiawatha," with relative success. Laemmle proved to be more of a resourceful than an innovative filmmaker. But he managed to get along by hiring away talent from the Trust's studios and keeping production costs under $1,500.

The Edison Trust struck back in 1910, founding the General Film

Exchange to monopolize film distribution and force out smaller companies. Laemmle, always an avid gambler, played his cards well and founded the competing Motion Picture Distributing and Sales Company with an alliance of independent distributors. The company bought only independently produced films and rented solely to independent exhibitors. Laemmle used his European connections to buy foreign films outside the Trust's jurisdiction. The Trust's seventeen attorneys slammed Laemmle with 289 lawsuits, garnering $300,000 in fines. Armed with only two lawyers and a shrewd anti-Trust publicity campaign spearheaded by his old advertising associate, Robert Cochrane, Laemmle created a public backlash and became a hero for the independent cause. In 1912 the Trust's power declined. Courts eventually backed Laemmle's company over the monopoly. "I won," Laemmle said later in life, " . . . and secured the freedom of film."

On the heels of his triumph, Laemmle and his cohorts consolidated the Independent Motion Picture Company into the Universal Film Manufacturing Company. "I've got the name," Laemmle said at a board meeting, "Universal. That's what we're supplying—universal entertainment for the universe." When asked how he came up with the idea, Laemmle admitted with a grin to appropriating the name from a truck painted with "Universal Pipe Fitting" that passed his office window. Laemmle shortened the company's name to Universal Studios.

In the 1910s, New York reigned as the film industry's Mecca. Laemmle helped change all that as well. Blessed with abundant sunshine, affordable land, and sympathetic federal courts, southern California beckoned. According to film historian Bernard Dick, other studios "knocked the producer's wild idea to move his operations to the West" and called his proposal "Laemmle's Folly." Universal Studios operated studios in Hollywood and Edendale, California, by 1912. Two years later, Laemmle consolidated the studios and purchased 230 acres in the San Fernando Valley for $165,000 (almost $4 million in 2014 dollars). As an all-encompassing studio city, Universal City included a telegraph office, post office, police and fire departments, a sawmill, blacksmith, café, a bank, electrical department, nursery, greenhouse, hospital, living quarters, 900 sets, sixty stages, and a small zoo. By 1913, Laemmle earned $100,000 yearly and was worth $1 million (about $23.5 million in 2014 dollars).

A pioneer in the industry, Laemmle implemented several inventive new business strategies. He generated interest for Hollywood's "star system" by including the names of actors and actresses in the credits (a movie first) and sending their autographed photos to exhibitors. Universal City efficiently mass-produced films by segmenting low-budget, medium-budget, and large-budget productions. Laemmle insisted upon producing as many low-budget films as possible in order to provide small exhibitors with affordable "program packages." He offered a popular nine-film package, the Complete Service Plan, thus enabling exhibitors to change marquees frequently. Laemmle published *Universal Weekly* to keep exhibitors and distributors informed of upcoming releases and included ready-made film posters with blank spaces for run dates and theater names. In 1915 the producer invented the idea of opening his studio for public tours, charging twenty-five cents and building a bandstand to give attendees a better view of film production. Under Laemmle's leadership, Universal became the largest studio in the world.

Unlike other Hollywood moguls, Laemmle enjoyed warm relations with his rank-and-file employees. Always sporting a carnation in his lapel, the boss spread his quirky, contagious, self-deprecating humor. "Uncle Carl" Laemmle was also a devoted family man, notorious for sometimes hiring relatives instead of more qualified candidates. He had a propensity for gambling, often visiting casinos and racetracks. However, Laemmle's reputation as a calculated risk-taker worked in Universal's favor more often than not.

Declining health and the Great Depression finally checked Laemmle's fortunes. Cost overruns on the 1936 production *Show Boat* caused Wall Street creditors to call in their loans. Unable to raise the capital to cover a $750,000 dollar debt, Laemmle forfeited his Universal shares, valued at an estimated $5 million (about $84 million in 2014 dollars). A perpetual optimist, Laemmle chose not to dwell on his loss, fixing instead on his immensely successful career. Laemmle generously bestowed his good fortune on others. His sponsorship enabled 300 Jewish-German immigrants to escape Nazi persecution, and he provided the immigrants and their families with start-up money in America. He died from cardiovascular disease at his house in Beverly Hills on September 24, 1939.

German immigrant Carl Laemmle had changed his life's direction at age forty by purchasing a Chicago nickelodeon and within six years changed the direction of America's nascent film industry. He founded one of the world's largest, and now oldest, motion picture studios. As one of the first producers to move his studio to southern California, Laemmle helped bridge the Old West and the New, establishing in the minds of millions of viewers worldwide a popular image of the American West.

Drinkwater, John. *The Life and Adventure of Carl Laemmle*. New York: Arno Press, 1978.

Gabler, Neal. *An Empire of Their Own: How the Jews Invented Hollywood*. New York: Anchor Books, 1988.

Gordon, Nancy. "Carl Laemmle Opened Universal Studios Versus Long Odds." *Business Investors Journal*. 8 August 2012.

Films Media Group. *100 Years of Hollywood: Carl Laemmle and Universal Studios*. German United Distributors: 2011.

BUFFALO BILL CODY

WESTERN SHOWMAN TO THE WORLD {1846–1917}

During the past century, one westerner outshone many of the others on the world stage, at least in terms of publicity and exposure. He taught other nations to think of America as the American West. Thanks largely to him, generations of children grew up playing cowboys and Indians, a game that often started with a squabble to see who would play the hero—Buffalo Bill. During his lifetime, he became the hero of stage plays, countless newspaper stories, fifteen movies, 557 dime novels, and his own Wild West Show. Long after his death in 1917, Buffalo Bill comic books, board games, puzzles, tin whistles, and toy guns sold worldwide.

Cody also advanced the art of advertising. He mastered the sales pitch. His unforgettable show posters rivaled those of Toulouse-Lautrec. Cody opened his show programs to advertisers so fans not only read about their hero and his show but found ads for everything from Quaker Oats to overalls. For a few dollars more, businesses could get the personal endorsement of Colonel Cody himself. He wore and endorsed Stetson hats and testified that he always used "Winchester rifles and Winchester ammunition." Long before the Lone Ranger offered a similar assortment of endorsements and branded products on his radio and television programs, Buffalo Bill taught Madison Avenue a trick or two.

Praised as the finest-looking man of his time, Cody strolled and rode tall, ramrod straight, and full-chested. He wore his hair in long curls and grew a goatee in 1869 when that became the vogue. Men imitated him, women adored him, and children idolized him.

For rapt, sold-out audiences, William Frederick "Buffalo Bill" Cody made a business of presenting history to the masses. He pioneered the "westerns" that would become a mainstay of Hollywood films, of enthusiastically read novels such as those of Zane Grey and Louis L'Amour, and of art that would give the world unforgettable images of the American West.

Cody's Wild West show was big business. He organized it in 1883 and added the Congress of Rough Riders of the World in 1893, expanding the narrative from the American West to world history. Some six hundred performers, roustabouts, and other employees traveled in fifty-two railroad cars. Before the show, Buffalo Bill often led a grand parade to showcase all performers, especially stars such as Annie "Little Miss Sure Shot" Oakley, and to drum up business. Astride his prancing white stallion, the handsome showman rode magically, so much at one with his horse that observers called them a centaur. After dashing to center stage, Cody swept his Stetson hat from his beautiful long hair, bowed to the audience, and bellowed (he needed no microphone): "Ladies and gentlemen. I give you the Wild West and Congress of Rough Riders of the World!"

The Rough Riders of the World were one of the first American attempts to respectfully reach out culturally to many peoples. The Congress featured Cossacks from Russia, Mexican vaqueros, African American buffalo soldiers, Peruvian galloping gauchos, Arabs, various European cavalries, American Indians, and Gypsies.

At a time when many Americans were concerned with the masses of exotic immigrants pouring in from all over the world, Cody's

Congress of Rough Riders showcased positively the most exotic peoples, especially if equestrians. A century before "multicultural diversity" became a byword, Cody paraded it before audiences worldwide. Frederick Remington noted that "The great interest which attaches to the whole show is that it enables the public to take sides on the question of which people ride best." Like modern-day Olympics or World Cup Soccer matches, Cody's spectacle inclusively and positively introduced athletes from all over the earth to the general public.

As nations headed toward World War I, Cody, as historian Louis L. Warren emphasized, "advanced international arbitration as a means to keep the peace." He reached out to many countries, even those hostile to each other. If Cody could gather all these diverse peoples of the world under his big tents, why could not his Congress become a model for the rest of the world? In the United States, immigrants flocked to the Wild West Shows, which they saw as a ritual of Americanization and inclusiveness as well as a chance to enjoy a diverse spectacle.

Attempted internationalism did not save Cody from criticism. Although perhaps the best known and most idolized American of his age, Cody came under unkind scrutiny. Critics asked if he was in real life the great American hero portrayed in dime novels, plays, films, and his Wild West Show. Although some called him and his show a fraud, Mark Twain, one of the most honest and cutting writers of the age, wrote that Cody "brought vividly back" the vanishing West. "Down to the smallest details, the show is genuine—cowboys, vaqueros, Indians, stage coach, costumes and all," Twain wrote, "and distinctly American."

Cody transformed show business into an international product. His entrepreneurial spirit made his name and show one of the world's best known brands. At a time when most Americans made fortunes in extractive industries, he was perhaps the first to realize that entertainment would become one of the largest and most exported of American products. To make a living, to create a new industry, required an innovative spirit and willingness to learn from setbacks. An estimated 90 percent of American business failed between the crashes of 1873 and 1893. To hurdle the busts, businessmen had to be nimble and explore a full range of prospective endeavors that the capitalist system offered. No one outdid Cody when it came to capitalizing on show business.

Cody also appreciated the need to diversify the places where he invested his dollars. Besides his own show, he bought bonds in a British railroad and an American coffee company, renamed in 1893 the Cody-Powell Coffee Company. He offered guiding services for hunters in Wyoming and purchased the *Duluth Press,* a newspaper in Minnesota. He also invested in other theatrical productions beyond his own shows and studied audience patterns.

Realizing that New Yorkers had already seen the Wild West summer outdoor show, Cody rearranged his performances for a winter season production inside Madison Square Garden. His new production, The Drama of Civilization, aimed to become middle- and upper-class entertainment, respectable educational fare that might even attract culture mavens. The show began with America's eastern seaboard colonization before marching westward. Huge artistic backdrops did duty for the great western outdoors. Panorama brought the wonders of Yellowstone to New York City. To present old history, Cody used many new techniques: elaborate backdrops, spectacular lighting, smoke, and, yes, mirrors, to made the old Wild West Show a novel visual treat. Cody's show may have dealt with historical happenings but technically it pioneered futuristic technical innovations.

From childhood, Cody had looked for and seized entrepreneurial opportunities. His career began when he left home at age thirteen looking for work to help his widowed mother and siblings. Born on a family farm in LeClaire, Iowa, on February 26, 1846, he found work in Leavenworth with Russell, Majors & Waddell, the lead freighting firm of the Great Plains and Rockies. His horsemanship, endurance, and courage led that firm to hire him as one of its famous Pony Express riders. Some scholars doubt Cody worked as a Pony Express rider, but historian Don Russell in *The Lives and Legends of Buffalo Bill*, offers convincing evidence that he did, as he claims in his various autobiographies, ride with the most famous of all U.S. mailmen. Indeed, it was Cody's association with the Pony Express that made that short-lived venture a prime piece of Americana. Cody boasted in one autobiography that, as a pony express rider, he once covered 322 miles in twenty-one hours and forty minutes, using twenty-one horses.

In his *Life & Adventures of Buffalo Bill* (1917), Cody claims railroad construction crews gave him the nickname after he fed them by killing, according to his own count, 4,280 buffalo. Although Cody, the most celebrated buffalo killer, helped endanger that species, he also preserved breeding herds that he shared with zoos in London, Montreal, and New York City. He helped save bison, enabling them to make a dramatic comeback during the twentieth century. A prime example is the healthy herd that grazes in Genesee Denver Mountain Park near the Buffalo Bill Grave and Museum atop Lookout Mountain in Golden, Colorado.

Cody has been dismissed as a poor actor by critics. A *New York Times* writer disagreed after seeing Cody first play himself in *Buffalo Bill: The King of Border Men*. The April 1, 1873 review praised Cody's "surprising aplomb, notable ease of gesture and delivery, and vocal power quite sufficient to fill a large theater . . . . His use of the revolver and the rifle indicated extensive practice, and were vastly relished by the audience [which showered Cody] with torrents of applause."

Even Queen Victoria became a fan. She tried to put him and the show up at Windsor Castle but it was not big enough so the show went on at Earl's Court. When Cody paraded the American flag, as was his custom at the beginning of each show, Queen Victoria rose from her seat. It was the first time a British sovereign saluted the banner of the rebellious colonies.

Other nations also cheered the first presentation of American life to tour Europe. In 1889 the Wild West Show toured not only London, but also Paris, Lyon, Marseille, Barcelona, Florence, Bologna, Milan, Verona, Munich, Vienna, Berlin, Dresden, Liepzig, Bonn, Frankfurt, and Stuttgart.

Cody married Louisa "Lulu" Maude Frederici Cody in her hometown of St. Louis in 1866. As his fame climbed, their relationship deteriorated. Mrs. Cody correctly complained of her husband's financial ineptness. Although a terrific showman, Cody proved to be a poor businessman. By 1913, his show had become the possession of Fred Bonfils and Harry Tammen, co-owners of *The Denver Post.* Tammen loaned Cody $20,000 and later foreclosed on the bankrupt, aging showman. In U.S. Bankruptcy Court, his Wild West Show's estimated value, animals and all, was $75,000. Tammen bought everything he wanted at auction and kept Cody the star, although the creaky, arthritic, bewigged hero had to be lifted onto his horse. Of Tammen, Cody wrote: "This man is driving me crazy. I can easily kill him . . . "

On January 10, 1917, uremic poisoning sent the Sir Galahad of the Plains over the great divide. An estimated 18,000 people viewed his body as it lay in state inside the gold-domed Colorado State Capitol. Others lined up outside in the January cold hoping to get to see their hero one last time. At the request of Cody and his family, he was later buried atop Lookout Mountain. An estimated 25,000 joined the funeral procession on June 3, 1917.

Millions of pilgrims have climbed the mountain to visit Cody's grave and the adjacent museum. They come to pay homage to the world's best known and most admired American performer of his day. They toss coins through the iron fence guarding his tomb, and single girls traditionally throw in hairpins to bring them good luck in finding a man as handsome as Bill Cody. Although not the best businessman, Cody proved to be the West's favorite showman and salesman.

Buffalo Bill, as historian Louis Warren has pointed out, represented not only the rise of the United States as an economic and entertainment power but also as a cultural force. Europe had long maintained cultural dominance and conceded to America only its fantastic natural attractions, its Niagara Falls and Grand Canyon. Cody shrewdly picked up on the natural themes with the use of "wild" buffalo, deer, elk, and with Indian actors and dramatic natural backdrops. Going further, he also used theatrical art, advertising, and appeals to mass audiences to compete internationally in the cultural marketplace. A century after his death, Buffalo Bill's memorable marketing still keeps him atop the cast of wild westerners.

Cody, William F. *Life and Adventures of "Buffalo Bill."* Chicago: John R. Stanton Publishers, 1917.

East, John H. "Interesting Bits of History," in *Colorado Magazine,* May 1944, p. 112.

Fees, Paul, Former Director of the Buffalo Bill Historical Center, Cody Wyoming, interview with T. J. Noel.

Friesen, Steve, Director of the Buffalo Bill Grave and Museum, Lookout Mountain, interviews with T. J. Noel.

Friesen, Steve. Buffalo Bill: Scout, Showman, Visionary. Golden, CO: Fulcrum Publishing, 2010.

Rosa, Joseph G. and Robin May. *Buffalo Bill and His Wild West: A Pictorial Biography.* Lawrence, KS: University Press of Kansas, 1989.

Russell, Don. *The Lives and Legends of Buffalo Bill.* Norman: University of Oklahoma Press, 1960.

U.S. Bankruptcy court Cases, Bankruptcy 2556, filed August 11, 1913. National Archives & Records Center, Denver.

Warren, Louis. *Buffalo Bill's America: William Cody and the Wild West Show.* New York: Alfred A. Knopf, 2005.

Wetmore, Helen Cody. *Last of the Great Scouts: The Life Story of Col. William F. Cody.* Duluth, MN: The Duluth Press Printing, Co., 1899.

Yost, Nellie Snyder. *Buffalo Bill: His Family, Friends, Fame, Failures, and Fortunes.* Chicago: The Swallow Press, 1979.

INDEX

Image sources: Ashley: Reconstruction from the advertisement. Astor: ©CORBIS; Bent, Charles: Denver Public Library; Bent, William: Denver Public Library; Boettcher: Denver Public Library; Carnegie: ©CORBIS; Cheesman: Denver Public Library; Cody: Denver Public Library; Colt: Public Domain (PD); Cooke: PD / Engraving 1839-49, Century magazine, vol. 73; Coors: Tom Noel Collection; Crocker: PD / by Stephen W. Shaw, pre-1872. Original painting Crocker Art Museum, E.B. Crocker Collection; Doheny: Library of Congress; Durant: ©Bettmann/CORBIS; Evans: History Colorado; Fargo: PD; Ford: Henry Ford Museum; Giannini: ©Bettmann/CORBIS; Goodnight: History Colorado; Guggenheim: The New York Times; Harvey: PD; Hearst: PD; Hill, James: Minnesota Historical Society; Hill, Nathaniel: Tom Noel Collection; Holladay: Oregon Historical Society; Holliday: PD; Hopkins: PD; Huntington, Collis: ©Bettmann/CORBIS; Huntington, Henry: The Huntington Library; Iliff: Denver Public Library; Judah: The Cooper Collection of North American Railroadiana; Lisa: Missouri Historical Society; Laemmle: ©John Springer Collection/CORBIS; McCormick: ©CORBIS; Miller: Gilroy Museum, CA; Morgan: ©CORBIS; Otis: The Bancroft Library; Palmer: History Colorado; Penrose: History Colorado; Pillsbury: Minnesota Historical Society; Pullman: PD; Rockefeller: ©Hulton-Deutsch Collection/CORBIS; St. Vrain: Tom Noel collection; Stanford: ©Bettmann/CORBIS; Strauss: PD; Swift: ©Bettmann/CORBIS; Wells: ©Bettmann/CORBIS; Weyerhaeuser: Minnesota Historical Society; Young: History Colorado.